THE CAMBRIDGE BIBLE COMMENTARY

NEW ENGLISH BIBLE

GENERAL EDITORS

P. R. ACKROYD, A. R. C. LEANEY
J. W. PACKER

ECCLESIASTICUS

ECCLESIASTICUS

OR
THE WISDOM OF JESUS
SON OF SIRACH

COMMENTARY BY

JOHN G. SNAITH

University Lecturer in Hebrew and Aramaic
University of Cambridge

CAMBRIDGE UNIVERSITY PRESS

Published by the Syndics of the Cambridge University Press
Bentley House, 200 Euston Road, London NW1 2DB
American Branch: 32 East 57th Street, New York, N.Y.10022

© Cambridge University Press 1974

Library of Congress Catalogue Card Number: 73–82459

ISBNS:
0 521 086574 hard cover
0 521 097754 paperback

Printed in Great Britain
at the University Printing House, Cambridge
(Brooke Crutchley, University Printer)

GENERAL EDITORS' PREFACE

The aim of this series is to provide the text of the New English Bible closely linked to a commentary in which the results of modern scholarship are made available to the general reader. Teachers and young people have been especially kept in mind. The commentators have been asked to assume no specialized theological knowledge, and no knowledge of Greek and Hebrew. Bare references to other literature and multiple references to other parts of the Bible have been avoided. Actual quotations have been given as often as possible.

The completion of the New Testament part of the series in 1967 provides a basis upon which the production of the much larger Old Testament and Apocrypha series can be undertaken. The welcome accorded to the series has been an encouragement to the editors to follow the same general pattern, and an attempt has been made to take account of criticisms which have been offered. One necessary change is the inclusion of the translators' footnotes since in the Old Testament these are more extensive, and essential for the understanding of the text.

Within the severe limits imposed by the size and scope of the series, each commentator will attempt to set out the main findings of recent biblical scholarship and to describe the historical background to the text. The main theological issues will also be critically discussed.

Much attention has been given to the form of the volumes. The aim is to produce books each of which will be read consecutively from first to last page. The introductory material leads naturally into the text, which itself leads into the alternating sections of the commentary.

The series is accompanied by three volumes of a more general character. *Understanding the Old Testament* sets out to provide the larger historical and archaeological background, to say something about the life and thought of the people of the Old Testament, and to answer the question 'Why should we study the Old Testament?'. *The Making of the Old Testament* is concerned with the formation of the books of the Old Testament and Apocrypha in the context of the ancient near eastern world, and with the ways in which these books have come down to us in the life of the Jewish and Christian communities. *Old Testament Illustrations* contains maps, diagrams and photographs with an explanatory text. These three volumes are designed to provide material helpful to the understanding of the individual books and their commentaries, but they are also prepared so as to be of use quite independently.

P. R. A.
A. R. C. L.
J. W. P.

CONTENTS

The footnotes to the N.E.B. text   *page* ix

  ✷   ✷   ✷   ✷   ✷   ✷   ✷   ✷   ✷   ✷   ✷   ✷

How the book was written   1
The discovery of Hebrew fragments   2
What the book is about   3

  ✷   ✷   ✷   ✷   ✷   ✷   ✷   ✷   ✷   ✷   ✷   ✷

Preface   5
The ways of wisdom   9
Man's life under divine providence   53
Maxims of prudence and self-discipline   96
The praise of wisdom   119
Counsels upon social behaviour   129
True piety and the mercy of God   167
Man in society   176
The wonders of creation   208
Heroes of Israel's past   214
Epilogue   256

  ✷   ✷   ✷   ✷   ✷   ✷   ✷   ✷   ✷   ✷   ✷   ✷

NOTES ON FURTHER READING   263

INDEX   265

THE FOOTNOTES TO THE
N.E.B. TEXT

The footnotes to the N.E.B. text are designed to help the reader either to understand particular points of detail – the meaning of a name, the presence of a play upon words – or to give information about the actual text. Where the Hebrew text appears to be erroneous, or there is doubt about its precise meaning, it may be necessary to turn to manuscripts which offer a different wording, or to ancient translations of the text which may suggest a better reading, or to offer a new explanation based upon conjecture. In such cases, the footnotes supply very briefly an indication of the evidence, and whether the solution proposed is one that is regarded as possible or as probable. Various abbreviations are used in the footnotes.

(1) Some abbreviations are simply of terms used in explaining a point: *ch(s).*, chapter(s); *cp.*, compare; *lit.*, literally; *mng.*, meaning; *MS(S).*, manuscript(s), i.e. Hebrew manuscript(s), unless otherwise stated; *om.*, omit(s); *or*, indicating an alternative interpretation; *poss.*, possible; *prob.*, probable; *rdg.*, reading; *Vs(s).*, version(s).

(2) Other abbreviations indicate sources of information from which better interpretations or readings may be obtained.

Aq. Aquila, a Greek translator of the Old Testament (perhaps about A.D. 130) characterized by great literalness.

Aram. Aramaic – may refer to the text in this language (used in parts of Ezra and Daniel), or to the meaning of an Aramaic word. Aramaic belongs to the same language family as Hebrew, and is known from about 1000 B.C. over a wide area of the Middle East, including Palestine.

Heb. Hebrew – may refer to the Hebrew text or may indicate the literal meaning of the Hebrew word.

Josephus Flavius Josephus (A.D. 37/8–about 100), author of the *Jewish Antiquities*, a survey of the whole history of his people, directed partly at least to a non-Jewish audience, and of various other works, notably one on the *Jewish War* (that of A.D. 66–73) and a defence of Judaism (*Against Apion*).

Luc. Sept. Lucian's recension of the Septuagint, an important edition made in Antioch in Syria about the end of the third century A.D.

Pesh. Peshitta or Peshitto, the Syriac version of the Old Testament. Syriac is the name given chiefly to a form of Eastern Aramaic used by the Christian community. The translation varies in quality, and is at many points influenced by the Septuagint or the Targums.

Sam. Samaritan Pentateuch – the form of the first five books of the Old Testament as used by the Samaritan community. It is written in Hebrew in a special form of the Old Hebrew script, and preserves an important form of the text, somewhat influenced by Samaritan ideas.

Scroll(s) Scroll(s), commonly called the Dead Sea Scrolls, found at or near Qumran from 1947 onwards. These important manuscripts shed light on the state of the Hebrew text as it was developing in the last centuries B.C. and the first century A.D.

Sept. Septuagint (meaning 'seventy'); often abbreviated as the Roman numeral (LXX), the name given to the main Greek version of the Old Testament. According to tradition, the Pentateuch was translated in Egypt in the third century B.C. by 70 (or 72) translators, six from each tribe, but the precise nature of its origin and development is not fully known. It was intended to provide Greek-speaking Jews with a convenient translation. Subsequently it came to be much revered by the Christian community.

Symm. Symmachus, another Greek translator of the Old Testament (beginning of the third century A.D.), who tried to combine literalness with good style. Both Lucian and Jerome viewed his version with favour.

Targ. Targum, a name given to various Aramaic versions of the Old Testament, produced over a long period and eventually standardized, for the use of Aramaic-speaking Jews.

Theod. Theodotion, the author of a revision of the Septuagint (probably second century A.D.), very dependent on the Hebrew text.

Vulg. Vulgate, the most important Latin version of the Old Testament, produced by Jerome about A.D. 400, and the text most used throughout the Middle Ages in western Christianity.

[...] In the text itself square brackets are used to indicate probably late additions to the Hebrew text.

(Fuller discussion of a number of these points may be found in *The Making of the Old Testament* in this series)

ECCLESIASTICUS

OR
THE WISDOM OF JESUS
SON OF SIRACH

✳ ✳ ✳ ✳ ✳ ✳ ✳ ✳ ✳ ✳ ✳ ✳ ✳

HOW THE BOOK WAS WRITTEN

Ecclesiasticus was originally written in Hebrew about 190 B.C. by Jesus ben ('son of') Sira, an experienced Jewish teacher who lived in Palestine, probably in Jerusalem. The book seems to be a collection of his teaching material, and became so popular that his grandson, on emigrating to Egypt about 132 B.C., translated it into Greek for the benefit of Jews who could not read Hebrew, even adding a preface (pp. 5–6) to explain the reasons for his translation. This Greek translation together with the translator's preface was accepted by the early Christian church as part of the Bible under its Greek title 'The Wisdom of Ben Sirach', and forms the text for the N.E.B. translation. 'Sirach' is the Greek form of the original Hebrew name 'Sira' used in this commentary. The title Ecclesiasticus appeared first in the Latin translations and was given to the book possibly either because of its frequent use in the Christian church or because of its superficial similarity to Ecclesiastes. Although, as described below, Hebrew texts have been discovered for many chapters, reflecting an earlier stage of development than the Greek, the Greek continued to be used by the Christian church. This is partly because the Hebrew text is incomplete, partly because the early popularity of the book led to many different, unreliable changes in the text and partly because the Greek text had become traditional. So popular

I

was the book that later copyists added more verses to emphasize certain religious precepts, verses which often appear in
the footnotes of the N.E.B. The Hebrew was never accorded
scriptural authority by the Jews and, although it was popular
reading matter, the rabbis frequently warned against giving
the book too great importance or authority.

THE DISCOVERY OF HEBREW FRAGMENTS

In 1896 the store-room (*genizah*) of an ancient synagogue in
Cairo was excavated, and four manuscripts of a Hebrew text
of Ben Sira's work were discovered, covering most of
3: 6 – 16: 26, 30: 11 – 38: 27 and 39: 15 – 51: 30, together
with small parts of other chapters. More fragments of the
Genizah text were published in 1930 and in 1957–9, some
found by relatives among the papers of a famous Hebrew
scholar after his death in New York. Several small fragments
of scrolls from Qumran near the Dead Sea (discovered soon
after 1948) have been identified as parts of the 'Wisdom of
Jesus Son of Sirach' or 'Ben Sira', and in 1964 a scroll containing 39: 27 – 43: 30 was discovered in the excavations at
Masada. Different manuscripts of the Hebrew, Greek and
Syriac texts vary considerably, and the textual study of this
book is probably harder and more complicated than that of
anything in the Old Testament. The Qumran and Masada
manuscripts of the Hebrew probably date from the first
century A.D. and, although the Genizah manuscripts are copies
from probably the eleventh or twelfth century and show signs
of careless copying, comparison with the earlier texts and
with the Greek and Syriac suggest that the Genizah texts
basically reflect a stage of development prior to the Greek
translation. Some scholars would therefore prefer to use the
Hebrew as the basis for translation rather than the Greek.

WHAT THE BOOK IS ABOUT

The life-time scrap-book of a lecturer or teacher always contains a variety of material – so too this book. Like Proverbs it contains many sayings handed down in poetic form through the centuries on all kinds of secular subjects: family life, relations with friends, treatment of old people, discipline of children, borrowing and lending money, mourning for the dead, business partnerships, behaviour of guests and hosts at banquets, the value of medicine and doctors, the evils of gossip, etc. Sayings on particular subjects are grouped together more than in Proverbs. Like Proverbs, Ecclesiasticus shows many points of contact with the international proverbial literature of the Ancient Near East, particularly with Egyptian books like the *Instruction of Ani* and the *Instruction of Amen-em-opet* (both probably dating from between the tenth and sixth centuries B.C.), and the passage contrasting manual workers and learned scholars in 38: 24 – 39: 11 seems to have been based on a satirical passage in the Egyptian *Maxims of Duauf* popular from the thirteenth century onwards. Such works were probably used in Egypt for training civil servants and administrative officials, and Ben Sira's stress on foreign travel, first-hand experience and behaviour in positions of responsibility in society suggests that the education he tried to provide was of a similar kind. The occasional interruption of series of proverbs with hymns or doctrinal passages (like ch. 24) recalls the Egyptian rather than the Hebrew style of proverbial book, and it is in these passages that the author's own attitude to life and theology appears most prominently.

The teaching of the hymns and doctrinal poems is unmistakably Jewish, and prepares the way for much later rabbinic (and Christian) doctrine. The poem on God's ordering of creation in 33: 7–15 offers an explanation of the existence of good and evil in the world side by side. The passage on pursuit of wisdom in 4: 11–19 encourages man with almost evangelical fervour to persevere in seeking wisdom until he receives the sudden joy of possession and enlightenment. In 16: 24 – 17: 24 a description of God's control of the world, with tremendous emphasis on his all-seeing providence, is followed by a passionate appeal for repentance in 17: 25–32. In ch. 24, with its personification of wisdom as a semi-divine female figure reminiscent of Prov. 8, wisdom's home on earth is in Jerusalem and the temple, and the self-consciousness of the Jews as God's chosen people breaks through the internationalism; in 24: 23 wisdom is further identified with the 'covenant-book of God Most High, the law which Moses enacted', encouraging the reader to view the law as the revealed will of God as did the later Pharisees. Ben Sira's Jewish consciousness is shown most of all in his recital of the history of the Jews through the Old Testament period in chs. 44–50, which are full of phrases echoing biblical narratives, and in particular his description of the return of Elijah (48: 10) shows anticipation of later rabbinic teaching. Even the secular portions of the book frequently mention 'the fear of the Lord', particularly at the end of sections; in chs. 1 and 2 Ben Sira describes this phrase as denoting a warm personal relationship of trust towards God which underlies all his advice and teaching on doctrinal and secular matters alike.

This mixture of social advice and Jewish doctrinal exposition explains the later popularity of the book, and seems to represent a certain stage in the development of rabbinic Judaism. The sayings of Ben Sira often sound like the sayings handed down in *Pirqe Aboth* ('The Sayings of the Fathers', abbreviated *Aboth* in this commentary), the earliest tractate (division) of the *Mishnah*, the oral Jewish law, considered by the Pharisees to be as authoritative as the written law (the first five books of the Old Testament from Genesis to Deuteronomy, often called the Pentateuch). The Mishnah, collected from originally oral sources and written up by the middle of the second century A.D., formed the basis for later Judaism. The Mishnah has been translated into English by H. Danby (*The Mishnah* (O.U.P., 1933)), and all references to the Mishnah in this

4

commentary refer to this volume. One verse is identical in Ecclus. 7: 17 and *Aboth* 4: 4. *Aboth* 1: 2 reads: 'By three things the world is sustained: by the Law, by the (Temple-) Service, and by deeds of loving-kindness' – a saying which superficially seems to sum up certain aspects of Ben Sira's own work, although Ecclesiasticus is much richer in its material than this statement would imply. Later Jewish teaching collected in the Babylonian Talmud (an expansion of the earlier Mishnah completed by the middle of the sixth century A.D. but reflecting several centuries' development) often shows strong similarities with Ben Sira's thought. Thus Ben Sira's wide-embracing work, written about 190 B.C., illustrates the development of main-stream Judaism at a time when the composition of the books of the Old Testament had just about ceased and most surviving Jewish literature is either highly sectarian (like the scrolls from the religious community that lived at Qumran) or concentrated on particular aspects of belief (like the apocalyptic works dealing with the future). But, whereas in many respects he seems progressive (as in the section on medicine and doctors in 38: 1–15), in other respects he clings to the past (as in his refusal to believe in life after death). The work provides an admirable link between the Old Testament and the later Judaism appearing in the New Testament.

* * * * * * * * * * * *

Preface

THE AUTHOR'S GRANDSON EXPLAINS HIS TRANSLATION

A LEGACY of great value has come to us through the law, the prophets, and the writers who followed in their steps, and for this Israel's traditions of discipline and wisdom deserve recognition. It is the duty of those who study the scriptures not only to become expert themselves, but also to use their scholarship for the benefit of the outside world through both the spoken and the written word. So my grandfather Jesus, who had applied himself industriously to the study of the law, the prophets, and the other writings of our ancestors, and had gained a considerable proficiency in them, was moved to compile a book of his own on the themes of discipline and wisdom, so that, with this further help, scholars might make greater progress in their studies by living as the law directs.

You are asked then to read with sympathetic attention, and make allowances if, in spite of all the devoted work I have put into the translation, some of the expressions appear inadequate. For it is impossible for a translator to find precise equivalents for the original Hebrew in another language. Not only with this book, but with the law, the prophets, and the rest of the writings, it makes no small difference to read them in the original.

When I came to Egypt and settled there in the thirty-eighth year of[a] the reign of King Euergetes, I found great scope for education; and I thought it very necessary to spend some energy and labour on the translation of this book. Ever since then I have been applying my skill night and day to complete it, and to publish it for the use of those who have made their home in a foreign land, and wish to become scholars by training themselves to live according to the law.

[a] *Or* there at the age of thirty-eight in...

✻ Just as the preface of a modern book often explains the
author's purpose in writing, so this preface explains why this
translator translated into Greek the Hebrew book of his
grandfather, Jesus ben Sira.

The translator says he emigrated from Palestine to Egypt
in the thirty-eighth year (probably 132 B.C.) *of the reign of King
Euergetes* (Ptolemy VII Euergetes Physcon, whose dates are
usually given as 145–117 B.C. but who had been joint king
since 170 B.C.). In Egypt he joined a considerable Egyptian–
Jewish population. Early in the sixth century Jeremiah and
other refugees had fled to Egypt for asylum from Babylonian
invaders; in the fifth century there had been a contingent of
Jewish soldiers and their families near Aswan at Elephantiné,
guarding the southern border of Egypt; when the high priest
Onias was exiled from Jerusalem in 162 B.C., he built a replica
of the Jerusalem temple at Leontopolis in the north-eastern
part of the Nile delta. Indeed, the Ptolemies, the descendants
of one of Alexander the Great's Greek generals and the rulers
of Egypt from 323 to 30 B.C., depended on Jewish military
help to maintain their authority over the native Egyptian
population, and encouraged Jewish immigration to this end.
Many Greek papyri fill in day-to-day details of the life of Jews
in most parts of Egypt who had taken over Greek ways of life
and become hellenized. According to the Jewish Alexandrian
writer Philo there were nearly a million Jews living in Egypt
in his time (the first century A.D.).

Many Jews, living in a Greek environment in Egypt, forgot
both colloquial and religious Hebrew, and were in danger of
not *living as the* Jewish *law* directed. Already in the third
century B.C. translation of the Old Testament into Greek was
started with a rendering of the Pentateuch, commonly called
the Septuagint. Ben Sira's grandson was fired by missionary
enthusiasm to bring to Greek-speaking Jewry the riches of
Palestinian Jewish learning and piety, which he found repre-
sented in his grandfather's book. Otherwise, he felt, *Israel's
traditions of discipline and wisdom* would not gain the *recognition*

they deserved. It was not enough for Hebrew-speaking rabbis and scribes *to become expert themselves*, but they should also *use their scholarship for the benefit of* Jews who had *made their home in a foreign land*, the Jews of the Dispersion. This translation stands in a succession of similarly 'evangelistic' Jewish works in the Graeco-Roman world together with the Wisdom of Solomon. The Roman Jewish historian Josephus wrote his long book *Antiquities* to show that the Jews had as distinguished a history and ancestry as had the Greeks, and he also tried to defend Judaism against criticism and attack in his *Contra Apionem* ('Against Apion', a particularly fierce critic of the Jews). Similarly Philo wrote many philosophical works presenting Jewish belief in Greek philosophical terms.

Translation from one language to another poses problems at any level and at any time. Here the translator shows in his preface that, because of the difficulties of translation, the Greek is necessarily inferior to *the original Hebrew*. It is impossible for us to assess the accuracy of the Greek translation in view of the problems of the Hebrew manuscripts previously discussed, but the preface shows how responsibly the translator approached his task.

When this book was published in its Greek form, the Jewish *scriptures* had already fallen into three divisions. Two were complete: *the law*, containing the first five books from Genesis to Deuteronomy, and *the prophets*, both the former prophets, containing Joshua, Judges and the books of Samuel and Kings, and the latter prophets, containing Isaiah, Jeremiah, Ezekiel and the twelve minor prophets (as indicated in 49: 10). The contents of *the writings* were not yet completely defined; the Psalms, Job, Proverbs and possibly the books of Chronicles, Ezra and Nehemiah were probably regarded as scripture, but some books, for example, Ecclesiastes and Esther, remained of doubtful status until the end of the first century A.D. ✳

8

The ways of wisdom

WISDOM AS GOD'S CREATION

ALL WISDOM IS from the Lord; **1**
wisdom is with him for ever.
Who can count the sand of the sea, **2**
the drops of rain, or the days of unending time?
Who can measure the height of the sky, **3**
the breadth of the earth, or the depth of the abyss*a*?
Wisdom was first of all created things; **4**
intelligent purpose has been there from the beginning.*b*
Who has laid bare the root of wisdom? **6**
Who has understood her subtlety?*c*
One alone is wise, the Lord most terrible, **8**
seated upon his throne.
It is he who created her, surveyed and measured her, **9**
and infused her into all his works.
To all mankind he has given her in some measure, **10**
but in plenty to those who love him.

✵ This belief in the divine origin of wisdom is found in the Old Testament proverbial literature, notably in Prov. 8: 22–4; wisdom does not represent the accumulated knowledge of man's experience in the world but was created by God even before the world, and is therefore peculiarly his own. Everything in the world is governed by the 'intelligent purpose' (verse 4) which is God's wisdom. This doctrine,

[a] *Some witnesses add* or wisdom. [b] *Some witnesses add* (5) The fountain of wisdom is God's word on high, and her ways are the eternal commandments. [c] *Some witnesses add* (7) Who has discovered all that wisdom knows, or understood her wealth of experience?

basic to the book, is later developed by the identification of
wisdom with the Jewish law.

2–3. God's majesty is stressed, as in some other Hebrew
poems (Job 38–41; Isa. 40: 12–14), by rhetorical questions
which, unanswerable by man, are intended to humble him
and make him aware of God's greatness. The second question
reflects the ancient view of the world as flat, of subterranean
waters and of *the sky* as of limited extent. The parts of divine
wisdom which are beyond man's understanding are called its
'subtlety' (verse 6), and form the 'root' and most important
part of it.

5–7. Verses 5 and 7 (printed in the footnotes) are found only
in some manuscripts. Verse 5 was probably added as a note to
refer readers to the later identification of wisdom with the
law, and verse 7 presents an alternative version of verse 6.

8–10. *One alone is wise:* Jewish monotheism became more
dogmatic as the Jewish faith competed with the many different
religions and philosophies of the Graeco-Roman world. Any
rational principle observable in creation was created by, and
subject to, the one transcendent God. But, whereas the one
creator sustains the life of *all mankind*, he is especially generous
to those who love him, i.e. the Jews, the people through whom
he chose to reveal his law and wisdom. This doctrine of the
special love of God for the Jews, sometimes called his 'election
love', appears from time to time in Ecclesiasticus side by side
with proverbial lore common to many nations.

The statement that *the Lord* is *most terrible* leads on to a
description of the reverence for God that men must have if
they are to receive wisdom. ✵

THE FEAR OF GOD AS THE WAY TO WISDOM

11 The fear of the Lord brings honour and pride,
   cheerfulness and a garland of joy.
12 The fear of the Lord gladdens the heart;

it brings cheerfulness and joy and long life.

Whoever fears the Lord will be prosperous at the last;   13
blessings will be his on the day of his death.

The essence of wisdom is the fear of the Lord;   14
she is created with the faithful in their mother's womb,

she has built an everlasting home among men,   15
and will keep faith with their descendants.

Those who fear the Lord have their fill of wisdom;   16
she gives them deep draughts of her wine.

She stocks her home with all that the heart can desire   17
and her storehouses with her produce.

Wisdom's garland is the fear of the Lord,   18
flowering with peace and health.

She showers down knowledge and ability,   19
and bestows high honour on those who hold fast to her.

Wisdom is rooted in the fear of the Lord,   20
and long life grows on her branches.[a]

✱ 'The fear of the Lord' in this book implies neither childish
terror of what God may do nor formal respect for one in
highest authority; it is to be understood rather as a warm,
personal trust and reverence. Orthodox Jews observe the
restrictions of the sabbath day, repressive to many of us, yet
find relaxation and joy in such observance. Reverence for the
law means for them 'cheerfulness' and a festive 'garland of
joy'. Ben Sira adds this kind of personal warmth to the traditional phrase 'fear of the Lord', which in earlier Hebrew
literature, for example in Proverbs, seems so colourless and
insipid. For him this new concept of the fear of the Lord is
the basis of the Jew's search for wisdom.

12–13. That God gives *long life* and prosperity in this life to

[a] *Some witnesses add* (21) The fear of the Lord drives away sins, and
wherever it dwells it averts his anger.

the pious is a doctrine well known in the Old Testament, and appears frequently in Ecclesiasticus. In this passage the 'wine' of verse 16 and the well-stocked 'storehouses' of verse 17 are both images for this prosperity. Ben Sira was one of the last Jewish writers of biblical times to hold this view, writing before the Maccabean revolt (167 B.C.) when martyrdoms such as those described in 2 Macc. 6-7 proved that the pious might die young and poor. Nevertheless, the book of Job, almost certainly known to Ben Sira, had already criticized the traditional doctrine severely, and that Ben Sira remained so staunchly traditional shows him to have been ultra-conservative. He was similarly conservative over life after death, as will appear.

14. The Greek word translated *essence* can equally mean 'starting-point'. Play on the two meanings cannot be brought out in English; the author means that reverence for God is both the most central thing in wisdom and the starting-point for obtaining it.

20. The warm personal relationship intended by the phrase *the fear of the Lord* does not only work one way, from man to God. As a tree draws sustenance through its roots, so a man's wisdom draws sustenance from his relationship with God, and *long life* develops as the fruit – according to the traditionalist Ben Sira. Later the Pharisees believed that reward came after death in resurrection. Tree imagery is often used elsewhere in this way, for example in Ps. 1 and Ecclus. 24: 13-19. Verse 21 is inserted in some manuscripts to provide a stronger link with what follows. *

ON SELF-CONTROL, OBEDIENCE AND HYPOCRISY

22 Unjust rage can never be excused;
   when anger tips the scale it is a man's downfall.
23 Until the right time comes, a patient man restrains himself,
   and afterwards cheerfulness breaks through again;

until the right moment he keeps his thoughts to himself,   24
and later his good sense is on everyone's lips.

In wisdom's store are wise proverbs,   25
but godliness is detestable to a sinner.

If you long for wisdom, keep the commandments,   26
and the Lord will give it you in plenty.

For the fear of the Lord is wisdom and discipline,   27
fidelity and gentleness are his delight.

Do not disregard the fear of the Lord   28
or approach him without sincerity.

Do not act a part before the eyes of the world;   29
keep guard over your lips.

Never be arrogant, for fear you fall   30
and bring disgrace on yourself;
the Lord will reveal your secrets
and humble you before the assembly,
because it was not the fear of the Lord that prompted you,[a]
but your heart was full of hypocrisy.

---

* In spite of the doctrinal theme underlying the whole book, much material is gathered together in the apparently random way common to the proverbial literature of the ancient Near East. This is understandable if the book represents in any way the subject-matter and method of what a scribe like Ben Sira may have taught in his school. In these three groups of verses much seems to consist of commonplace sayings that Ben Sira may have taken over from traditional lore without placing his own imprint upon them. The link with what precedes is not clear.

22–4. Self-control is necessary to keep the correct balance in holding back one's words, whether of *anger* (verse 22) or of advice to an angry person (verses 23–4). Presumably it is through possessing wisdom that one knows the right time to speak.

[a] *Or* because you had no concern for the fear of the Lord.

25–7. Both *wisdom* and *the fear of the Lord* are here used in traditional senses without Ben Sira's particular slant. *wisdom* means not divine pre-existent wisdom but the accumulation of wise sayings over the centuries. The *fear of the Lord* is described in non-personal terms as something given in teaching, not as a personal relationship of trust. Similar verses advocating faithful obedience can be found in many passages in Proverbs and Ecclesiasticus.

28–30. The author turns to give the reader direct advice which draws together verses 22–7 and makes them his own. Unless the true, personal *fear of the Lord* involves the whole person, a man will have a divided, or even deceitful, mind, because he will pretend to be other than he is and *act a part before the eyes of the world* as a religious person. Thus it is dangerous to misunderstand or *disregard* the true, personal *fear of the Lord*, as otherwise you fall into *hypocrisy*. No particular *assembly* is envisaged in verse 30; the meaning is that any evil *secrets* about yourself which you wish to keep hidden will be made quite public knowledge by God. ✻

ON TESTS TO BE ENDURED

2 My son, if you aspire to be a servant of the Lord,
   prepare yourself for testing.
2 Set a straight course, be resolute,
   and do not lose your head in time of disaster.
3 Hold fast to him, never desert him,
   if you would end your days in prosperity.
4 Bear every hardship that is sent you;
   be patient under humiliation, whatever the cost.
5 For gold is assayed by fire,
   and the Lord proves men in the furnace of humiliation.
6 Trust him and he will help you;
   steer a straight course and set your hope on him.

* Hypocrisy as described in 1: 28–30 can only be uncovered by testing, so the faithful believer must face the necessity for this, and be prepared to submit humbly to such testing, just as Job's faithfulness was tested by Satan (Job 1–2). Like Job's friends many Jews still regarded illness and disaster as punishments for sin, and were all too apt to lose their heads 'in time of disaster' (verse 2). Thus personal 'hardship' could lead to misunderstanding and contempt from other people and considerable 'humiliation' for the devout Jew (verse 4). Here, however, as in 44: 20, Ben Sira presents another explanation of human suffering as testing the strength of a person's faith in God.

1. The reader is addressed as *my son* often in this book in a way typical of wisdom teaching, like 'Listen, my sons, to a father's instruction...for it is sound learning I give you' (Prov. 4: 1–2). The phraseology denotes a teacher–pupil relationship common in Babylon and Egypt also, and is here transferred from confrontation of teacher and pupil in the school to author and reader of a book.

5. *gold is assayed by fire:* the image of refining *gold* and silver to separate what is precious from what is worthless was popular with ancient Jewish writers. This verse is probably a traditional proverb around which Ben Sira built this section on testing.

6. The section closes with an appeal for personal faith in God as the way in which to withstand the unpleasant process of testing. *

ASSURANCE OF SUCCESS TO THE FAITHFUL

You who fear the Lord, wait for his mercy;   7
do not stray or you will fall.
You who fear the Lord, trust in him,   8
and you shall not miss your reward.
You who fear the Lord, expect prosperity,   9

lasting happiness and favour.

10 Consider the past generations and see:

was anyone who trusted the Lord ever disappointed?

was anyone who stood firm in the fear of him ever
    deserted?

did he ever neglect anyone who prayed to him?

11 For the Lord is compassionate and merciful;

he forgives sins and comes to the rescue in time of trouble.

✶ 7–9. Reassurance is felt to be necessary, perhaps to cover
the time-lag between faith in times of testing and the later
reward. So the promise of verse 6 is expanded and defined more
closely as God's *mercy* and material *prosperity*. By God's *mercy*
is probably meant the strong personal bond formed between
two people who have faced difficulties together – here the
devout Jew and God, the strength in the partnership coming
from God.

10. *was anyone who trusted the Lord ever disappointed? was
anyone...deserted? did he ever neglect anyone...?:* in answer to
these questions historians might well suggest several persons
who certainly *trusted the Lord* but were *disappointed*: Josiah,
king of Judah, for example, who was most faithful to the law,
purified the temple in Jerusalem, and yet died in battle in
609 B.C. (2 Kings 22: 1 – 23: 30). But for Ben Sira the only
answer is 'not one'. From the standpoint of his faith he looked
back at his nation's history as recorded in the Old Testament
and saw massive support for faith in God. He sets out his
evidence for this in chs. 44–50.

11. The section closes, as in 1: 10 and 2: 6, with a description
of God's help to the believer; the phrase *compassionate and
merciful* was familiar to Jews from various sources as, for
example, Exod. 34: 6 and Ps. 103: 8 (N.E.B. 'compassionate
and gracious'). ✶

THREEFOLD WOES AND ASSURANCES

Woe to faint hearts and nerveless hands   12
and to the sinner who leads a double life!
Woe to the feeble-hearted! they have no faith,   13
and therefore shall go unprotected.
Woe to you who have given up the struggle!   14
What will you do when the Lord's reckoning comes?

Those who fear the Lord never disobey his words;   15
and all who love him keep to his ways.
Those who fear the Lord try to do his will;   16
and all who love him steep themselves in the law.
Those who fear the Lord are always prepared;   17
they humble themselves before him and say:
'We will fall into the hands of the Lord, not into the hands 18
      of men,
for his majesty is equalled by his mercy.'

✻ Verses starting with the same words are a great help when
learning by heart. Here one group of verses (verses 12–14)
starting with 'Woe to . . .' and expressing condemnation is set
between two groups of verses expressing reassurance to the
faithful, one (verses 7–9) starting with 'You who fear the
Lord . . .', the other (verses 15–17) with 'Those who fear the
Lord . . .' Such patterns of words show that the verses were
originally handed on from teacher to pupil by oral repetition.
These teaching methods are found in non-Israelite proverbial
literature and were used in Jewish schools and synagogues to
teach the 'oral law' or, as the New Testament calls it, the
'tradition of the elders' – authoritative Jewish law supplemen-
tary to the Pentateuch which was later collected in writing
in the Mishnah (see p. 4).

12–14. It is easy to be faithful to God when all goes well but to abandon one's faith when trouble comes; this is what is meant by the *double life* or, literally in the Greek, 'two paths' of *the sinner*. Such indecisive people forfeit their right to God's protection (verse 13), and disaster is unavoidable *when the Lord's reckoning comes* (verse 14). By this the author does not mean judgement and retribution after death – the later Jewish and Christian belief – but rather sudden illness and disaster while alive when, Ben Sira believed, faith in God made all the difference between winning through to a happy and prosperous old age or falling into sorrow, poverty and an early death.

15–16. For Ben Sira one of the ways to the personal relationship with God described in 1: 11–12 was obedience to the Jewish law: the *words* and *ways* which God had prescribed for the Jews in the Pentateuch and in the 'tradition of the elders'. Steeping yourself thus in God's revealed will made sure you lived as God wished – not, in Ben Sira's view, in hope of reward but because of personal faith and love.

18. '*We will fall into the hands of the Lord . . .*': the faithful here quote (inaccurately) the words of David in 2 Sam. 24: 14. The sense is the same but, whereas David had done wrong and was submitting himself humbly to punishment, here the faithful have done no wrong and are only preparing themselves for times of difficulty. The quotation is used to round off the whole section (chs. 1 and 2) by stressing God's protective love to those who trust him. ✳

ON RESPECT FOR ONE'S PARENTS

3 Children, listen to me, for I am your father;
   do what I tell you, if you wish to be safe.

2 It is the Lord's will that a father should be honoured by
   his children,
   and a mother's rights recognized by her sons.

Respect for a father atones for sins, 3
and to honour your mother is to lay up a fortune. 4
A son who respects his father will be made happy by his 5
    own children;
when he prays, he will be heard.
He who honours his father will have a long life, 6
and he who obeys the Lord comforts his mother;
he obeys his parents as though he were their slave. 7
My son, honour your father by word and deed, 8
so that you may receive his blessing.
For a father's blessing strengthens his children's houses, 9
but a mother's curse uproots their foundations.
Never seek honour at the cost of discredit to your father; 10
how can his discredit bring honour to you?
A man is honoured if his father is honoured, 11
and neglect of a mother is a disgrace to children.
My son, look after your father in his old age; 12
do nothing to vex him as long as he lives.
Even if his mind fails, make allowances for him, 13
and do not despise him because you are in your prime.
If you support your father it will never be forgotten, 14
but be put to your credit against your sins;
when you are in trouble, it will be remembered in your 15
    favour,
and your sins will melt away like frost in the sunshine.
To leave your father in the lurch is like blasphemy, 16
and to provoke your mother's anger is to call down the
    Lord's curse.

✻ Family relationships form one of many areas of everyday
life which Ben Sira, always practical, describes as spheres for
the practice of that devotion to God which he calls 'the fear

of the Lord' as in 1: 11. Whereas in 30: 1-13 and 42: 9-14 he discusses parents' duties in bringing up children, here he deals with children's attitudes to their parents. As the fifth of the Ten Commandments the command to 'honour your father and mother' (Exod. 20: 12) was prominent in ancient Judaism not only in law and narrative but also in proverbs (Prov. 19: 26) and moral tales (Ruth 1: 16; Tobit 4: 3-4), and has been highly valued ever since. Respect for parents is not, of course, limited to Judaism and is found as frequently in the proverbs of other nations in ancient times, especially in those of Egypt.

1. This section on natural parentage is introduced by the widespread comparison of teacher and pupils to father and children noted on 2: 1. *if you wish to be safe:* the desire for safety referred to here is not to be taken in any Christian sense of salvation from sin or from hell; it is rather safety from disastrous consequences in times of crisis as described in the note on 2: 12-14.

2. *It is the Lord's will that a father should be honoured by his children:* other translations keep the order of the Greek words and differ in interpretation: 'The Lord honours the father in his children' (Jerusalem Bible), possibly by their large number; 'the Lord honoured the father above the children' (Revised Standard Version). The N.E.B. here as often paraphrases the Greek to bring out a sense which is clear and definite although uncertain and debatable in the original.

3. There are several ways, according to Ben Sira, of removing the bad effect of human sin before God. Sacrifices may be offered in the temple as prescribed in the Old Testament; but also good deeds which fulfil God's commandments help to destroy the effect of sin: *Respect for* one's *father*, almsgiving (that is giving money to the poor) (3: 30), forgiveness of others (28: 2), fasting (34: 26) and even mere avoidance of evil (35: 3). In this he anticipated the sayings of later Jewish rabbis recorded in the Talmud. However, as in 34: 18-26 (see notes there), neither sacrifices nor good deeds were effective with-

out sincere repentance. As a rabbi of the second century A.D. said, 'repentance and good works are a shield against retribution' (*Aboth* 4: 11).

5. *when he prays:* the reference is to prayer in times of trouble 'when the Lord's reckoning comes' (2: 14) – the critical moments in life for Ben Sira.

7. The words *as though* are important. Although Ben Sira believed in strong parental authority, he never supports the right of parents to sell their children into slavery as was assumed in the regulations of Exod. 21: 7 and practised in the depressed period after the exile (Neh. 5: 5). Later rabbis stated that a son stood to his father in the same relation as a *slave* to his master.

9. As often in Hebrew poetry the verse must be taken as a whole: both *father* and *mother* are referred to in both parts of the verse.

10. When a son seeks to assert his independence, rivalry with his father can sometimes lead him to let his father down in public and spoil his reputation. Such action could sometimes lead to financial loss.

13–15. The context, that of a father's old age, is set by verse 13. *If you support your father:* for this the Hebrew and the Greek both use the technical term for 'almsgiving' or giving to the poor, as in 3: 30. The Pharisees later believed that good deeds counted for credit, sins for debit, before God. To criticize this belief as a system of theological accounts is too crude. Many Christians have believed that salvation may be earned by good deeds, and the Jewish belief is founded on a strong sense of God's inspiration of man which makes man able to perform good deeds. Nevertheless, whether salvation was to be earned by good deeds or granted through a relationship of faith in God was a major point of conflict between Jews and Christians in the New Testament.

16. Care is taken to place the whole discussion of children's attitudes to parents in a religious context at the end of the section. ✲

ON HUMILITY AND PRIDE

17 My son, be unassuming in all you do,
   and those the Lord approves will love you.

18 The greater you are, the humbler you must be,
   and the Lord will show you favour.*a*

20 For his power is great,
   and he is honoured by the humble.

21 Do not pry into things too hard for you
   or examine what is beyond your reach.

22 Meditate on the commandments you have been given;
   what the Lord keeps secret is no concern of yours.

23 Do not busy yourself with matters that are beyond you;
   even what has been shown you is above man's grasp.

24 Many have been led astray by their speculations,
   and false conjectures have impaired their judgement.*b*

26 Stubbornness will come to a bad end,
   and the man who flirts with danger will lose his life.

27 Stubbornness brings a load of troubles;
   the sinner piles sin on sin.

28 When calamity befalls the arrogant, there is no cure;
   wickedness is too deeply rooted in him.

* Section 3: 17 – 4: 10 is another section dealing with what
seems on the surface to be a purely social matter: humility
and generosity to the poor and the oppressed. But as in 3: 16
the section closes with a clear reference to God's love in 4: 10,

[a] *Some witnesses add* (19) Many are high and mighty; but he reveals
his secrets to the modest.
[b] *Some witnesses add* (25) Without eyes you will be deprived of light;
if you have no knowledge, do not lay claim to it.

22

echoing the religious tone of 3: 17–20 and putting the whole
section in a religious context. Humility and generosity are
part of Ben Sira's picture of the faithful Jew and arise from
desire for relationship with God: thus in verse 20 the humble
are identified with the faithful. Humility saves people in times
of crisis (18: 21) because God exalts the humble (10: 14,
which is very like the tearing of 'monarchs from their
thrones' and the lifting 'high' of 'the humble' in Luke 1: 52).
After verses 17–20 verses 21–4 condemn intellectual arrogance
and verses 25–8 stubbornness.

19 (in the footnotes) is omitted in some important manuscripts and is probably an alternative form of verse 20.

21–4. Since the campaigns of Alexander the Great in 334–
323 B.C. Greek influence had become very strong in the
Middle East and threatened traditional Judaism. The Jews
based their doctrine and practice on God's will as revealed
in the written and oral law (Pentateuch and Mishnah):
human reasoning was entirely subjected to divine revelation.
The faithful were to meditate on what they had been given
(verse 22). Certain subjects, dangerous for the amateur, were
barred from general discussion, such as the complicated
forbidden decrees for marriage in Lev. 18: 6–18, the story of
creation and the mystical interpretation of the heavenly
chariot in Ezek. 1: 4–28. If God had wished his people to
probe into the creation of the world and universe, he would
have said so in his law. The Greeks, however, encouraged free
inquiry and full use of human reasoning with no thought of
revelation or sacred book; no questions were barred. Thus in
science (study of the natural world and the universe) and morality Jewish and Greek thought came into increasing conflict,
and later rabbis warned against 'speculations, and false
conjectures' (verse 24), often quoting verses 21 and 22 as the
first shots fired in this defensive battle. This is one important
respect in which Ben Sira anticipates the attitudes of much later
Jewish writers. To desert the revealed tradition of the past and
use one's own imagination was intellectual pride for Ben Sira

for whom it was 'Better to be godfearing and lack brains than to have great intelligence and break the law' (19: 24).

22. *Meditate on the commandments you have been given:* the Greek text runs literally: 'Meditate on what has been assigned to you.' Neither Greek nor Hebrew mentions *commandments* which the N.E.B. has introduced for explanation. The author probably intended the whole of the law as the sphere for meditation.

25 (in the footnotes) occurs in different positions in Hebrew and Greek manuscripts, and is omitted in some of the most reliable. It was probably added in the margin as an illustration of verses 21–4.

26–8. We pass from intellectual pride to stubborn arrogance of character, equated with wickedness because of undue reliance upon oneself rather than upon God. The N.E.B. translation in verse 27 (*brings a load of troubles*) is particularly clever, the literal sense of the Greek being 'is weighed down with troubles'. The *calamity* referred to in verse 28 is probably, as indicated by the Hebrew 'wound', a physical injury – one of the crises in which Ben Sira believed God helped the faithful. ✳

ON GIVING TO THE NEEDY

29 A sensible man will take a proverb to heart;
   an attentive ear is the desire of the wise.

30 As water quenches a blazing fire,
   so almsgiving atones for sin.

31 He who repays a good turn is mindful of the future;
   when he falls he will find support.

4 My son, do not cheat a poor man of his livelihood
   or keep him waiting with hungry eyes.

2 Do not tantalize a starving man
   or drive him to desperation in his need.

If a man is desperate, do not add to his troubles   3
or keep him waiting for the charity he asks.

Do not reject the appeal of a man in distress   4
or turn your back on the poor;

when he begs for alms, do not look the other way   5
and so give him reason to curse you,

for if he curses you in his bitterness,   6
his Maker will listen to his prayer.

Make yourself popular in the assembly,   7
and show deference to the great.

When a poor man speaks to you, give him your attention   8
and answer his greeting politely.

Rescue the downtrodden from the oppressor,   9
and be firm when giving a verdict.

Be a father to orphans   10
and like a husband to their mother;
then the Most High will call you his son,
and his love for you will be greater than a mother's.

✻ Everyone knows of the needs of the underprivileged
today, and many individuals and institutions contribute, but
in the ancient world special emphasis was necessary. The gap
between rich and poor had greatly increased in the third
century B.C. when Palestine was administered from Egypt;
taxes were collected by middle-men who gave the required
amount to the Egyptian authorities and made as much extra
as they wished. This situation led Ben Sira to increase the
importance already given to care for the poor and oppressed
in the Old Testament (for example, in Deut. 15: 7–8 and
Amos 2: 6–7). He viewed generosity to the less fortunate as
a means of atonement – an attitude continued in later Judaism
which has always highly valued giving to the poor. Credit
must be given to the Jews for seeking to break down this

barrier of wealth to some extent, although ostentatious charity clearly existed and was bitterly attacked in the New Testament (Matt. 6: 2–4). Rabbi Akiba of the second century A.D. once remarked: 'God placed the poor on earth in order to save the rich from hell.'

4: 1–2. 'Do not defraud' is cited as a commandment in Mark 10: 19. Too many took advantage of their wealth to oppress the poor unfairly, as seems to have been the practice of Egyptian and Roman tax-collectors.

7–9. Popularity *in the assembly* (probably the synagogue) refers, in this context, to fame for open-handed generosity rather than to ingratiating oneself with the leaders. The second line is in contrast to the first and reveals Ben Sira's fear of those in authority – he felt that even judges were in danger of intimidation by powerful men (7: 6), and must therefore resist all the pressures of the wealthy and powerful *and be firm when giving a verdict* (verse 9).

10 sums up the section. *then the Most High will call you his son:* the Greek runs 'you will be like a son of the Most High', which the N.E.B. rejects in favour of a closer rendering of the Hebrew. ✶

WISDOM REVEALS HERSELF AS A TEACHER

11 Wisdom raises her sons to greatness
and cares for those who seek her.
12 To love her is to love life;
to rise early for her sake is to be filled with joy.
13 The man who attains her will win recognition;
the Lord's blessing rests upon every place she enters.
14 To serve her is to serve the Holy One,
and the Lord loves those who love her.
15 Her dutiful servant will give laws to the heathen,
and because he listens to her, his home will be secure.

If he trusts her, he will possess her   16
and bequeath her to his descendants.
At first she will lead him by devious ways,   17
filling him with craven fears.
Her discipline will be a torment to him,
and her decrees a hard test
until he trusts her with all his heart.[a]
Then she will come straight back to him again and   18
    gladden him,
and reveal her secrets to him.
But if he strays from her, she will desert him   19
and abandon him to his fate.

* After sections discussing particular themes we have a
collection of mixed proverbs on private and public relationships (4: 20 – 6: 17) enclosed by two passages praising wisdom
(4: 11–19 and 6: 18–37). In 4: 11–19 wisdom is personified
and is referred to as 'she'. The Hebrew even makes 'her'
speak in the first person in verses 14–19 as in 24: 3–22 and
Prov. 8: 34–6. Elsewhere the divine power which instructs man
in both manual skill and religious understanding, here wisdom
is sometimes called God's spirit. Both the personification of
wisdom and the concept of wisdom instructing the faithful
lead up to the New Testament understanding of the personal
'Holy Spirit' who 'will teach you everything' (John 14: 26).

11–12. With these links in subject-matter it is not surprising
to find an echo of the earlier book of Proverbs; thus verse 11,
Wisdom raises her sons to greatness, resembles Prov. 4: 8
('cherish her (wisdom), and she will lift you high'). Such
echoes of phrases used in the Old Testament occur fairly
frequently in Ecclesiasticus, and particularly in the survey of
Israel's history in chs. 44–50. This has led to some describing
the book as written in the style of a mosaic.

[a] *Or* until she can trust him.

14. *the Holy One* is a favourite expression for God in later Jewish writings.

15. *Her dutiful servant will give laws to the heathen:* the original Hebrew probably meant 'whoever obeys her (wisdom) judges rightly' (Hebrew *'emet*, 'aright, truly'). The translator, however, living in gentile Egypt, translated the Hebrew *'emet* as *'ummot* ('the nations, gentiles'), both words having the same consonants. The former interpretation fits the context better, but the latter illustrates the Greek translator's purpose of encouraging Jews in an alien environment to bear faithful witness *to the heathen*.

17. Serving God by following wisdom and fulfilling the law is at first mere obedience, demanding, perplexing and discouraging; but at a certain point the penny will drop, the faithful will find himself in a relationship of understanding and love with God. Then joy takes the place of *torment* when *he trusts* wisdom *with all his heart*. The subject of the verb *trusts* in the Greek may be *he* (the believer) or *she* (wisdom, as in the footnote). The N.E.B. rightly follows the Hebrew, interpreting the verse as human faithfulness. ✳

ON UNDUE SELF-EFFACEMENT IN PUBLIC

20 Watch your chance and defend yourself against wrong,
   and do not be over-modest in your own cause;
21 for there is a modesty that leads to sin,
   as well as a modesty that brings honour and favour.
22 Do not be untrue to yourself in deference to another,
   or so diffident that you fail in your duty.
23 Never remain silent when a word might put things right,
24 for wisdom shows itself by speech,
   and a man's education must find expression in words.
25 Do not argue against the truth,
   but have a proper sense of your own ignorance.

Never be ashamed to admit your mistakes,   26
nor try to swim against the current.
Do not let yourself be a doormat to a fool   27
or curry favour with the powerful.
Fight to the death for truth,   28
and the Lord God will fight on your side.

☆ The long section on public and private relationships
(4: 20 – 6: 17) begins with a collection of verses on behaviour
in public affairs: some people, too self-effacing, do not speak
out when they should (4: 20–8), others, over self-reliant, push
themselves too confidently (5: 1–7). Notice how each short
section closes with a reference to God's help (4: 28) or judgement (5: 7), putting the advice against a background of religious commitment.

After describing generally the danger of excessive modesty
(verses 20–1), the author describes various situations in which
modesty, usually thought to be a good thing, can destroy
personal integrity. Most politicians have at some time to
choose between their duty to follow their conscience and the
deference to others required by the electoral system and party
membership. Ben Sira knew public life well (see 39: 1–11)
and also its problems of personal honesty to oneself (42: 1)
and too much 'diffidence' (20: 22). Although there was in
Palestine no electoral system or formal party organization,
law courts, governors' courts and official entertaining pre-
sented similar challenges.

Wise men of the Middle East frequently started their
proverbs with prohibitions ('Do not...') as may be seen in
Egyptian literature and in the book of Proverbs. Here sixteen
verses start with 'Do not...' up to 6: 4, when the tone changes
from negative to positive advice (see also 7: 1–20 and 8: 1–
9: 11).

23. The words *when a word might put things right* illustrate the
N.E.B.'s translation technique. There is doubt about the

original Greek: all manuscripts have the words 'time of salvation', but many scholars think the original was 'time of need'. Whereas the Revised Standard Version translates 'crucial time' and notes the alternative in the footnotes, the N.E.B., instead of making a decision between the two readings, seems to combine both in a smooth, but not quite accurate, translation.

26. *Never...try to swim against the current:* some commentators, following a proverb in the *Story of Ahiqar* (a 'wisdom' book well known in Ben Sira's time, originating probably in Mesopotamia) and the saying of a later Jewish rabbi, think this verse refers to the impossibility of resisting a river in flood. Others suggest that the author means it is easier to stop *the current* of a river (a very difficult thing) than to conceal one's sins from God (quite impossible!). But the simple explanation is best: if the course of events is running so that *your mistakes* will appear anyway, *admit* them readily without trying to deny them – thus you will keep your self-respect.

28. Religion and politics are not separate for Ben Sira. Maintenance of the civil rights of every citizen comes before the self-interest of public officialdom and should form part of the public responsibility of the religious person. ✶

ON UNDUE SELF-CONFIDENCE

29 Do not be forward in your speech
   but slack and neglectful in your work.
30 Do not play the lion in your home
   or swagger*a* among your servants.
31 Do not keep your hand open to receive
   and close it when it is your turn to give.

5 Do not rely upon your money
   and say, 'I am independent.'

[a] *Possible meaning; Gk. obscure.*

Do not yield to every impulse you can gratify 2
or follow the desires of your heart.
Do not say, 'I am my own master'; 3
you may be sure the Lord will call you to account.
Do not say, 'I sinned, yet nothing happened to me'; 4
it is only that the Lord is very patient.
Do not be so confident of pardon 5
that you sin again and again.
Do not say, 'His mercy is so great, 6
he will pardon my sins, however many.'
To him belong both mercy and wrath,
and sinners feel the weight of his retribution.
Come back to the Lord without delay; 7
do not put it off from one day to the next,
or suddenly the Lord's wrath will be upon you,
and you will perish at the time of reckoning.

* Too much self-confidence leads to false views of the balance
in certain aspects of life: giving and receiving (verse 31), one's
position in the household (verse 30), conversation and hard
work (verse 29).

29. That Jews preferred hard *work* to *forward speech* is
clear from a saying of Shammai, a Jerusalem rabbi of about
30 B.C. to A.D. 10, who said, 'say little and do much, and
receive all men with a cheerful countenance' (*Aboth* 1: 15).

30. *or swagger among your servants:* the Greek seems to mean
'nor be a faultfinder with...' (Revised Standard Version);
but the two surviving Hebrew manuscripts differ from the
Greek and from each other, all the well-known English
translations differ and the footnote rightly says that the meaning is obscure. The N.E.B.'s *swagger among* follows one of the
Hebrew manuscripts, and the Greek is probably an incorrect
paraphrase of this.

31

31. That Ecclesiasticus influenced not only Judaism but also Christianity is shown by the quotation of this verse in the *Didaché* (4: 5), a manual on church order and discipline written perhaps at the end of the first century A.D. which shows many signs of contact with Ecclesiasticus.

5: 1. Wealth, although doctrinally considered by the Jews to represent God's reward for piety, is seen often to lead in practice to materialism rather than to gratitude to, and greater trust in, God. Certainly a miser's lust is never satisfied, and ostentatious display of wealth is condemned, especially in religious contexts (see 34: 18–24 and 35: 12–17), just as the rich man and the kingdom of God are opposed to each other in Matt. 19: 23. The social oppression referred to in the commentary on 3: 29 – 4: 10 would naturally lead Ben Sira to lay greater emphasis on this than previous authors.

2–3. To regard oneself as all-powerful over one's possessions is to put oneself in the place of God who gave them to you and can take them away whenever he pleases.

4–7. The time-lag between sin and punishment (i.e. calamity in this life) led eventually in Judaism to belief in retribution after death. Ben Sira, however, was still trying to counter the arguments of those who, believing in retribution before death and observing the prosperity of the wicked, ceased to believe in God's retribution at all (verse 4). He also opposes those who wrongly presumed upon his continual forgiveness (verses 5–6). The former would find that *the time of reckoning* would come so quickly that no time was left for repentance. The latter were continually criticized in Judaism for cheapening God's forgiveness. If a man repents 'and goes and does the same again...what has he gained by his penance?' (34: 26). The Mishnah warns against presuming on God's mercy: 'if a man said, "I will sin and repent, and sin again and repent," he will be given no chance to repent. If he said, "I will sin and the Day of Atonement will effect atonement," then the Day of Atonement effects no atonement' (*Yoma* 8: 8–9). In the New Testament situation Paul

had to argue against those who found in Christian views of
forgiveness opportunity to 'persist in sin, so that there may
be all the more grace' (Rom. 6: 1). ✶

AGAINST DUPLICITY WITH OTHERS

Do not rely upon ill-gotten gains,	8
for they will not avail in time of calamity.	
Do not winnow in every wind	9
or walk along every path.[a]	
Stand firmly by what you know	10
and be consistent in what you say.	
Be quick to listen,	11
but take time over your answer.	
Answer a man if you know what to say,	12
but if not, hold your tongue.	
Honour or shame can come through speaking,	13
and a man's tongue may be his downfall.	
Do not get a name for being a gossip	14
or lay traps with your tongue;	
for as there is shame in store for the thief,	
so there is harsh censure for duplicity.	
Avoid the little faults as well as the great.	15
Do not change from a friend into an enemy,	**6**
for a bad name brings shame and disgrace,	
and this is the mark of duplicity.	

✶ Living for momentary gain, whether by making quick
money (verse 8) or by agreeing automatically with the most
influential person (verses 9–10), does not affect God's long-
standing will for you.

[a] *Gk. adds* this is the mark of duplicity (*from 6: 1*).

9–10. Ben Sira probably quotes a country proverb in verse
9 (*Do not winnow in every wind*). To separate corn and chaff,
both were thrown into the air on the shovel; the *wind* carried
away the light chaff, and the heavier corn fell onto the thresh-
ing floor. It was nonsensical to *winnow* in a changing *wind*
because it tended to blow the chaff back again. Thus it is
nonsensical to change opinions with every pressure put upon
you. As verse 10 and the Greek addition quoted in the footnote
('this is the mark of duplicity') show, the author is encouraging his readers to take time to think out his own position
and then *Stand firmly* by it. Better to wait and keep your self-
respect than to say quickly what other people want you to
say (verses 12–13).

14. In what sense does the *gossip...lay traps with* his
tongue? By posing as a friend and encouraging others to talk
freely, and then telling unpleasant stories about them. The
gossip features in many old proverbs, and everyone knows
people with whom you have to be careful what you say.

15. *Avoid the little faults as well as the great:* the Greek means
literally 'do not be ignorant in great or small matters', that
is, in all *faults*. The Hebrew and Syriac ('do not act wrongly')
make better sense. With the help of the Hebrew the N.E.B.
has produced a clear and relevant paraphrase which is not
very close to the Greek. ✻

ON BLIND PASSION

2 Never be roused by violent passions;
   they will tear you apart like a bull,[a]
3 they will eat up your leaves, destroy your fruit,
   and leave you a withered tree.
4 Evil passion ruins the man who harbours it,
   to the delight of his gloating enemies.

[a] they. . .bull: *probable meaning; Gk. and Heb. both obscure.*

✳ Remarks on *violent passions* link the opportunism condemned in the previous passage with the advice on friendship to follow in verses 5–17. The meaning of verse 2 is doubtful, but the reference to the *bull* seems certain: just as an enraged *bull* blindly destroys anything near him, so a sudden, blind bad temper can destroy all one's trustworthiness. The author then changes his image from the blindness of passion to its heat which scorches one's whole life like the sun in the height of a Palestinian summer scorching the vegetation. ✳

ON TRUE FRIENDSHIP

Pleasant words win many friends,   5
and an affable manner makes acquaintance easy.

Accept a greeting from everyone,   6
but advice from only one in a thousand.

When you make a friend, begin by testing him,   7
and be in no hurry to trust him.

Some friends are loyal when it suits them   8
but desert you in time of trouble.

Some friends turn into enemies   9
and shame you by making the quarrel public.

Another sits at your table,   10
but is nowhere to be found in time of trouble;

when you are prosperous, he will be your second self   11
and make free with your servants,

but if you come down in the world, he will turn against 12
     you
and you will not see him again.

Hold your enemies at a distance,   13
and keep a wary eye on your friends.

A faithful friend is a secure shelter;   14
whoever finds one has found a treasure.

35

15 A faithful friend is beyond price;
    his worth is more than money can buy.
16 A faithful friend is an elixir of life,
    found only by those who fear the Lord.
17 The man who fears the Lord keeps his friendships in
        repair,
    for he treats his neighbour as himself.

* Ben Sira presents no doctrine of friendship, but from practical experience of life deduces that trustworthiness is the most important thing in a friend. Like many earlier Egyptian teachers he advises the testing of friends, believing true friends hard to find, but lifts the quality of trustworthiness to a new level by stating that true friendship arises only from one's faithful relationship with God (verses 16–17). His advice on friendship was valued highly by later Jewish teachers, for verse 6 is quoted twice in the Talmud and verses 6–8 by Saadia Gaon, a Jewish teacher of the ninth or tenth century A.D.

A general proverb, 'Pleasant words win many friends' (verse 5), introduces a discussion of the problems in choosing friends. Negative advice (verses 6–13) again precedes positive (verses 14–17), and the section again concludes by relating the problem to basic religious attitudes.

9. Some feel that true *friends* should always agree on everything. True friendship consists rather in respecting the other's different opinion and not letting him down in public, maintaining the bond of trust.

11–12 enlarge on the meaning of verse 10, that some are friends when receiving hospitality but never stand by to help. As the Babylonian Talmud remarks: 'At the door of the rich all are friends; at the door of the poor there are none' (*Shabbath* 32a).

16. An *elixir of life* is 'a liquor supposed to have the power of indefinitely prolonging life', according to the dictionary.

The Greek uses the word for 'medicine', and probably meant no more than 'restorative medicine'. It is likely, however, that the translator misread the Hebrew *tserōr ḥayyīm* ('bundle of life') for *tsorī ḥayyīm* ('medicine of life'). *tserōr ḥayyīm* is used in 1 Sam. 25: 29 as an image expressing God's care for those whom he loves. Just as the tramp in a fairy tale puts all his possessions in a bag and looks after it with the greatest care, so God is pictured as treasuring the lives of his chosen ones. So in 1 Sam. 25: 29 David is told, 'the LORD your God will wrap your life up and put it with his own treasure, but the lives of your enemies he will hurl away like stones from a sling'. The Hebrew here probably uses the phrase to denote a most precious possession *found only by those who fear the Lord.* *

THE SEARCH FOR WISDOM

My son, seek wisdom's discipline while you are young,   18
and when your hair is white, you will find her still.
Come to her like a farmer ploughing and sowing;   19
then wait for her plentiful harvest.
If you cultivate her, you will labour for a little while,
but soon you will be eating her crops.
How harsh she seems to the undisciplined!   20
The fool cannot abide her;
like a stone she is a burden that tests his strength,   21
but he is quick to toss her aside.
Wisdom well deserves her name,   22
for she is not accessible to many.

Listen, my son, accept my judgement;   23
do not reject my advice.
Put your feet in wisdom's fetters   24
and your neck into her collar.

25 Stoop to carry her on your shoulders
and do not chafe at her bonds.

26 Come to her whole-heartedly,
and keep to her ways with all your might.

27 Follow her track, and she will make herself known to
you;
once you have grasped her, never let her go.

28 In the end you will find the relief she offers;
she will transform herself into joy for you.

29 Her fetters will become your strong defence
and her collar a gorgeous robe.

30 Her yoke[a] is a golden ornament
and her bonds a purple cord.

31 You shall put her on like a gorgeous robe
and wear her like a splendid crown.

32 If it is your wish, my son, you can be trained;
if you give your mind to it, you can become clever;

33 if you enjoy listening, you will learn;
if you are attentive, you will grow wise.

34 When you stand among your elders,
decide who is wise and join him.

35 Listen gladly to every godly argument
and see that no wise proverb escapes you.

36 If you discover a wise man, rise early to visit him;
let your feet wear out his doorstep.

37 Ponder the decrees of the Lord
and study his commandments at all times.
He will strengthen your mind
and grant your desire for wisdom.

[a] *So Heb.; Gk.* Upon her.

✶ The section 6: 18–37 takes up in greater detail the disciplined training and subsequent reward in studying wisdom already mentioned in 2: 1–6 and 4: 17–19. Verses 18–22 stress the need for seemingly unrewarding perseverance and hard work; verses 23–31 then show how the seeker is suddenly rewarded with understanding after a period of hard work; verses 32–7 give directions to encourage the eager student. The section ends in verse 37 with a reminder of God's strength to assist.

19. *Come to her like a farmer:* wisdom is viewed as a plot of productive land which requires much hard work before results appear. As in agriculture such disciplined labour may be a 'torment' (4: 17) at first to the student of wisdom, but he will win through to satisfying results in the end as surely as the *farmer.*

20–1. By *fool* is meant one who cannot see beneath the surface of things, who does not look beyond the passing moment and therefore gives no thought to the future. He drops *a* large *stone* because it is heavy, without remembering his purpose in carrying it.

22. It is not clear why wisdom *deserves her name.* Two explanations have been suggested. Some have thought that, as in the ancient world names were thought to express the inner nature of a person, so the author is referring to the hidden essence of wisdom which, by its very nature, is not for the majority and has to be sought out. But none of the Hebrew words for 'wisdom' or 'training' mean 'hidden'. More probably some kind of play on words is intended – perhaps *mūsār* ('discipline, training') and *mōsēr* ('bond, halter'), thus providing a link with the 'fetters' of verse 24. But such a pun is not very apparent in the Hebrew – let alone the Greek translation.

23–31. The change from wearisome labour to joy, forecast in 4: 18, is here illustrated by the balance of metaphors in verses 24–5 and 29–31: the *fetters, collar* and *bonds* of servitude are transformed into defensive armour, *a gorgeous*

39

robe and ornaments, and wisdom, instead of weighing heavily on the student's shoulder as a burden, becomes *a splendid crown* on his head. The figure of putting on a yoke is used of discipleship to the law in the Mishnah (*Aboth* 3: 5) and to Jesus in the New Testament (Matt. 11: 28–30, which may imitate this passage and 51: 25–6).

30–1. The metaphors not only balance those of verses 24–5 but also have symbolic significance, linking discipleship of wisdom with study of the law. The *purple cord* here translates the same words as 'violet thread' in Num. 15: 38–9 where the phrase refers to the command to the Hebrews to bind a 'violet thread' in the tassels of their garments so that 'whenever you see this in the tassel, you shall remember all the LORD's commands and obey them'. For the link between wisdom and the law, see further 19: 20 and 24: 25.

'Upon her' (footnote): the translator has misread the Hebrew *'ullāh* ('her yoke') for *'āleyhā* ('upon her') through similarity of consonants.

32–7. As such learning was for the few, students of wisdom and the law became a professional class as described in 39: 1–11. Various ways of learning are outlined in verses 34–7, the most important – study of the law – coming last. Further advice to students is given in 9: 14–16.

34. In the Near East proverbs had always been handed down in the open air where the *elders* met together, often in the open space near the town gate; these are the places where wisdom raises her voice, as in Prov. 1: 20–1. Ben Sira takes over much of the traditional language, but nevertheless encourages pupils to go to the houses of particular teachers who they feel are helpful (*decide who is wise and join him*). Thus later different schools grew up under the leadership of famous rival rabbis such as Hillel and Shammai (about 30 B.C. – A.D. 10). ✳

MANY WARNINGS IN MORAL AND SOCIAL LIFE

Do no evil, and evil will not come upon you;   **7**
turn away from wrong, and it will avoid you.   2
Do not sow in the furrows of injustice,   3
for fear of reaping a sevenfold crop.

Do not ask the Lord for high office   4
or the king for preferment.
Do not pose as a righteous man before the Lord   5
or play the sage in the king's presence.
Do not aspire to be a judge,   6
unless you have the strength to put an end to injustice;
for you may be intimidated by a man of rank
and so compromise your integrity.
Do not commit an offence against the community   7
and so incur a public disgrace.

Do not pile sin upon sin,   8
for even one is enough to make you guilty.
Do not say, 'My liberality will be taken into account;   9
when I make an offering to God Most High he will
      accept it.'
Do not grow weary of praying   10
or neglect the giving of charity.
Never laugh at a man in his bitter humiliation,   11
for there is One who both humbles and exalts.
Do not plot to deceive your brother   12
or pay back a friend in his own coin.
Refuse ever to tell a lie;   13
it is a habit from which no good comes.

14 Never be garrulous among your elders
   or repeat yourself when you pray.
15 Do not resent manual labour or farm-work,
   for it was ordained by the Most High.
16 Do not enlist in the ranks of sinners;
   remember that retribution will not delay.
17 Humble yourself to the uttermost,
   for the doom of the impious is fire and worms.

✻ Between 7: 1 and 10: 3 come many small collections of sayings on various types of human relationship. The connections between them are sometimes extremely loose. No less than thirty-nine sayings begin with 'Do not...', twelve of these being in 7: 1–17; it seems therefore more suitable to begin the new section at 7: 1 rather than at 7: 4 with the N.E.B. The first section begins with a general statement giving the trend of the whole section like 4: 20. Verse 1 seems ordinary enough, but it was quoted many times in later Jewish literature.

3. Metaphors from sowing and *reaping* are used to express good results and to contrast good and bad results.

4–6. These verses express the need to know one's own capabilities and the honesty to acknowledge one's limitations rather than to pretend to be clever – similar thoughts to those in 10: 26–8. Likewise *strength* of character is an important qualification for *a judge*: the rich and influential would often try to bribe him and tempt him to *compromise* his *integrity*. For similar thoughts see 4: 7–9.

8–10. As in 5: 4–7 Ben Sira attacks repeated sin and the temptation to try and compensate by making a religious *offering* (see also 34: 19–26). Verse 10 follows as a warning not to let one's faith fail and to keep *the giving of charity* closely connected with prayer.

11. *a man in his bitter humiliation:* before laughing at such a person, remember that God is in control and the last laugh may be on you!

14. If thoughtless speech to other men is to be avoided, how much more to God in prayer! Length of recited prayer does not count for sincerity.

15. Judaism had a high respect for *manual* work; *it was ordained by* God, according to Gen. 2: 15, that man should work the garden of Eden even before he went wrong. The Mishnah states that study of the law should always be mixed with worldly occupation and that study of the law without worldly labour 'brings sin in its train' (*Aboth* 2: 2). Paul, the early Christian missionary who had been brought up as a Pharisee, earned his living by making tents (Acts 18: 3). The Babylonian Talmud remarks that every man was to teach his son some handicraft by which to earn his living (*Kiddushin* 99 b).

17. *Humble yourself to the uttermost, for the doom of the impious is fire and worms:* humility as a way of turning aside God's retribution was a sufficiently noteworthy idea for the original Hebrew of this verse to be quoted in the Mishnah: 'Be exceedingly lowly of spirit, for the hope of man is but the worm' (*Aboth* 4: 4). The worm is used elsewhere to express man's mortal nature and the decay of his body in the grave (10: 11; 19: 3; Job 25: 6) – quite consistent with Ben Sira's belief in the finality of death. The addition of *fire* in the Greek translation shows how Jewish ideas on life after death had changed between Ben Sira's time and that of his grandson. Partly due to the experience of persecution many Jews had begun to believe in a judgement for all, live and dead, at some future time, preceded by fire – an idea probably taken over from Persian religion in the last two centuries B.C. ✴

ON CORRECT ATTITUDES WITHIN THE HOUSEHOLD

Do not part with a friend for gain,[a]   18
or a true brother for all the gold of Ophir.
Do not lose the chance of a wise and good wife,   19

[a] *Probable reading (compare 27: 1), supported by Vss.; Gk. for a trifle.*

for her attractions are worth more than gold.

20 Do not ill-treat a slave who works honestly
   or a hired servant whose heart is in his work.

21 Love a good slave from the bottom of your heart
   and do not grudge him his freedom.

22 Have you cattle? Take care of them,
   and if they bring you profit, keep them.

23 Have you sons? Discipline them
   and break them in from their earliest years.

24 Have you daughters? See that they are chaste,
   and do not be too lenient with them.

25 Marry your daughter, and a great load will be off your
      hands;
   but give her to a sensible husband.

26 If you have a wife after your own heart, do not divorce
      her;
   but do not trust yourself to one you cannot love.

27 Honour your father with all your heart
   and do not forget your mother's birth-pangs;

28 remember that your parents brought you into the world;
   how can you repay what they have done for you?

✻ This selection of proverbs deals with relationships with
friends (verse 18), wife (verses 19 and 26), slaves (verses 20–1),
cattle (verse 22), children (verses 23–5) and parents (verses
27–8). Some of these groups are given more attention elsewhere (friends in 6: 5–17 and 22: 19–26, wives in 26: 13–18
sons in 30: 1–13 and daughters in 26: 10–12 and 42: 9–14).
They are brought together here under a developing theme;
discussion of the value of different members of the household
leads on in verse 23 to advice on how to treat them.

18. *gain:* the N.E.B. translation assumes that in the copying
of the Greek manuscripts one letter was accidentally added:

44

instead of the correct *diaphorou* ('profit, gain' as in 27: 1) the copyist wrote *adiaphorou* ('something paltry, a trifle').

20–1. At a time when different social classes were moving further apart, Ben Sira condemned all looking down on the poor and slaves; everyone was a person in his own right, and it was his character that mattered, as shown further in 10: 19–25. *do not grudge him his freedom:* Ben Sira here commends sincere implementation of the law in Deut. 15: 12 where a fellow-Hebrew slave was to be set free in the seventh year and given lavish gifts. It is possible that he here envisages an extension of the law to non-Jews as well.

23–5. Elsewhere Ben Sira advises fathers to 'whip' their sons 'often' (30: 1) and to 'Keep close watch' on daughters (26: 10, repeated in 42: 11); the emphasis on strict discipline seems overdone to us.

26. In Judaism divorce was the decision of the husband and, as it was simply accomplished by writing a bill of divorce (almost at whim), the only safeguard the wife had was responsible behaviour on the part of her husband, who should think carefully before he contracts either marriage or divorce.

27–8 recall the author's remarks on respect for parents in 3: 1–16. ✻

ON RELIGIOUS DUTIES

Fear the Lord with all your heart   29
and reverence his priests.
Love your Maker with all your might   30
and do not leave his ministers without support.
Fear the Lord and honour the priest   31
and give him his dues, as you have been commanded,
the firstfruits, the guilt-offering, and the shoulder of the
        victim,
the dedication sacrifice, and the firstfruits of holy things.

32 Be open-handed also with the poor,
   so that your own well-being may be complete.

33 Every living man appreciates generosity;
   do not withhold your kindness even when a man is dead.

34 Do not turn your back on those who weep,
   but mourn with those who mourn.

35 Do not hesitate to visit the sick,
   for by such visits you will win their affection.

36 Whatever you are doing, remember the end that awaits
      you;
   then all your life you will never go wrong.

⁂ This section is concerned with religious duties – some
liturgical (supporting priests and making temple offerings),
others in family life. The latter were no less religious in nature,
in that generosity to the poor, mourning with the bereaved
and visiting the sick are all viewed today by orthodox Jews
as following God's revealed will and therefore as religious
as any synagogue service. All these actions were expressions
of the true, personal fear of God referred to in 1: 11 – 2: 6.

31. Ben Sira had a strong interest in the priesthood and the
temple ritual, as shown by the attention given in his historical
survey (chs. 44–50) to Aaron (45: 6–22) as compared with
Moses (45: 1–5). Priests were forbidden in the law to possess
any land (Num. 18: 20); other means of maintenance were
devised to coincide with the offerings brought by the people.
Certain offerings were mainly for the priests as, for example,
the grain offering (Lev. 6: 14–18) here called, probably wrongly, *the dedication sacrifice*. The first grain and fruit to be harvested
(Num. 18: 11–13) was given to the priests, and also the shoulders of bulls and sheep offered, together with the cheeks and
stomach (Deut. 18: 3). But the Hebrew and Greek texts differ
over the specific offerings mentioned here, and *the guilt-
offering* seems not to have been given to the priests (Lev. 5: 6).

It is likely that Ben Sira was referring to maintenance of priests in a general way, using technical terms imprecisely, without much reference to current practice. The cost of maintaining the clergy was certainly very heavy on devout Jews, as we see from the diligent activity of Tobit described in Tobit 1: 6–8. When the public grew lax, the priests suffered as in Nehemiah's time in the fifth century B.C., but by the second century the priests had become quite wealthy.

33–4. *kindness even when a man is dead:* such generous *kindness* is likely to be more than decent burial and lamentation and to include *generosity* to the mourners and friends of the dead man. Ben Sira expands on mourning for the dead in 22: 11–12.

36. *remember the end that awaits you:* the section finishes with a challenge. Although Ben Sira did not believe in life after death, he thought the last moment of life very important, as he explains in 11: 26–8. Again the Greek translation, written when belief in life after death was more widespread, emphasizes *the end that awaits* man more than the Hebrew. *

WARNINGS AGAINST WRONG ATTITUDES
TO OTHERS

Do not pit yourself against a great man,   **8**
for fear of falling into his power.
Do not quarrel with a rich man;   2
you may be sure he will outbid you.
For money has been the ruin of many
and has misled the minds of kings.
Do not argue with a long-winded man,   3
and so add fuel to his fire.
Never make fun of an ill-mannered man,   4
or you may hear your ancestors insulted.
Do not rebuke a man who is already penitent;   5

remember that we are all guilty.

6 Despise no man for being old;
some of us are growing old as well.

7 Do not be smug over another man's death;
remember that we must all die.

8 Do not neglect the studies of the learned,
but apply yourself to their maxims;
from these you will learn discipline,
and how to be the servant of princes.

9 Do not ignore the discourse of your elders,
for they themselves learned from their fathers;
they can teach you to understand
and to have an answer ready in time of need.

10 Do not kindle a sinner's coals,
for fear of being burnt in the flames of his fire.

11 Do not let a man's insolence bring you to your feet;
he will only sit waiting to trap you with your own words.

12 Do not lend to a man with more influence than yourself,
or, if you do, write off the loan as a loss.

13 Do not stand surety beyond your means,
and, when you do stand surety, be prepared to pay.

14 Do not go to law with a judge,
for in deference to his position they will give him the
verdict.

15 Do not go travelling with a reckless man:
you may find him a burden on you.
He will do as he fancies,
and his folly will bring death on you as well.

Do not fall out with a hot-tempered man　　16
or walk with him in unfrequented places;
he thinks nothing of bloodshed,
and where no help is at hand he will set upon you.

Never discuss your plans with a fool,　　17
for he cannot keep a secret.

Do nothing private in the presence of a stranger;　　18
you do not know what use he will make of it.

Do not tell what is in your mind to all comers　　19
or accept favours from them.

---

* Apart from verses 8 and 9 ch. 8 contains further warnings against foolish action of various kinds: mistaken attitudes to other people (verses 1–7), too eager readiness to fall in with other people's suggestions (verses 10–13) and unwise trust of others (verses 14–19). Verses 8 and 9 more positively give guidance how to learn wisdom through study of tradition.

1–2. Both Hebrew and Greek use a legal term in verse 1 – *Do not pit yourself against* is more literally 'Do not litigate against...' The setting is Palestine of the third century B.C. where the power of influence and money was growing.

5. To think of strict Jews as continually reproving with no sympathetic understanding is quite wrong. Ben Sira is here in line with later Pharisaism; as the Mishnah states, 'if a man has repented they may not say to him, "remember thy former deeds"' (*Baba Metzia* 4: 10).

8–9. Candidates for the Egyptian civil service under the Pharaohs had been trained in 'wisdom' schools for centuries, reared in the study of manners and relationships such as are contained in many Egyptian collections of proverbs and Ben Sira's own manual. We need only compare Ben Sira's own description of the ideal wise man in 39: 1–11. Before manuals of proverbs and traditions were written down they would have been handed on by word of mouth for a very long time.

12–13. The author deals with lending and standing *surety* (i.e. giving guarantees for people) again in 29: 1–20 where it is discussed in greater detail.

14–19. Before you start dealings with anyone, consider his character and the likely end result. Juries may be prejudiced and give verdicts in favour of a man as powerful as *a judge*; *a hot-tempered man* is unpredictable, and *a stranger* is unreliable because you do not know him well enough to forecast what he will do. ✻

ON DANGEROUS WOMEN

9 Do not be jealous over the wife you cherish,
and so put into her head the idea of wronging you.

2 Do not surrender yourself to a woman
and let her trample down your strength.

3 Do not go near a loose woman,
for fear of falling into her snares.

4 Do not keep company with a dancing-girl,
or you may be caught by her tricks.

5 Do not let your mind dwell on a virgin,
or you may be trapped into paying damages for her.

6 Never surrender yourself to prostitutes,
for fear of losing all you possess,

7 nor gaze about you in the city streets
or saunter in deserted corners.

8 Do not let your eye linger on a woman's figure
or your thoughts dwell on beauty not yours to possess.
Many have been seduced by the beauty of a woman,
which kindles passion like fire.

9 Never sit at table with another man's wife
or join her in a drinking party,
for fear of succumbing to her charms
and slipping into fatal disaster.

* Warnings against the wiles of unscrupulous women were frequent in Egyptian and Israelite proverbs as, for example, in Prov. 6: 24–6. Later rabbis became almost neurotic about this, and condemned all excitement of lustful thoughts through the senses: they even said that no man should walk behind a woman, even his own wife! The Babylonian Talmud twice quotes parts of verses 3, 8 and 9 in support of such views. More guidance on dangerous women, contrasted with faithful wives, is found in 25: 13 – 26: 27.

3–7. *loose* women and dancing-girls in wealthy houses often sought to exploit the rich, who could find such associations very expensive. If a man raped *a virgin* he was liable for *damages* as assessed by the law (Deut. 22: 28–9, where he is required to pay fifty pieces of silver to the girl's father and marry her). To *saunter in* lonely places and to *gaze about* the *streets* could be interpreted as looking for *prostitutes*, who would take advantage.

9. *fatal disaster* refers to capital punishment prescribed by the law for adulterers in Lev. 20: 10. How far such severe punishments were carried out in Ben Sira's day is uncertain. Certainly by the time of the writing of the Mishnah humanitarianism had caused the rabbis to hedge capital penalties around with so many safeguards that it must have been impossible to reach the point where they were carried out. One has the feeling it was largely theoretical, but had to be treated seriously because it was in the written law. *

ON OTHER MEN AND POLITICIANS

Do not desert an old friend;   10
a new one is not worth as much.
A new friend is like new wine;
you do not enjoy drinking it until it has matured.
Do not envy a bad man his success;   11
you do not know what fate is in store for him.

12 Take no pleasure in the pleasures of the wicked;
   remember that they will not go scot-free all their lives.
13 Keep clear of a man who has power to kill,
   and you will not be haunted by the fear of death.
   If you do approach him, make no false step
   or you will risk losing your life.
   Tell yourself that you are making your way among pitfalls,
   or walking on the battlements of the city.
14 Take the measure of your neighbours as best you can,
   and accept advice from those who are wise.
15 Let your discussion be with intelligent men
   and all your talk about the law of the Most High.
16 Choose the company of good men at table,
   and take pride in fearing the Lord.

17 A craftsman is recognized by his skilful hand
   and a councillor by his words of wisdom.
18 A gossip is the terror of his town,
   detested for his unguarded talk.
10 A wise ruler trains his people,
   and gives them sound and orderly government.
2 Like ruler, like ministers;
   like sovereign, like subjects;
3 a king untutored is the people's ruin,
   but wise rulers make a city fit to live in.

✻ From women Ben Sira turns to men and later (verses 13
and 17 onwards) to politicians. This section illustrates the
difficulties of dividing this book into sections. 9: 17 – 10: 3
is clearly concerned with government, but so are 10: 4–5, and
the 'man who has power to kill' (9: 13) is probably a ruler.
Different translators and commentators divide differently,

usually taking 10: 1–5 as a section on government. The N.E.B.
prefers to separate 9: 17 – 10: 3 from 10: 4–5 which are
taken as a link passage introducing the second major division
of the book.

10. Comparing old, mature *wine* which you can trust with
new acid *wine* with its tendency to burst skins is traditional
proverbial material, used elsewhere in Luke 5: 37–9.

13. *a man who has power to kill:* probably a reference to
dictators, again a traditional theme appearing in Prov. 16: 14.
As shown by 10: 1–3 Ben Sira believed in an honourable
ruler, well trained in wisdom, who would base his power on
intelligent exercise of justice rather than on bloodshed. As
noted in 10: 2, the type of leader determines the type of
cabinet and government.

14. The author again stresses the importance of testing
acquaintances, as in 6: 7, 34.

15–16 are parallel verses: *fearing the Lord* is thus the equiva-
lent of following *the law of the Most High* as in 21: 11. *at table:*
wise men handed on teaching in conversation over meals as
well as in gatherings in the open air (see 6: 34).

17–18. The politician accomplishes with *words* what the
craftsman accomplishes with his hands. In both cases lack of
control spoils the result, although this is not immediately
obvious with words. ✲

Man's life under divine providence

AGAINST HUMAN PRIDE

THE GOVERNMENT of the world is in the hand of 4
the Lord;
at the right time he appoints the right man to rule it.
In the Lord's hand is all human success;   5
it is he who confers honour on the legislator.

6 Do not nurse a grievance against your neighbour for every
      offence,
   and do not resort to acts of insolence.
7 Arrogance is hateful to God and man,
   and injustice is offensive to both.
8 Empire passes from nation to nation
   because of injustice, insolence, and greed.
9 What has man to be so proud of? He is only dust and ashes,
   subject even in life to bodily decay.[a]
10 A long illness mocks the doctor's skill;
   today's king is tomorrow's corpse.
11 When a man dies, he comes into an inheritance
   of maggots and vermin and worms.
12 The origin of pride is to forsake the Lord,
   man's heart revolting against his Maker;
13 as its origin is sin,
   so persistence in it brings on a deluge of depravity.
   Therefore the Lord sends upon them signal punishments
   and brings them to utter disaster.

14 The Lord overturns the thrones of princes
   and enthrones the gentle in their place.
15 The Lord pulls up nations by the roots
   and plants the humble instead.
16 The Lord lays waste the territory of nations,
   destroying them to the very foundations of the earth.
17 Some he shrivels away to nothing,
   so that all memory of them vanishes from the earth.
18 Pride was not the Creator's design for man
   nor violent anger for those born of woman.

   [a] subject...decay: *probable meaning, based on Heb.; Gk. obscure.*

* According to the N.E.B.'s division the author turns from the first part of the book (1: 1 – 10: 3 – mainly on personal behaviour and the search for wisdom) to the second part (10: 4 – 18: 29 – dealing mainly with man's community life). The first two verses (verses 4 and 5) state generally that all man's community life is regulated ultimately by God. Ben Sira then condemns arrogance in verses 6–13: one's own feelings of pride and resentment are to be resisted in public life, and one should fulfil one's task in humility.

6. For *insolence* the Greek uses *hybris*, often translated 'overweening pride', and used frequently by the Greek tragedians, Aeschylus, Sophocles and Euripides, who often demonstrated in their plays how disaster fell on men who overreached themselves, for example in *King Oedipus* by Sophocles.

8. *Empire passes from nation to nation:* some see here a reference to the transfer of Judaean sovereignty from Ptolemy V of Egypt to Antiochus III of Syria after the battle of Panium in 198 B.C. But Ben Sira nowhere refers to precise events of his time. As bloodbaths between contenders for thrones were frequent in ancient near eastern empires on the death of a ruler, Ben Sira's reference is more probably quite general.

9–11. *subject even in life to bodily decay:* the N.E.B. follows the Hebrew as noted in the footnote, but very discreetly. The Hebrew ('his guts are full of worms') may refer to some disease involving *worms* internally or, less probably, figuratively to spiritual corruption through the practice of violence. *A long illness mocks the doctor's skill* (verse 10): the Greek manuscripts have *doctor* as subject: 'the doctor makes light of the disease' as trifling, but next day the patient is nevertheless dead. The N.E.B. follows the common change, and takes *doctor* as object; the *illness mocks the doctor's* attempts to heal it, even though the patient be a *king*. The *maggots, vermin* (so the Hebrew; the Greek has 'wild beasts') *and worms* of verse 11 refer to corruption after death.

12–13. *The origin of pride:* the Greek word *archē* means more than *origin* as here translated. It is used in 1: 14 for 'essence'. Thus, just as 'the essence of wisdom is the fear of the Lord', so the essence of pride *is to forsake the Lord*, and *persistence* in *pride* escalates *depravity*.

14–17 contain examples of some of the 'signal punishments' (verse 13) which God brings upon the proud.

17. As Ben Sira did not believe in life after death, the only immortality possible lay in the *memory* of one's family or nation. For the *memory* of a person to vanish meant therefore complete extinction, as implied in 44: 8–9. ✳

THE HIGHEST HONOUR IS THE FEAR OF THE LORD

19 What creature is worthy of honour? Man.
   What men? Those who fear the Lord.
   What creature is worthy of contempt? Man.
   What men? Those who break the commandments.
20 As the members of the family honour their head,
   so the Lord honours those who fear him.[a]
22 The rich, the famous, and the poor—
   their only boast is the fear of the Lord.
23 It is unjust to despise a poor man who is intelligent,
   and wrong to honour a man who is a sinner.
24 The prince, the judge, and the ruler win high honours,
   but none of them is as great as the godfearing man.
25 The wise slave will have free men to wait on him,
   and a man of sense will not grumble at it.

✳ Man is to be honoured by his wisdom and fear of God rather than his station in life; religious and moral character is more important than social conventions and the power

[a] *Some witnesses add* (21) Fear the Lord, and you will be accepted; be obstinate and proud, and you will be rejected.

money brings. Later rabbis here agreed with Ben Sira. The section starts in verse 19 with a characteristically Jewish catechetical form such as children might recite in the synagogue school. This general statement is then illustrated by various comparisons. In verses 22, 24 and 25 various social classes are mentioned to show how 'the god-fearing man' is to be preferred above all.

20. *As the members of the family. . . so the Lord. . .*: a strange comparison, as one expects *the Lord* to be praised as *head* of all. But the point here is not the Lord's greatness, but the link between honour and loyal love.

21 (in the footnote) was included in some manuscripts and contains some later Greek theological terms. It was probably added later as a theological comment. ✻

ON BEING YOURSELF AND NOT PRETENDING

Do not be too clever to do a day's work	26
or boast when you have nothing to live on.	
It is better to work and have more than enough	27
than to boast and go hungry.	
My son, in all modesty, keep your self-respect	28
and value yourself at your true worth.	
Who will speak up for a man who is his own enemy,	29
or respect one who disparages himself?	
A poor man may be honoured for his wisdom,	30
a rich man for his wealth;	
if a man is honoured in poverty, how much more in wealth!	31
And if he is despised in wealth, how much more in poverty!	
A poor man with wisdom can hold his head high	**11**
and take his seat among the great.	

2 Do not overrate one man for his good looks
  or be repelled by another man's appearance.
3 The bee is small among winged creatures,
  yet her produce takes first place for sweetness.
4 Do not pride yourself on your fine clothes
  or be haughty when honours come to you;
  for the Lord can perform marvels
  which are hidden from the eyes of men.
5 Many kings have been reduced to sitting on the ground,
  while a mere nobody has worn the crown.
6 Many rulers have been stripped of their honours,
  and great men have found themselves at the mercy of
      others.

✶ If to be godfearing brings the greatest honour, and social
class does not matter before God, it is foolish to pretend to be
what you are not. Do not pretend to be 'too clever' for
manual 'work' 'when you have nothing to live on' (verses
26–7 – a motto for unemployed university graduates?). The
rabbis thought it important not to despise work; see the note
on 7: 15. It sounds well that you must 'value yourself at your
true worth' (verse 28), but Ben Sira does not explain how you
assess this – a considerable problem – except for warnings
against excessive self-depreciation in verse 29.

30–1. The respect given to many later rabbis illustrates this
verse. Riches increase respect for the wise, *poverty* increases
the scandal of fools.

11: 2–3. The author now condemns all who judge by
appearances, using *The bee* as an illustration. The same likeness is drawn in Egyptian wisdom books but not in the Old
Testament book of Proverbs.

4–5. The *marvels* to be performed refer to sudden reversal of
fortune, seen as judgement for boasting in prosperity. Verse 5
is then added as an example of such reversal of fortune. ✶

SOME PRACTICAL ADVICE

Do not find fault before examining the evidence;   7
think first, and criticize afterwards.
Do not answer without first listening,   8
and do not interrupt when another is speaking.
Never take sides in a quarrel not your own   9
or become involved in the disputes of rascals.

* Some practical hints are now added to help people avoid
finding 'themselves at the mercy of others' (verse 6). Such
encouragement to caution is frequently given in proverbial
sayings, and one of the marks of a wise man described in
Aboth 5: 7 is that he 'does not break in on the words of his
fellow'. *

ON ATTITUDES TO WORK AND FINANCIAL
PROSPERITY

My son, do not engage in too many transactions;   10
if you attempt too much, you will come to
     grief.
When you are in pursuit, you will not overtake;
when you are in flight, you will not escape.
One man slaves and strains and hurries   11
and is all the farther behind.
Another is slow-witted and in need of help,   12
lacking in strength and abounding in poverty;
but the Lord turns a kindly eye upon him
and lifts him up out of his miserable plight.
He raises him to dignity   13
to the amazement of all.

14 Good fortune and bad, life and death,
   poverty and wealth, all come from the Lord.[a]

17 His gifts to the devout are lasting;
   his approval brings unending success.

18 A man may grow rich by stinting and sparing,
   but what does he get for his pains?

19 When he says, 'I have earned my rest,
   now I can live on my savings',
   he does not know how long it will be
   before he must die and leave his wealth to others.

20 Stand by your contract and give your mind to it;
   grow old at your work.

21 Do not envy a rogue his success;
   trust the Lord and stick to your job.
   It is no difficult thing for the Lord
   to make a poor man rich in a moment.

22 The Lord's blessing is the reward of piety,
   which blossoms in one short hour.

23 Do not say, 'What use am I?
   What good[b] can the future hold for me?'

24 And do not say, 'I am independent;
   nothing can ever go wrong for me.'

25 Hardship is forgotten in time of success,
   and success in time of hardship.

26 Even on the day a man dies it is easy for the Lord
   to give him his deserts.

[a] *Some witnesses add* (15) From the Lord come wisdom, understanding,
and love, knowledge of the law, and the doing of good works. (16)
Error and darkness have been with sinners from their birth, and evil
grows old along with those who take delight in it.
[b] *Or* 'What more do I need? What greater success . . .

One hour's misery wipes out all memory of delight, 27
and a man's end reveals his true character.
Call no man happy before he dies, 28
for not until death is a man known for what he is.[a]

✻ Although the later rabbis required religious students to practise a trade they recognized that too much interest in business could push study of the law out. Rabbi Meir of the second century A.D. advised 'Engage not overmuch in business but occupy thyself with the Law' (*Aboth* 4: 10). In any case both prosperity and poverty are gifts of God rather than human achievements, and God can transform a man's circumstances suddenly. The correct attitude, as shown in verses 20–8, is to concentrate on the task you have committed yourself to. Whereas verses 10–19 emphasize the dangers of concentrating too much on the mercenary side of work, verses 20–8 stress conscientious application to one's work even if it isn't very profitable.

10. This advice is directed to poor people who try to improve their standard of living by aiming at quick success in business. They may become so entangled in shady *transactions* that they find that they can neither beat the other man nor withdraw. The phrase *you will come to grief* is an idiomatic translation; a literal translation of the Greek is: 'you will not be free of guilt' – in other words, you are bound to be involved in wrongdoing if you take on too many business interests.

11 illustrates the fate of the man who, unable to 'overtake' or 'escape' (verse 10), finds that, once involved, he slips *behind* in spite of all his efforts.

12–14. The authors of Job and Ecclesiastes also noticed that one man slipped behind all the time while another was suddenly raised to prosperity and dignity, and questioned the justice of God's control of human life. Ben Sira, however,

[a] not. . .he is: *so Heb.; Gk.* a man is known by his children.

does not give way to scepticism but rather wonders at the sudden and unforeseen nature of God's rewards. For all three the future is unpredictable, but, whereas for Ecclesiastes 'There is nothing better for a man to do than to eat and drink and enjoy himself in return for his labours' (Eccles. 2: 24), for Ben Sira the answer is to 'trust the Lord and stick to your job' (verse 21), for you never know either when you will receive sudden reward or when you will die. Ben Sira's answer to the problem is thus deeply religious.

15–16 (in the footnote) appear only in some Greek manuscripts – possibly to agree with the Hebrew text where they were probably added to complete the list of God's gifts (verse 15) and to give some account of the presence of evil in men (verse 16).

20. Older commentaries translated 'covenant' rather than *contract*, and interpreted it as commitment in the religious life. But the phrase probably refers to secular *work* and is typical of the practical advice often given in wisdom books.

22–3. The *one short hour* probably refers to the speed of the change of fortune rather than to the short time spent enjoying it. If *The Lord's blessing* can blossom *in one short hour*, then one must be hopeful and not complain gloomily that *the future* holds no *good* for you: this shows lack of faith. The alternative translation in the footnote duplicates verse 24, referring to feelings of self-sufficiency coming before a fall. The two verses are contrasted: verse 23 condemns the man who forgets the possibility of change for the *good*, verse 24 the man who forgets the possibility of change for the bad. Verse 25 then sums up this contrast.

26–8. These verses describe possible change of fortune at the time of *death* rather than retribution afterwards. Ben Sira believed that the circumstances of a person's death often revealed his true character, and verse 27 was quoted by Saadia Gaon, a Jewish teacher of the tenth century A.D. Final assessment of a man's character should not be made *until* after his *death* because circumstances can change so greatly. This is

commonly held, and is one of the main themes of tragedies
whether they be written by Aeschylus, Shakespeare or
Ibsen.

28. *not until death:* the Greek translator misunderstood the
Hebrew word *'aḥarītō* to mean 'his future descendants' rather
than 'his latter end' or his *death*. This is an easy mistake as
elsewhere Ben Sira suggests that the only immortality open to
man lies in the creation of children. ✲

ON INVITATIONS TO ONE'S HOME
AND GIFTS TO OTHERS

Do not invite all comers into your home;   29
dishonesty has many disguises.

A proud man's mind is like a decoy-partridge in its cage,   30
or like a spy watching for a false step.

He waits for a chance to twist good into evil   31
or to cast blame on innocent actions.

A small spark kindles many coals,   32
and the insinuations of a bad man end in bloodshed.

Beware of a scoundrel and his evil plots,   33
or he may ruin your reputation for ever.

Admit a stranger to your home and he will stir up trouble 34
     for you
and make you a stranger to your own flesh and blood.

If you do a good deed, make sure to whom you are doing **12**
     it;
then you will have credit for your kindness.

A good turn done to a godfearing man will be rewarded,   2
if not by him, then by the Most High.

No good comes to the persistent wrong-doer   3

or to the man who never gives alms;[a]
5 refuse him bread; give him nothing at all;
he will only use your gifts to get the better of you,
and you will suffer a double wrong
in return for the favours you have done him.
6 The Most High himself hates sinners
and sends bad men what they deserve.
7 Give to a good man, but never help a sinner;
keep your good works for the humble, not the insolent.[b]

☆ Uncertainty over the true character of a person (verse 28) leads Ben Sira to discuss inviting people into the intimacy of one's home (11: 29–34) and helping other people by gifts and good deeds (12: 1–7). Great caution is necessary to ensure that the person invited or helped is trustworthy as 'dishonesty has many disguises' (11: 29), and in both cases an unscrupulous person can take advantage of your kindness and do you harm.

30 refers to the practice of trapping birds by placing a bird and food in a *cage* constructed in such a way that a second bird can fly in for the food but cannot fly out again and is thus trapped. Jer. 5: 26–7 speaks of 'wicked men' who 'set deadly traps to catch men', and whose 'houses are full of fraud, as a cage is full of birds'. Drawn in by the thought of quick gain, a man cannot get himself out of dishonesty. The *decoy-partridge in its cage* does not fit the Ecclesiasticus passage as well; perhaps intimacy with *A proud man* is attractive to the poor who then find that they are tricked and their reputation is ruined (verse 33).

34. The section on invitations to one's *home* is concluded with a reference back to the original problem (verse 29),

[*a*] *The order of the following verses has been disturbed in all versions; Gk. reads* . . .gives alms; (4) give to a godfearing man, but never help a sinner; (5) keep your good works for the humble, not the insolent; refuse him. . . (*compare verse 7*).

[*b*] keep. . .insolent: *this is the beginning of verse 5 in Gk.*

just as the section on helping others starts and finishes with a
reference to doing a good deed (12: 1 and 12: 7).

12: 4–7. The order of verses differs in the ancient versions
(see footnote). The N.E.B. follows the order in the Hebrew
manuscript and places verse 4 and the first line of verse 5
after verse 6 as verse 7, where the two lines provide a general
summary to close the section verses 1–7. The *double wrong*
(verse 5) consists of the original wrong done by 'the persistent
wrong-doer' (verse 3) and also of the manipulation of the gift
by him to the hurt of the giver. Better to leave all giving to
such people in the hands of God who knows best *what* people
deserve. ✳

ON FRIENDS AND ENEMIES

Prosperity does not reveal your friends; 8
adversity does not conceal your enemies.
When all goes well a man's enemies are friendly,[a] 9
but in hard times even his friend will desert him.
Never trust your enemy; 10
he will turn vicious as sure as metal rusts.
If he appears humble and obsequious, 11
take care! Be on your guard against him!
Behave towards him like a man who polishes a mirror
to make sure that it does not corrode away.
Do not have him at your side, 12
or he will trip you up and supplant you.
Do not let him sit at your right hand,
or he will soon be wanting your own seat;
and in the end you will see the force of my words
and recall my warning with regret.
Who sympathizes with a snake-charmer when he is bitten, 13
or with a tamer of wild animals?

[a] *So Heb.; Gk.* grieve.

65

14 No more does anyone pity the man who keeps bad
    company
and involves himself in another's wickedness.
15 He may stand by you for a while,
but, if you falter, his friendship will not last.

16 An enemy has honey on his lips,
but in his heart he plans to trip you into the ditch.
He may have tears in his eyes,
but give him a chance and he will not stop at bloodshed.
17 If disaster overtakes you, you will find him there ahead
    of you,
ready, with a pretence of help, to pull your feet from
    under you.
18 Then he will nod his head and rub his hands
and spread gossip, showing his true colours.
13 Handle pitch and it will make you dirty;
keep company with an arrogant man and you will grow
    like him.

✻ This section gives more guidance on the handling of
personal relationships in traditional proverbial form and
language. Note the continual contrasts between good and
evil and between kind words and wicked thoughts, and the
metaphors drawn from everyday life: metal mirrors, snake-
charming and handling dirty substances ('pitch', 13: 1).

8–9. You cannot tell who *your friends* are when you are
prosperous because then even *your enemies* pose as friends.
Verse 9 makes this point if correctly translated (*When all goes
well a man's enemies are friendly*): the Greek translator has
misread the original Hebrew *rea*' 'friend' for *ra*' 'be sad' –
easily done, as the Hebrew text would have had the consonants
but no vowels marked.

10–11. Mirrors were made of metal, not glass, and, if not polished carefully and often, lost their shine and became rusty; constant care was necessary. The author means that constant care was necessary with enemies also to avoid the malice and danger behind the *humble and obsequious* face. But only extreme watchfulness is indicated here – to say that you must please your enemy and thus polish his malice away (butter him up!) pushes the likeness too far and anticipates verse 13.

12. The *right hand* place was the seat of honour.

13–14. To treat an enemy with undue favour to try and stop his wickedness is like charming a snake. An English proverb puts it: those who play with fire must expect to get burned!

15–16. Only while your prosperity lasts (see verse 8) will your enemy stand by you as a friend. When disaster comes he may pretend to be sympathetic but will in fact be plotting your ruin.

18. Nodding the *head* is often used in the Old Testament for mocking: in Ps. 22: 6–7 the author is 'scorned by the people' and 'All who see' him 'wag their heads'. But, as this context describes an enemy pretending to be friendly, nodding the *head* here may be intended as a sign of sympathy in contrast to the malicious *gossip* of the next line. ✳

ON MIXING WITH THE RICH

Do not lift a weight too heavy for you,   2
keeping company with a man greater and richer than
      yourself.
How can a jug be friends with a kettle?
If they knock together, the one will be smashed.
A rich man does wrong, and adds insult to injury;   3
a poor man is wronged, and must apologize into the
      bargain.

4 If you can serve his turn, a rich man will exploit you,
   but if you are in need, he will leave you alone.

5 If you are in funds, he will be your constant companion,
   and drain you dry without a twinge of remorse.

6 He may need you; and then he will deceive you,
   and will be all smiles and encouragement,
   paying you compliments and asking, 'What can I do for
        you?',

7 embarrassing you with his hospitality,
   until he has drained you two or three times over;
   but in the end he will laugh at you.
   Afterwards, when he sees you, he will pass you by,
   nodding his head over you.

* After discussing behaviour before possible enemies Ben
Sira turns to behaviour with other groups of society: rich
men (verses 2–7) and the aristocracy (verses 8–13); he then
describes his own views on the different levels of society
(verses 15–23). Some have seen in these verses echoes of
excessive social oppression in Palestine during the Greek-
dominated third century B.C. But serious oppression is a well-
worn theme in the proverbial literature of the ancient Near
East, and Ben Sira's language is full of traditional forms and
imagery, so that it is unnecessary to see contemporary conditions behind his words.

2–3. When two pots fall against each other, the more
fragile one – here the clay *jug* rather than the iron *kettle* –
breaks. So the *poor man* always comes off worse in a clash with
the *rich*, as verse 3 explains.

7. The rich man invites you to his home so many times that
you ruin yourself in returning *hospitality* as custom demands.
nodding his head here plainly indicates mocking. *

ON MIXING WITH THE ARISTOCRACY

Take care not to be led astray   8
and humiliated when you are enjoying yourself.
If a great man invites you, be slow to accept,   9
and he will be the more pressing in his invitation.
Do not be forward, for fear of a rebuff,   10
but do not keep aloof, or you may be forgotten.
Do not presume to converse with him as an equal   11
or be over-confident if he holds you long in talk.
The more he speaks, the more he is testing you,
examining you even while he smiles.
The man who cannot keep your secrets is without   12
    compunction
and will not spare you harm or imprisonment;
so keep your secrets to yourself and be very careful,   13
for you are walking on the brink of ruin.*a*

☆ From caution with the rich Ben Sira passes to modesty and
self-restraint with the politically powerful. The advice given
is extremely sensible, but guided by self-preservation rather
than any high moral standard.

11–12 recall a more pointed warning given in the Mishnah:
'Be heedful of the ruling power for they bring no man nigh
to them save for their own need' (*Aboth* 2: 3). Nervousness
may lead to overfamiliarity and temptation to speak too
freely, unthinkingly revealing your secrets to someone who
will not keep them but use them against you.

14. Some Greek manuscripts add the words translated in the
footnote. They do not appear in the major Greek, Hebrew or
Syriac manuscripts, and are certainly a later addition inserting
some religious message into a completely secular passage. ☆

[a] *Some witnesses add* When you hear this in your sleep, wake up. (14)
Love the Lord all your life and appeal to him for salvation.

69

THE DIVISIONS OF SOCIETY

15 Every animal loves its like,
and every man his neighbour.

16 All creatures flock together with their kind,
and men form attachments with their own sort.

17 What has a wolf in common with a lamb,
or a sinner with a man of piety?

18 What peace can there be between hyena and dog,
what peace between rich man and pauper?

19 As lions prey on the wild asses of the desert,
so the rich batten on the poor.

20 As humility disgusts the proud,
so is the rich man disgusted by the poor.

21 If a rich man staggers, he is held up by his friends;
a poor man falls, and his friends disown him as well.

22 When a rich man slips, many come to his rescue;
if he says something outrageous, they make excuses for
him.
A poor man makes a slip, and they all criticize him;
even if he talks sense, he is not given a hearing.

23 A rich man speaks, and all are silent;
then they praise his speech to the skies.
A poor man speaks, and they say, 'Who is this?',
and if he stumbles, they give him an extra push.

✶ Ben Sira was no socialist; he believed that the various
classes of society should remain and that there was no benefit
in mixing freely. It was better for each to keep to his own level.
This is illustrated freely from the animal world (verses 15-20)
– a source of illustration well used in ancient lore – and then

verses 21–3 conclude the whole section by drawing even more sharply the contrast in treatment by others between the rich and the poor already described in verses 2–7.

15. The author does not mean the later concept of loving one's *neighbour* as oneself. Rather, just as one member of a species consorts with other members of the same species because they are alike, so a man consorts with someone of similar character and level in society. ✶

ON HAPPINESS

Wealth is good, if sin has not tainted it;   24
poverty is a crime only to the ungodly.
It is a man's heart that changes the look on his face   25
either for better or worse.
The sign of a happy heart is a cheerful face,   26
but the invention of proverbs involves wearisome thought.
Happy the man who has never let slip a careless word,   **14**
who has never felt the sting of remorse!
Happy the man whose conscience does not accuse him,   2
whose hope has never been disappointed!

✶ A series of couplets on wealth (13: 24 – 14: 19) is here introduced by some remarks on the connexion between wealth and happiness. As verse 24 shows, it is the character, not wealth, of a person that makes him happy. Happiness does not therefore come automatically with much money.

25. Several remarks on true happiness are now added, as the subject has been raised. In material originally transmitted orally mere mention of another topic often led to a cluster of proverbs on that topic, even though they were irrelevant to the main topic (here, money). By *a man's heart* is meant his inward, moral and spiritual, state, here opposed to the amount of money he has.

26. *the invention of proverbs involves wearisome thought:* this is not Ben Sira's own reflexion on his work (though some find his book boring enough to think this!), but rather a general comment on discretion, as the next verse (14: 1) speaks of not letting 'slip a careless word'. The Hebrew text has clearly been copied wrongly, and the original may have meant something like 'thinking of distress brings worry and anxiety' – which would fit the next two verses better. ✻

ON MISERS

3 It is not proper for a mean man to be rich:
what use is money to a miser?

4 He deprives himself only to hoard for other men;
others will live in luxury on his riches.

5 How can a man be hard on himself and kind to others?
His possessions bring him no enjoyment.

6 No one is worse than the man who is grudging to himself:
his niggardliness is its own punishment.

7 If ever he does good, it is by mistake,
and then in the end he reveals his meanness.

8 It is a hard man who has a grudging eye;
he turns his back on need and looks the other way.

9 A covetous man's eye is not satisfied with his share;
greedy injustice shrivels the soul.

10 A miser grudges bread
and keeps an empty table.

✻ Ben Sira believed that men should play a full part in society as his portrait of an ideal man (see 39: 1–11) shows. A rich man should use his money for his own 'enjoyment' and 'innocent pleasure' (verse 14) but also for doing good, helping the needy (verses 7–8) and sharing hospitality generously (verse 10). Money that is not being used for one's own pleasure or for helping others is out of circulation and, in Ben Sira's view, a waste.

5. This applies specifically to the miser as the context shows. Many a good man would *be hard on himself and kind to others* with Ben Sira's approval.

7. The miser's real nature is revealed *in the end*, partly because of the money he leaves, partly because 'a man' is 'known for what he is' and 'his true character' is revealed at death (11: 27–8). ✳

ON WEALTH AND DEATH

My son, if you can afford it, do yourself well,	11
always offering to the Lord the sacrifice due to him.	
Remember that death is not to be postponed;	12
the hour of your appointment with the grave is	
undisclosed.	
Before you die, do good to your friend;	13
reach out as far as you can to help him.	
Do not miss a day's enjoyment	14
or forgo your share of innocent pleasure.	
Are you to leave to others all you have laboured for	15
and let them draw lots for your hard-earned wealth?	
Give and receive; indulge yourself;	16
you need not expect luxuries in the grave.	
Man's body wears out like a garment;	17
for the ancient sentence stands: You shall die.	
In the thick foliage of a growing tree	18
one crop of leaves falls and another grows instead;	
so the generations of flesh and blood pass	
with the death of one and the birth of another.	
All man's works decay and vanish,	19
and the workman follows them into oblivion.	

✻ Ben Sira believed in no life after death except in Sheol, a neutral, non-personal existence in a shadowy place beneath the earth. His belief is not strong, but seems to have been taken over automatically with other traditional concepts from the Old Testament. There rich and poor, good and evil were treated alike: 'one and the same fate befalls every one, just and unjust alike' (Eccles. 9: 2) without distinction. Why should the rich man not enjoy his wealth, provided he is generous to the poor and oppresses no one? Happiness lay in this life only, as there was no distinctively individual life to follow. Thus Ben Sira shows a positive attitude to this life which contrasts with the more negative attitude later when persecution and martyrdom in Jewish revolts led to increasing emphasis on the doctrines of the resurrection of the dead and of reward for good and punishment for evil after death. It was considered by some later to be worth rejecting the wealth and happiness of this world to ensure happiness in the world to come, whatever form this might take.

13. *Before you die, do good to your friend* refers either to ordinary social hospitality or to verbal instructions (like a will) about distribution of property just before death. If no instructions were given the relatives seem to have drawn lots for their shares (verse 15).

16. The emphasis on enjoying wealth is not as selfish in Ben Sira as in Ecclesiastes: Ben Sira regards the use of wealth for the benefit of others as natural for the good man as use for oneself.

17. Ben Sira's attitude to life often seems secular and only superficially religious because – in the wisdom tradition – he deals primarily with life as it is; occasionally he shows his orthodoxy by basing teaching on scriptural authority as here – as did later rabbis and Christian fathers. The 'appointment with the grave' (verse 12) refers to the story of the garden of Eden in Genesis where God decrees to Adam that 'on the day that you eat from it' (the fruit of 'the tree of the

knowledge of good and evil') 'you will certainly die' (Gen.
2: 16–17).

18. The term *flesh and blood* became in rabbinical literature
a technical term for 'human'. ✲

ANOTHER PSALM ON WISDOM

Happy the man who fixes his thoughts on wisdom	20
and uses his brains to think,	
the man who contemplates her ways	21
and ponders her secrets.	
Stalk her like a hunter	22
and lie in wait beside her path!	
The man who peers in at her windows	23
and listens at her keyhole,	
who camps beside her house,	24
driving his tent-peg into her wall,	
who pitches his tent close by her,	25
where it is best for men to live –	
he will put his children in her shade	26
and camp beneath her branches,	
sheltered by her from the heat,	27
and dwelling in the light of her presence.	

The man who fears the Lord will do all this,	**15**
and if he masters the law, wisdom will be his.	
She will come out to meet him like a mother;	2
she will receive him like a young bride.	
For food she will give him the bread of understanding	3
and for drink the water of knowledge.	
He will lean on her and not fall;	4
he will rely on her to save him from disgrace.	

5 She will promote him above his neighbours,
and find words for him when he speaks in the assembly.

6 He shall be crowned with joy and exultation;
lasting honour shall be his heritage.

7 Fools shall never possess wisdom;
sinners shall catch no glimpse of her.

8 She holds aloof from arrogance,
far from the thoughts of liars.

9 Worship is out of place on the lips of a sinner,
unprompted as he is by the Lord.

10 Worship is the outward expression of wisdom,
and the Lord himself inspires it.

✻ The links between this section and Ps. 1 are striking in both subject-matter and order: both start by praising the happiness of a man whose life they then describe as rich in meditation and learning in the (religious) law; both contrast him with the wicked and finish by stressing God's care for good and faithful followers. The poem is thus based on a well-known pattern. The two halves (14: 20–7 and 15: 2–10) are joined by 15: 1 – a key verse which emphasizes Ben Sira's particular viewpoint, already discussed on 1: 1–20, that the personal relationship with God which he calls 'the fear of the Lord' leads a man to study the law and to seek for wisdom which God gives 'in plenty to those who love him' (1: 10); 'The essence of wisdom' for him 'is the fear of the Lord' (1: 14; see notes on 1: 1–20). Man's search for wisdom through personal faith, already expounded in 1: 1–20; 4: 11–19 and 6: 18–37, is developed here and also in 38: 24 – 39: 11, where the ideal follower of God s wisdom is described in detail.

22–5. In 6: 24–30 young followers of wisdom were encouraged to enslave themselves by putting their limbs 'in wisdom's fetters' and by wearing wisdom's yoke. The picture here is of a young man courting a girl. Lying in wait, peeping through *windows* and listening at keyholes hardly show the propriety expected of a decent young man, but the stress is not on the wooer's moral propriety but rather on his thoroughly determined pursuit of his bride-to-be. Thus 'happy' is 'the man who' is similarly determined to win close knowledge of wisdom and thus of God (verse 20).

26. *her shade. . .her branches:* wisdom is pictured as a tree also in 1: 20 where she is 'rooted in the fear of the Lord and long life grows on her branches'. The author refers us back deliberately to a key passage for his theological thought.

15: 2. After describing man's search for wisdom (14: 20–7) Ben Sira now turns to what man receives when he has found her (15: 2–6).

3. The terms *water* and *bread* are often used in later Jewish literature for spiritual sustenance received through religious faith: one rabbi said that non-Jews converted to Judaism would 'find in Israel the bread of the Torah (law)'. Already one prophet of the Old Testament had appealed to those spiritually hungry and thirsty to come and listen to the prophet's words: 'have good food to eat' and 'have life' (Isa. 55: 1–3).

5. As frequently in Ecclesiasticus, practical life (here in public law-courts) creeps into passages of spiritual content. Personal religion cannot be kept separate from man's duties in society.

7–8 contrast *sinners* who are excluded from sharing God's *wisdom* – they can't even *catch* a *glimpse of* it, let alone *possess* it.

9–10. Ben Sira's interest in worship appears for the first time – often overrated by commentators who have felt that his long descriptions of the high priests Aaron (45: 6–22) and Simon (50: 1–21) show that the worship of the temple was of tremendous importance to him. However, personal faith and behaviour in public and private life take up much more of his attention and in the last resort 'Keeping the law is worth many offerings' (35: 1). Worship is part of a much wider observance of God's will. ✳

77

ON SIN AND FREE WILL

11 Do not say, 'The Lord is to blame for my failure';
  it is for you to avoid doing what he hates.

12 Do not say, 'It was he who led me astray';
  he has no use for sinful men.

13 The Lord hates every kind of vice;
  you cannot love it and still fear him.

14 When he made man in the beginning,
  he left him free to take his own decisions;

15 if you choose, you can keep the commandments;
  whether or not you keep faith is yours to decide.

16 He has set before you fire and water;
  reach out and take which you choose;

17 before man lie life and death,
  and whichever he prefers is his.

18 For in his great wisdom and mighty power
  the Lord sees everything.

19 He keeps watch over those who fear him;
  no human act escapes his notice.

20 But he has commanded no man to be wicked,
  nor has he given licence to commit sin.

✻ Mention of sin in verses 8–9 leads to a discussion on sin and free will in the form of an answer to popular objections introduced in verses 11–12 by the words 'Do not say' as in 16: 17. The more modern form of the problem how man can choose evil if God knows and controls all things seems not to have arisen in Judaism until debates with Moslems over predestination (that is, that God fixed the future unalterably in advance) by Saadia Gaon in the tenth century A.D. We should probably assume here a reference to the 'evil tendency' (*yēṣer hārā'*) in man – a concept common in rabbinic Judaism which believed that God had implanted in man two tendencies, one for good and one for evil, and that it was man's free choice which he followed. The objector then means: 'God created the evil tendency in me; he is therefore responsible for the evil I do.' In answer Ben Sira stresses God's gift to man of freedom of choice and man's full responsibility for 'his own' evil 'decisions' (verse 14), but he himself comes near to the arguments he here rejects when he states later that 'the works of the Most High... go in pairs, one the opposite of the other', including good and evil (33: 14–15; see notes).

13. By *fearing the Lord* the author assumes that warm personal relationship already discussed in the notes on 1: 11–20 and 14: 20 – 15: 10.

14. As God created man and all that God created 'was very good' (Gen. 1: 31), he cannot have created him evil; if man follows evil it is then his own responsibility.

15. *the commandments* refers to the whole law in a general sense as an expression of the way of life God approves rather than in a detailed sense as a collection of detailed commands.

16–17. According to 37: 18 'Four kinds of destiny are offered to men, good and evil, life and death'. Both these passages echo Deut. 30: 15 where Moses offered the Hebrews 'the choice of life and good, or death and evil'.

18–20. Verses 18 and 19 are concessive in sense: although *the Lord sees everything* and nothing *escapes his notice*, yet *he has commanded no man to be wicked* – a summary of the argument to close the section. *

LARGE FAMILIES – NOT ALWAYS A SIGN OF GOD'S FAVOUR

Do not set your heart on a large family of ne'er-do-wells **16**
or be content if your sons are godless.
However many they are, do not think yourself happy,   2
unless the fear of the Lord is in them.

3 Do not count on their living to be old
  or rely on their numbers;
  for one son can be better than a thousand;
  better indeed to die childless than to have godless children.
4 Thanks to one man of good sense a city may be populous,
  while a tribe of lawless men becomes a desert.
5 Many a time have I seen this with my own eyes,
  and still weightier examples have come to my ears.

* Large families and old age were commonly considered as marks of prosperity and thus of God's favour. Ben Sira is at pains to correct this traditional view: character comes before number, and thus it is better even 'to die childless' than to have wicked children, however many. In this short section Ben Sira probably answers the objection: 'I am no sinner because I have a large family and this proves God favours me.' In verses 6–11 he goes on to illustrate the disastrous consequences of large gatherings of sinners from national history.

1. *ne'er-do-wells* is an idiomatic paraphrase for 'worthless'. The original Hebrew probably meant something like 'do not expect beauty from worthless sons', that is, do not boast in their number and assume that they will later improve because you think God favours you.

4. An illustration of how *one* can be 'better than a thousand'.

5 forms a link with the following section on national history. Usually the first person is used in Ecclesiasticus of the author as teacher as in other wisdom books, especially the Wisdom of Solomon and Ecclesiastes. Occasionally, as here, Ben Sira seems to use it in a more personal way of his own experience. The book is so full of traditional elements that we do not expect the personality of the author to appear. Yet there does seem to be a genuine personality behind it, and the book is signed (50: 27). *

GOD'S ANGER AGAINST SINNERS ILLUSTRATED

Where sinners gather, the fire breaks out;   6
retribution blazes up in a rebellious nation.

There was no pardon for the giants of old,   7
who revolted in all their strength.

There was no reprieve for Lot's adopted home,   8
abhorrent in its arrogance.

There was no mercy for the doomed nation,   9
exterminated for their sins –

those six hundred thousand warriors   10
marshalled in stubborn defiance.

Even if only one man were obstinate,   11
it would be a miracle for him to escape punishment.

For mercy and anger belong to the Lord;
he shows his power in forgiveness, or in the flood of his
        wrath.

His mercy is great, but great also is his condemnation;   12
he judges a man by what he has done.

He does not let the sinner escape with his loot   13
or try the patience of the godly too long.

He opens a way for every work of mercy,   14
and everyone is treated according to his own deserts.[a]

✶ Ben Sira lists examples from the national history in the Old
Testament to illustrate the disastrous results of large gatherings
of 'sinners' (verses 6–10). He then emphasizes that God's
anger is just as reliable as his mercy (verses 11–14).

6. *Where sinners gather, the fire breaks out:* this probably

[a] *Some witnesses add* (15) The Lord made Pharaoh too stubborn to
acknowledge him, so that his deeds might be published to the world.
(16) He displays his mercy to the whole creation, and has separated light
from darkness with a plumb-line.

refers to the rebellion of the sons of Korah and their supporters against Moses when 'fire had come out from the LORD' and burnt up two hundred and fifty of them in punishment (Num. 16: 1–35).

7. *the giants of old* or 'Nephilim' were the sons of illicit intercourse between 'the sons of the gods' and 'the daughters of men' (Gen. 6: 1–4). The story is brief and obscure, full of mythical allusions we cannot understand, but represents the last, most serious evil before the flood and, according to Genesis, led directly to God's decision to destroy all mankind except Noah and his family.

8. The destruction of Sodom, *Lot's adopted home*, is frequently cited, together with that of Gomorrah, as a warning of God's punishment for sinful rebellion. Gen. 18: 16 – 19: 29 tells the story of its destruction and of Abraham's prayers for its *reprieve*.

9. *the doomed nation* probably means the Canaanites who had earlier inhabited Palestine but, according to many passages in Deuteronomy and Joshua, were exterminated when the Hebrews settled there. This extermination was not as complete as Old Testament tradition often implies, but Ben Sira learned his history from the Old Testament without modern historical analysis.

10. The *six hundred thousand warriors* were not of 'the doomed nation' as the N.E.B. implies; the phrase should be translated 'likewise those six hundred thousand warriors. . .' It probably refers to those who are said to have left Egypt with Moses (Exod. 12: 37) and later became hungry and rebellious midway through the Sinai desert (Num. 11: 21). Ben Sira links this number with those who, as punishment for rebellion, were sentenced by God to die in the desert without seeing the promised land (Num. 14: 20–33).

11. The first two lines of this verse link the previous section on large, sinful families (verses 1–4) and the historical illustrations (verses 6–10) with the following verses which assure the reader of the reliability of both God's *mercy* and his *anger*.

14. The interpretation is doubtful. The N.E.B. seems to mean that, although condemnation is inevitable for the sinner, God *opens a way for every work of mercy* done by men until the very end. But the word *mercy* has been used in the last few verses only of God's mercy, and it may be that the Jerusalem Bible's interpretation is correct ('He allows free play to his mercy', that is, as free play as he possibly can). The section ends on a more hopeful note.

Verses 15–16 (in the footnote) appear in one Hebrew manuscript and a few witnesses in Greek and Syriac. Verse 15 was added by a copyist who felt Pharaoh should have been included among the sinners who were destroyed, and verse 16 introduces a reference to God's mercy in creation. ✣

FURTHER OBJECTIONS

Do not say, 'I am hidden from the Lord; 17
who is there in heaven to give a thought to me?
Among so many I shall not be noticed;
what is my life compared with the measureless creation?
Heaven itself, the highest heaven, 18
the abyss and the earth are shaken at his coming;
the very mountains and the foundations of the world 19
tremble when he looks upon them.
What human mind can grasp this, 20
or comprehend his ways?
As a squall takes men unawares, 21
so most of his works are done in secret.
Who is to declare his acts of justice 22
or wait for his remote decree?'
These are the thoughts of a small mind, 23
the absurdities of a senseless and misguided man.

✶ Whereas the earlier objection tried to throw responsibility for sin from man to God (15: 11–12), here another, again introduced by the words 'Do not say. . .', claims that God sees man's sin but is so busy maintaining the vast universe that he takes no notice. The objector's words probably continue to verse 22 and are followed by immediate rejection of them by the author (verse 23). A more detailed answer follows in 17: 15–20 after a doctrinal exposition of God's power in creation and maintenance of the universe (16: 24 – 17: 14).

18–19. As often in the poetry of the Old Testament, hymnic language is suddenly introduced to emphasize God's greatness. The Hebrew phrase for *Heaven itself, the highest heaven* and *the very mountains* seem to have been quoted directly from Solomon's prayer in 1 Kings 8: 27 and from the psalm of Jonah (Jonah 2: 6) (which is of doubtful translation). In theological arguments both sides use scriptural verses for support, and Ben Sira here has deliberately used psalmic language to give force to the objection. He is no doubt reflecting genuine objections of his day.

22. God's *remote decree* refers to 'the ancient sentence' of death mentioned in 14: 17. Retribution is a long way off, so it doesn't matter for the present.

23. *These are. . .absurdities:* an immediate rejection of the objector's arguments; a detailed argument will follow later. ✶

GOD'S CONTROL OF THE WORLD – THE UNIVERSE

24 Listen to me, my son, and learn sense;
    pay close attention to what I say;
25 I will show you exact discipline
    and teach you accurate knowledge.
26 When the Lord created his works in the beginning,
    and after making them defined[a] their boundaries,

[a] When. . .defined: *probable reading, based on Heb.; Gk.* The works of the Lord have been under his judgement from the beginning. . .he defined. . .

he disposed them in an eternal order   27
and fixed their influences for all time.
They do not grow hungry or weary,
or abandon their tasks;
one does not jostle another;   28
they never disobey his word.

* The next three sections belong together as a didactic poem
(that is one that teaches) expounding the doctrine of God's
control of the universe and revelation of his will to man
through Israel (16: 24 – 17: 14). The author then answers
the objections raised in verses 17–22 in the light of the poem.
God's creation of the universe is described in 16: 24–28, of the
earth and man in 16: 29 – 17: 10 and of Israel in 17: 11–14.
In this, the first of three passages dealing with the doctrine of
creation (see also 39: 12–35 and 42: 15 – 43: 33) the tone is
calm and philosophical, very different from the poetic
descriptions of Isa. 40–55 and Job where rhetorical questions
are piled up for effect. Ben Sira emphasizes 'exact discipline'
and 'accurate knowledge' – phrases reminding us strangely
of modern scientific study, which may have come from Greek
scientific and philosophical thought, possibly from the
Stoics.

24–5 introduce the poem with the teacher–pupil phraseology already noted on 2: 1.

26. *created:* the Greek word for 'creation' (*ktisei*) can easily
have been miswritten as 'judgement' (*krisei*) in a context that
has mentioned accuracy and discipline, the two Greek words
differing in only one letter. The Hebrew and what follows
make it clear that 'creation' is original, as the footnote suggests.

27. God's 'works' in the heavens include sun, moon and
stars as described in Gen. 1: 14–19. *their influences* fixed the
'festivals . . . seasons and years' (Gen. 1: 14) and the reliability
of their movements was a subject of much wonder. *

85

GOD'S CONTROL OF THE WORLD – THE EARTH AND MAN

29 The Lord then looked at the earth
and filled it with his good things.
30 With every kind of living creature he covered the ground,
into which they must all return.

17 The Lord created man from the earth
and sent him back to it again.
2 He set a fixed span of life for men
and granted them authority over everything on earth.
3 He clothed them with strength like his own,[a]
forming them in his own image.
4 He put the fear of man into all creatures
and gave him lordship over beasts and birds.[b]
6 He gave men tongue and eyes and ears,
the power of choice and a mind for thinking.
7 He filled them with discernment
and showed them good and evil.
8 He kept watch over their hearts,
to display to them the majesty of his works.[c]
10 They shall praise his holy name,
proclaiming the grandeur of his works.

☆ Ben Sira continues to base his poem on Genesis, which he interprets literally. 'his good things' (16: 29) probably refers

[a] *So one Vs.; Gk.* their own.
[b] *Some witnesses add* (5) The Lord gave them the use of the five faculties; as a sixth gift he distributed to them mind, and as a seventh, reason, the interpreter of those faculties.
[c] *Some witnesses add* (9) He has given them the right to boast for ever of his marvels.

to the vegetation (Gen. 1: 11–12), and 'every kind of living creature' (16: 30) to the animals, birds and fishes mentioned in Gen. 1: 20–5. He links the creation of 'man from the earth' (17: 1; cp. Gen. 2: 7) with the punishment of man after eating the forbidden fruit in Eden (Gen. 3: 19: 'Dust you are, to dust you shall return').

17: 2. The *fixed span of* man's *life* does not appear in Genesis where, before the flood, men are said to have lived hundreds of years. Ps. 90: 10 mentions 'seventy years' as a lifetime, 'eighty if our strength holds'. Ben Sira himself elsewhere refers to human life as 'numbered' contrasted to a 'good name' which 'lasts for ever' (41: 13). Man's *authority over* other creatures is described in Gen. 1: 28.

3–4. Gen. 1: 26–7 describes how 'God created man in his own image' which Ben Sira, using language reminiscent of Ps. 8: 6–9, interprets as giving men *strength like his own*, and repeats the point for emphasis in verse 4, adding a reference to other creatures' *fear of man* ordained in Gen. 9: 2.

6. Wisdom language takes over from scriptural quotation here. One group of manuscripts inserts verse 5 as a comment from Greek philosophy on this verse. The Stoics added to the usual five senses (sight, hearing, touch, taste and smell) *mind*, reason and an eighth, an obscure technical term of Stoic philosophy here omitted.

7. Scriptural quotation ended, the author ignores Gen. 2: 17, where man's possession of 'the knowledge of good and evil' is against God's will, but refers rather to the intuitive *discernment* that wisdom teachers tried to develop in their pupils.

The footnote adds verse 9, another version of verse 10 found in only a few manuscripts. ✻

GOD'S CONTROL OF THE WORLD – THE CHOSEN PEOPLE

He gave them knowledge as well   11
and endowed them with the life-giving law.

12 He established a perpetual covenant with them
and revealed to them his decrees.
13 Their eyes saw his glorious majesty,
and their ears heard the glory of his voice.
14 He said to them, 'Guard against all wrongdoing',
and taught each man his duty towards his neighbour.

✽ Although he does not mention Israel until verse 17, Ben Sira turns here to the chosen people and describes the 'covenant', the giving of the law and the theophany (that is, the appearance of God) at Mount Sinai (Exod. 19–20).

14. The author either gives a general summary of the whole law or summarizes some of the Ten Commandments. ✽

THE FURTHER OBJECTIONS ANSWERED

15 Their conduct always lies open before him,
never hidden from his scrutiny.*a*
17 For every nation he appointed a ruler,
but chose Israel to be his own possession.*b*
19 So whatever they do is clear to him as daylight;
he keeps constant watch over their lives.
20 Their wrongdoing is not hidden from the Lord;
he observes all their sins.*c*
22 A man's good deeds he treasures like a signet-ring,
and his kindness like the apple of his eye.

[a] *Some witnesses read* ... scrutiny. (16) Every man from his youth tended towards evil; they could not make themselves hearts of flesh in place of their hearts of stone. (17) When he distributed the nations over all the earth, for every ...

[b] *Some witnesses add* (18) He rears them with discipline as his first-born, imparting to them the light of love and never neglecting them.

[c] *Some witnesses add* (21) The Lord who is gracious and knows what they are made of has neither rejected nor deserted tham, but spared them.

In the end he will rise up and give the wicked their deserts, 23
bringing down their recompense on their own heads.
Yet he leaves a way open for the penitent to return to him, 24
and gives the waverer strength to endure.

* The objections raised in 16: 17–22 are now answered. God
cannot be disinterested in the world if he exercises as much
control over the universe, earth and Israel as the doctrinal
poem (16: 24 – 17: 14) has shown. No one can pretend they
are 'hidden from the Lord' (16: 17).

17. This statement of the traditional Jewish doctrine of the
election of Israel as his special people has been further empha-
sized in some Greek manuscripts by the addition of verses
18 and 21, here printed in the footnotes.

In Ben Sira's day the Jews had had no king of their own
since 586 B.C., and had been subject to the Babylonian,
Persian, Egyptian and Syrian empires. Ben Sira probably
refers to the view, long held in some circles, that any human
ruler over Israel was an act of rebellion against the true king
of Israel, God. When the Hebrews asked for a king 'like other
nations' in Samuel's time, the Lord is portrayed as saying to
Samuel: 'It is I whom they have rejected, I whom they will
not have to be their king' (1 Sam. 8: 5–7). However, the
ruler of this verse may not refer to a human ruler but to angels,
semi-divine beings whom it was believed God had appointed
to control other nations, like the 'angel prince of the kingdom
of Persia' (Dan. 10: 13). The Septuagint introduces this idea
into its translation of Deut. 32: 8, when it says 'God set the
bounds of the nations according to the number of the angels of
God.' The point here would be that, instead of appointing an
angel for Israel, God ruled directly himself.

20–2. Verses 20 and 22 answer directly the questions of
16: 21 and 22 respectively.

23–4. Verse 23 probably indicates the final judgement on
each man at the moment of death, for 'Even on the day a

man dies it is easy for the Lord to give him his deserts' (11: 26). Fears are dispelled by the offer of forgiveness *for the penitent* in verse 24, which leads naturally to an exhortation to repent in verses 25–9. Some felt that Ben Sira was too optimistic about man's nature and that man was in fact too sinful to repent without radical change; thus verse 16 was added in some manuscripts later, stressing man's need for a new spirit and a different 'heart of flesh' as declared in Ezek. 11: 19. ✶

APPEAL TO REPENT

25 Turn to the Lord and have done with sin;
  make your prayer in his presence, and so lessen your
    offence.
26 Come back to the Most High, renounce wrongdoing,
  and hate intensely what he abhors.
27 Who will praise the Most High in the grave
  in place of the living who give him thanks?
28 When a man is dead and ceases to be, his gratitude dies
    with him;
  it is when he is alive and well that he praises the Lord.
29 How great is the Lord's mercy
  and his pardon to those who turn to him!
30 Not everything is within man's reach,
  for the human race is not immortal.
31 Is anything brighter than the sun? Yet the sun suffers
    eclipse.
  So flesh and blood have evil thoughts.
32 The Lord marshals the armies of high heaven,
  but all men are dust and ashes.

✶ Later Judaism believed fervently in the need for repentance;
Ben Sira's remarks here lack fervency and his reasons for

commending repentance seem weak. Whereas later Jews spoke of love for God and experience of punishment as leading to repentance, Ben Sira speaks of turning to praise God while alive because you cannot after death. The section ends with further emphasis on man's imperfection compared with God.

27–8. Ben Sira follows earlier Jewish belief that man ceases to live in any vital, positive way after death. Good and bad go to Sheol, a shadowy, colourless place where there are no rewards and no punishments (described in the note on 14: 11–19). 'None talk of thee among the dead; who praises thee in Sheol?' (Ps. 6: 5). Man must therefore fulfil his duty to *praise* God before death.

31–2. The author uses *the sun* and stars (*the armies of high heaven*, the 'heavenly host' of earlier translations) to illustrate man's weakness. If even sun and stars have imperfections, how much more man! This remark leads on naturally to the following hymn on God's compassion for man. *

HYMN ON GOD'S COMPASSION FOR MAN'S WEAKNESS

He who lives for ever is the Creator of the whole universe; **18**
right belongs to the Lord alone.[a]   2
To no man is it given to unfold the story of his works;   4
who can trace his marvels to their source?
No one can measure his majestic power,   5
still less, tell the full tale of all his mercies.
Man can neither increase nor diminish them,   6
nor fathom the wonders of the Lord.
When a man comes to the end of them he is still at the   7
        beginning,
and when he has finished he will still be perplexed.

[a] *Some witnesses add* and there is none beside him, (3) who can steer the world with his little finger, so that all things obey his will; as king of the universe, he has power to fix the bounds between what is holy and what is profane.

8 What is man and what use is he?
  What do his good or evil deeds signify?
9 His span of life is at the most a hundred years;
10 compared with endless time, his few years
  are like one drop of sea-water or a single grain of sand.
11 This is why the Lord is patient with them,
  lavishing his mercy upon them.
12 He sees and knows the harsh fate in store for them,
  and therefore gives full play to his forgiveness.
13 Man's compassion is only for his neighbour,
  but the Lord's compassion is for every living thing.
  He corrects and trains and teaches
  and brings them back as a shepherd his flock.
14 He has compassion on those who accept discipline
  and are eager to obey his decrees.

---

* A hymn is inserted here to emphasize God's compassion, just as the hymn in 14: 20 – 15: 10 was added to emphasize the happiness of the wise man. After again stressing God's endless power (verses 1–7) and man's insignificance (verses 8–9), the author describes God's pity for man, particularly because his life is so short and his death so final, but at the end of the section limits God's compassion to 'those who accept discipline' (verse 14) and follow after wisdom.

1–2 are expanded in some manuscripts by verse 3, a marginal gloss added to describe further God's *right* to be obeyed.

7. However hard and long man tries to understand God's works, he always remains *perplexed*. For Ben Sira with his deep-rooted faith in God this is a further proof of God's greatness. To the author of Ecclesiastes it led to scepticism and the conclusion that 'God has so ordered it that man should not be able to discover what is happening here under the sun'

(Eccles. 8: 17). The problems of doubt that appear in Ecclesiastes and Job do not seem to have worried the traditionalist Ben Sira.

9. Ps. 90: 10 reckoned man's life as 'seventy years... eighty if our strength holds'. Ben Sira seems to follow Egyptian tradition in assessing man's maximum life-span as *a hundred years*.

12. *the harsh fate* awaiting man is death at an age early in God's reckoning.

13–14. God's apparently free-ranging forgiveness and *compassion* is quickly limited to those who seek true wisdom. This brings the passage into conformity with earlier parts of the book and forms a fitting close to the section. ✶

ON GENEROSITY

My son, do good without scolding;   15
do not spoil your generosity with hard words.
Does not the dew give respite from the sweltering heat? 16
So a word can do more than a gift.
A kind word counts for more than a rich present;   17
with a gracious man you will find both.
A fool cannot refrain from tactless criticism,   18
and a grudging giver makes no eyes sparkle.

✶ The traditional almsgiving (giving to the poor) of Jewish piety is to be performed in a truly generous spirit. Gifts accompanied by 'tactless criticism' and rebukes make the recipient feel ashamed; kind words with a gift achieve even more than the gift itself in helping the recipient. Thus the Babylonian Talmud says that 'he who gives a farthing is blessed sixfold, but he who adds words elevenfold'.

16. As *dew* lessens the effect of *heat*, so kind words lessen the effect of suffering more than mere gifts. ✶

ON THE NEED FOR FORESIGHT

19 Before you speak, learn;
   and before you fall sick, consult a doctor.
20 Before judgement comes, examine yourself,
   and you will find pardon in the hour of scrutiny.
21 Before you fall ill, humble yourself;
   show your penitence as soon as you sin.
22 Let nothing hinder the prompt discharge of your vows;
   do not wait till death to be absolved.
23 Before you make a vow, give it due thought;
   do not be like those who try the Lord's patience.
24 Think of the wrath you must face in the hour of death,
   when the time of reckoning comes, and he turns away his
       face.
25 In time of plenty remember the time of famine,
   poverty and need in days of wealth.
26 Between dawn and dusk times may alter;
   all change comes quickly, when the Lord wills it.
27 A wise man is always on his guard;
   when sin is rife, he will beware of negligence.
28 Every man of sense makes acquaintance with wisdom,
   and to him who finds her she gives cause for thankfulness.
29 Skilled speakers display their special wisdom
   by a flow of apt proverbs.

* Ben Sira closes the section on *Man's life under divine
providence* (10: 4 – 18: 29) by reminding readers of the need
for man to examine his life and repent before God's judgement
falls. As judgement could come in various forms – sickness,
death, famine, poverty – and such changes could come
'quickly, when the Lord wills it' (verse 26), 'A wise man'

must always be 'on his guard' (verse 27, which equates the wise man with the religious man again). Verses 28–9 then form a link with the *Maxims of prudence and self-discipline* which follow (18: 30 – 23: 27).

19–21. In Old Testament times sickness had been considered punishment from God for sin, and to call *a doctor*, as did King Asa when suffering from gangrene (2 Chron. 16: 12), was an act of rebellion against God. Here illness is still regarded as a time of *judgement* which can be forestalled by *penitence* at the time of sin, but consulting *a doctor* is no longer rebellion but rather a necessity to be avoided if possible. Later Ben Sira states that the doctor is to be honoured as one whom God has created and whose 'skill comes from the Most High' (38: 2). Thus he stands midway between old and new views on medicine.

22–4. *vows* were promises of action or money made in the Temple in return for God's help in some matter. Broken promises cause continual complaint in all life's circumstances, whether religious or secular, ancient or modern. Thus Deuteronomy urges people not to 'put off' the 'fulfilment' of a vow (23: 21), and Ecclesiastes thinks 'Better not vow at all than vow and fail to pay' (5: 5). Vows made without *due thought* challenged God's judgement unnecessarily as did the Hebrews at Massah (Deut. 6: 16).

29. *Skilled speakers display their special wisdom by a flow of apt proverbs* could almost be a motto for the book – or Ben Sira's own self-justification for such a lengthy display of professional skill! *

95

Maxims of prudence and self-discipline

ON THE RESULTS OF GIVING WAY TO PASSION AND LUXURY

30 Do not let your passions be your guide,
but restrain your desires.

31 If you indulge yourself with all that passion fancies,
it will make you the butt of your enemies.

32 Do not revel in great luxury,
or the expense of it may ruin you.

33 Do not beggar yourself by feasting on borrowed money,
when there is nothing in your purse.

19 A drunken workman never grows rich;
carelessness in small things leads little by little to ruin.

2 Wine and women rob the wise of their wits,
and a frequenter of prostitutes becomes more and more
reckless,

3 till sores[a] and worms take possession of him,
and his recklessness becomes his undoing.

* The major section on *Maxims of prudence and self-discipline* from 18: 30 to 23: 27 contains no doctrinal sections like 10: 4–25 and 14: 20 – 15: 10 in the previous major section on *Man's life under divine providence*, but rather proverbs based on secular life with only 'background' references to God in Ben Sira's own style. In 18: 30–1 passionate behaviour is discussed, followed in 18: 32 – 19: 3 by luxurious feasting, drunkenness and prostitution.

[a] *Or* decay.

96

31. If you give way to *passion*, in love or anger for example, you will make a fool of yourself, and *your enemies* will take malicious delight in making fun of you.

33. *feasting on borrowed money:* the point is not passionate greed but rather the moral failing of allowing love of luxury to lead you into debt.

19: 3. The Greek word translated *sores*, or 'decay' in the footnote, is uncertain. The N.E.B. clearly intends a reference to venereal diseases, the *sores* of which can be very painful; death can result from some of them, indicated here by the *worms* which corrupt the body in the grave. ✲

ON HANDLING MALICIOUS GOSSIP

To trust a man hastily shows a shallow mind,   4
and to sin is to do an injury to yourself.

To delight in wickedness is to court condemnation,   5
but evil loses its hold on the man who hates gossip.   6

Never repeat what you hear,   7
and you will never be the loser.

Tell no tales about friend or foe;   8
unless silence makes you an accomplice, never betray a
    man's secret.

Suppose he has heard you and learnt to distrust you,   9
he will seize the first chance to show his hatred.

Have you heard a rumour? Let it die with you.   10
Never fear, it will not make you burst.

A fool with a secret goes through agony   11
like a woman in childbirth.

As painful as an arrow through the thigh   12
is a rumour in the heart of a fool.

Confront your friend with the gossip about him; he may 13
    not have done it;

or if he did it, he will know not to do it again.

14 Confront your neighbour; he may not have said it;
or if he did say it, he will know not to say it again.

15 Confront your friend; it will often turn out to be slander;
do not believe everything you hear.

16 A man may let slip more than he intends;
whose tongue is always free from guilt?

17 Confront your neighbour before you threaten him,
and let the law of the Most High take its course.[a]

✶ Ben Sira here explores various ways of treating gossip – a favourite topic for the wise men of the ancient Near East. He devotes several verses to the very difficult matter of how to handle gossip about a friend, giving several reasons why it is best to confront him with it (verses 13–17). As often at the close of sections, verse 17 links the topic with religious faith. Some later editors felt that the reference to 'the law of the Most High' was too brief; thus some Greek manuscripts add verses 18 and 19 (here in the footnotes) to stress further the benefits of obedience to the law.

4. *To trust a man hastily* probably refers to trusting a gossip's word rather than to placing confidence in someone. The context leads us to define *sin* here as listening to gossip too easily – this is *an injury to* one's own self-esteem.

5. The *wickedness* referred to is the wickedness which the gossip attributes to the person talked about.

8. *silence* can make you *an accomplice* when you appear to condone sin by keeping silent about your friend's evil deed. 'If a person hears a solemn adjuration to give evidence as a witness to something he has seen or heard and does not

[a] *Some witnesses add* without giving way to anger. (18) The fear of the Lord is the way towards acceptance, and wisdom wins love from him. (19) The knowledge of the Lord's commandments is life-giving discipline, and those who do what pleases him eat from the tree of immortality.

declare what he knows, he commits a sin and must accept responsibility' (Lev. 5: 1).

10–12. Ben Sira uses three images to describe the well-known temptation to be first with a malicious piece of gossip. To *burst* with gossip is used commonly enough. Desire to gossip seems to hurt until the story is told just as *a woman in childbirth* is in pain until the baby is born and *an arrow through the thigh* hurts until it is extracted.

17. Mention of *the law of the Most High* closes the section with a religious reference, and probably recalls Lev. 19: 17 – 'You shall not nurse hatred against your brother. You shall reprove your fellow-countryman frankly and so you will have no share in his guilt.' ✳

ON GOOD AND BAD CLEVERNESS

All wisdom is the fear of the Lord   20
and includes the fulfilling of the law.[a]

The knowledge of wickedness is not wisdom,   22
nor is there good sense in the advice of sinners.

There is a cleverness that is loathsome,   23
and some fools are merely ignorant.

Better to be godfearing and lack brains   24
than to have great intelligence and break the law.

A meticulous cleverness may lead to injustice,   25
and a man may make himself offensive in order that right
    may prevail.

There is a scoundrel who stoops and wears mourning,   26
but who is a fraud at heart.

He covers his face and pretends to be deaf,   27
but when nobody is looking, he will steal a march on you;

[a] Some *witnesses add* and a knowledge of his omnipotence. (21) A servant who says, 'I will not do as you wish', even if he does it later, angers the man who feeds him.

89798

28 and if lack of strength prevents him from doing wrong,
   he will still harm you at the first opportunity.
29 Yet you can tell a man by his looks
   and recognize good sense at first sight.
30 A man's clothes, and the way he laughs,
   and his gait, reveal his character.

* After a typical 'background' remark on the connexion between secular wisdom and observance of 'the law' (verse 20), Ben Sira explains that intelligence is not the same as 'wisdom' or 'good sense', contrasting good and bad in the different halves of verses 22–6. A person of 'great intelligence' can be a great sinner and one who lacks brains can be good (verse 24). Verses 27–30 then give advice on telling the inward character of a person from his outward appearance.

20. All one's life should be lived in close personal relationship with God (*the fear of the Lord*), whereas *fulfilling of the law* is only part of one's life. *the fear of the Lord* and practice of *the law* are not here identified: the former *includes* the latter.

21 (in the footnote) was added in some Greek manuscripts by later Christians, and is based on the parable of the two sons in Matt. 21: 28–32.

23–4 should be taken together, contrasting *godfearing* fools who *lack brains* and are good through guilelessness with clever people of *great intelligence* who *break the law*.

25. The N.E.B. refers the second part of the verse to someone who is deliberately rude and *offensive in order* to get a good result: crooked cleverness can lead to good results as well as to bad. The contrast of the previous verses is then continued. *

ON DISCIPLINE IN SPEECH

A reproof may be untimely,   **20**
and silence may show a man's good sense.
Yet how much better it is to complain than to nurse a ₂
grudge,
and confession saves a man from disgrace.*ᵃ*
Like a eunuch longing to seduce a girl   ₄
is the man who tries to do right by violence.
One man is silent and is found to be wise;   ₅
another is hated for his endless chatter.
One man is silent, at a loss for an answer;   ₆
another is silent, biding his time.
The wise man is silent until the right moment,   ₇
but a swaggering fool is always speaking out of turn.
A garrulous man makes himself detested,
and one who abuses his position arouses hatred.   ₈

✻ 'wisdom shows itself by speech, and a man's education
must find expression in words' (4: 24). Speech of the right
quantity (verses 5 and 8) and at the right time (verses 6–7)
thus became for Ben Sira an important way of distinguishing
a wise man from a fool.

1–2 presupposes different circumstances: whereas often *A
reproof* will make matters worse (verse 1), sometimes it is
better to ask for explanations of bad conduct than silently
to nurse a grudge (verse 2): the offender then has a chance to
confess and save himself *from disgrace*. Ben Sira especially
valued the ability to recognize the right time for speech and
action, and frequently mentions this when giving advice:
for example, 'Until the right time comes, a patient man
restrains himself' (1: 23).

[a] *Some witnesses add* (3) How good it is to respond to reproof with
repentance, and so escape deliberate sin!

4 doesn't fit the context and is probably misplaced, unless it illustrates the wrong done by the offender of verse 2.

8. By *one who abuses his position* the author means people who rate themselves too highly and think they have more right to reprove others than anyone else. ✷

A SERIES OF PARADOXES

9 A man sometimes finds profit in adversity,
and a windfall may result in loss.

10 Sometimes liberality does not benefit the giver,
sometimes is brings a double return.

11 The quest for honour may lead to disgrace,
but there are those who have risen from obscurity to
eminence.

12 A man may make a good bargain,
but pay for it seven times over.

13 A wise man endears himself when he speaks,
but fools scatter compliments in vain.

14 A gift from a fool will bring you no benefit;
it looks bigger to him than it does to you.

15 He gives small gifts accompanied by long lectures,
and opens his mouth as wide as the town crier.
He gives a loan today and asks it back tomorrow,
obnoxious fellow that he is!

16 The fool says, 'I have no friends,
I get no thanks for my kindnesses;
though they eat my bread, they speak ill of me.'

17 How everyone will laugh at him – and how often!

✷ The method of contrasting one half of a couplet with another, used in 20: 1–8, is here continued in verses of varied content. The section closes with criticism of people who lack sensitivity in giving (verses 14–17). Most of the couplets show shrewd observation of people and explain themselves.

13. The point of the contrast is the way in which each person *speaks*: the *wise man* is liked because he shows tact and sympathy, whereas the unintelligent overdoes his *compliments* and seems insincere.

14–15. An unintelligent person has no idea of the (personal rather than financial) value of his gift to the recipient. ⁂

ON UNTIMELY SPEECH, DIFFIDENCE AND LIES

Better a slip on the stone floor than a slip of the tongue; 18
and the fall of the wicked comes just as suddenly.
An ill-mannered man is like an unseasonable story, 19
continually on the lips of the ill-bred.
A proverb will fall flat when uttered by a fool, 20
for he will produce it at the wrong time.

Poverty may keep a man from doing wrong; 21
when the day's work is over, conscience will not trouble
    him.
A man's diffidence may be his undoing, 22
or the foolish figure he cuts in the eyes of the world.
A man may be shamed into making promises to a friend 23
and needlessly turn him into an enemy.

A lie is an ugly blot on a man's name, 24
and is continually on the lips of those who know no better.
It is better to be a thief than a habitual liar, 25
but both will come to the same bad end.
A lying disposition brings disgrace; 26
the shame of it can never be shaken off.

✻ Miscellaneous proverbs follow. Verses 18–20 are linked by the theme of 'unseasonable' speech, verses 21–3 (probably) by the theme of financial or personal weakness and verses 24–6 by the dangers of telling lies – a favourite theme for Ben Sira.

18. *the wicked* may mean those who speak offensive words; but the couplet may be filled up with the familiar warning of sudden disaster falling on sinners.

20. The unintelligent man again speaks 'out of turn' (verse 7) – a habit which Ben Sira considered lacking in intelligence.

21. *conscience will not trouble* a poor man because he has worked too hard to think of ways of *doing wrong*!

22–3. The diffident man *may be his* own *undoing* because he does not openly admit his poverty; he thus turns his *friend . . . into an enemy* because he makes *promises* he knows he cannot fulfil. ✻

ON OPPORTUNE USE OF WISDOM

27 A wise man advances himself when he speaks,
and a man of sense makes himself pleasant to the great.
28 The man who tills his land heaps up a harvest,
and he who pleases the great reaps pardon for his
wrongdoing.
29 Hospitality and presents make wise men blind;
like a gag in the mouth they silence criticism.
30 Hidden wisdom and buried treasure,
what use is there in either?
31 Better a man who hides his folly
than one who hides his wisdom!*a*

✻ After a varied collection of advice on everyday situations we have a reminder that wisdom is to be used and not hidden

[a] *Some witnesses add* (32) Better to seek the Lord with unremitting patience than to be the masterless charioteer of one's own life.

away. 'The essence of wisdom' is here far from 'the fear of the Lord' (1: 14), but rather how to get on in life by winning influential friends in clever ways. The wise man praised by Ben Sira elsewhere would not allow himself to be blinded by *Hospitality and presents* or to be silenced by them as with *a gag* (verse 29). The passage is purely secular and lacks the deep religious content (which reappears in 21: 1) of passages like 4: 11–19, 14: 20 – 15: 8 and 24: 1–22 – an example of the strange variety of attitude within the book. No wonder some pious editor considered the methods here described as 'masterless' charioteering and felt obliged to add verse 32 (here in the footnote) and recall opportunists to the 'fear of the Lord'. ✶

ON CONTROLLING SIN   **21**

Have you done wrong, my son? Do it no more,
but ask pardon for your past wrongdoing.   2
Avoid wrong as you would a viper,
for if you go near, it will bite you;
its teeth are like a lion's teeth
and can destroy the lives of men.
Every breach of the law is like a two-edged sword;   3
it inflicts an incurable wound.
By intimidation and insolence a man forfeits his wealth;   4
thus a proud man will be stripped of his possessions.
The Lord listens to the poor man's appeal,   5
and his verdict follows without delay.
To hate reproof is to go the way of sinners,   6
but whoever fears the Lord will repent whole-heartedly.
A great talker is known far and wide,   7
but a sensible man is aware of his failings.
To build a house with borrowed money   8

is like collecting stones for your own tomb.[a]

9 A gathering of lawless men is like a bundle of tow,
which ends by going up in flames.

10 The road of sinners is smoothly paved,
but it leads straight down to the grave.

11 Whoever keeps the law keeps his thoughts under control;
the fear of the Lord has its outcome in wisdom.

✻ Here comes another passage which, like 19: 20, relates the
secular proverbs of this part of the book to theology. Two
orthodox rabbinic doctrines underlie the section, those of
repentance and forgiveness, and of man's evil tendency
(already discussed in the notes on 15: 11–20). The sinner is
encouraged to 'ask pardon' (verse 1) and to accept reproof and
'repent whole-heartedly' (verse 6). Further, only by obeying
the law can man keep his evil tendency 'under control'
(verse 11); wisdom is identified with 'the fear of the Lord'
and inner discipline.

2. The *viper* probably stands for the subtlety of temptation,
although a later rabbinic author likened man's evil tendency
to a serpent biting him. *lion's teeth* represent strength, and thus
subtlety, strength and destruction are cited as three functions
of sin.

7. *A great talker* may have a wide reputation, but he cannot
deceive a man of insight who sees the *failings* behind his
fluency.

8. Most Greek manuscripts liken building *a house with
borrowed money* to 'harvesting stones against the winter' (in
footnote) instead of wood – a particularly useless way to
prepare for the future. The N.E.B. selects the reading of a few
Greek manuscripts and the Syriac translation – *like collecting
stones for your own tomb:* that is, as you borrow *money* you
cannot pay back and *build* your *house*, you are helping to
create fatal disaster for yourself. ✻

[a] *Some witnesses read* like harvesting stones against the winter.

ON UNINTELLIGENT PEOPLE

A man who is not clever cannot be taught,   12
but there is a cleverness which only breeds bitterness.
A wise man's knowledge is like a river in full spate,   13
and his advice is a life-giving spring.
A fool's mind is a leaky bucket: 14
it cannot hold anything it learns.
If an instructed man hears a wise saying,   15
he applauds it and improves on it.
If a rake hears it, he is annoyed
and throws it behind his back.
Listening to a fool is like travelling with a heavy pack,   16
but there is delight to be found in intelligent conversation.
The assembly welcomes a word from the wise man,   17
and thinks over what he says.

A fool's wisdom is like a tumbledown house;   18
his knowledge is a string of ill-digested sayings.
To fools education is like fetters,   19
like a handcuff on the wrist.
To the wise education is a golden ornament   21
like a bracelet on the arm.
A fool laughs out loud;   20
a clever man smiles quietly, if at all.

A fool rushes into a house,   22
while a man of experience hangs back politely.
A boor peers into the house from the doorstep,   23
while a well-bred man stands outside.
It is bad manners to listen at doors;   24
a man of sense would think it a crushing disgrace.

25 The glib only repeat what others have said,
but the wise weigh every word.
26 Fools speak before they think;
wise men think first and speak afterwards.

☆ After a reference to theological background (verse 11), Ben Sira returns to secular proverbs until the prayer in 22: 27 – 23: 6. This section concerns 'the fool', a word used here not as a term of abuse (as often today) but merely to denote an unintelligent person. Throughout the section the reactions of wise and unintelligent in similar situations are contrasted with each other.

12. *there is a cleverness which only breeds bitterness:* this recalls that intelligence can be used for both good and bad ends as already stressed in 19: 23–4.

13–14. Water imagery was popular in proverbial literature throughout the ancient world, and Ben Sira's use of it here illustrates the universal character of the Jewish tradition. The later rabbis continue using the image of the person who studies the law 'for its own sake' and 'is made like to a never-failing spring and like to a river that ever flows more mightily' (*Aboth* 6: 1). Here the *wise man* has the resources to produce valuable thought, *advice* and action, whereas the unintelligent cannot retain knowledge and experience and thus acts inconsistently.

17. Wisdom 'finds words for' the man who fears the Lord 'when he speaks in the assembly' (15: 5).

19, 21. The two verses contrast each other and belong together – verse 21 was misplaced in copying at some stage of the manuscript tradition. *education* refers to training of the mind for public life and scholarly study rather than for practical skills.

22–3 are quoted in the Babylonian Talmud and later as an example of good manners. ☆

ON THREE KINDS OF IMMORAL BEHAVIOUR

When a bad man curses his adversary,[a]　　27
he is cursing himself.
A tale-bearer blackens his own character　　28
and makes himself hated throughout the neighbourhood.

An idler is like a filthy stone;　　**22**
everyone jeers at his disgrace.
An idler is like a lump of dung;　　2
whoever picks it up shakes it off his hand.

There is shame in being father to a spoilt son,　　3
and the birth of a daughter means loss.
A sensible daughter wins a husband,　　4
but an immodest one is a grief to her father.
A brazen daughter disgraces both father and husband　　5
and is despised by both.

✻ Into a long discourse on the difference between wise and
unintelligent people (21: 12–26; 22: 6–18) the author inserts a
passage deploring three kinds of morally bad behaviour: bad
use of words (21: 27–8), laziness (22: 1–2) and ingratitude in
children (22: 3–5).

27. It is unlikely that Ben Sira uses 'Satan' (footnote) as
a personal name in the sense of the head of cosmic evil powers
– a concept that became very popular from the second century
B.C. as shown in the Qumran scrolls and the New Testament.
Although the Hebrew word *sātān* was so used in 1 Chron.
21: 1, where 'Satan' incites David to evil, it was used also
of a purely human enemy. Ben Sira, very conservative in
theoretical theology as opposed to the practical, shows no

[a] *Or* curses Satan.

knowledge of any independent evil power in the universe, and here means that *When a bad man curses his adversary* he is merely cursing his own wrongdoing that led someone to opposing him, and therefore *is cursing himself.*

22: 1–2. Stones were sometimes used as toilet paper in the ancient world. *An idler* is thus as offensive as *dung.*

3–5. Elsewhere Ben Sira complains that *a daughter*, whether married or not, 'keeps him (her father) awake at night' (42: 9–14), a passage which illustrates further Ben Sira's mistrust of women. The Talmud instructs Jewish men to thank God daily for not making them a woman. Verses 4 and 5 further define verse 3 by showing how *brazen* and *immodest* daughters can mean 'loss'. ✻

MORE ON UNINTELLIGENT PEOPLE

6 Unseasonable talk is like music in time of mourning,
but the lash of wisdom's discipline is always in season.

7 Teaching a fool is like mending pottery with glue,
or like rousing a sleeper from heavy sleep.

8 As well reason with a drowsy man as with a fool;
when you have finished, he will say, 'What was that?'*[a]*

11 Mourn over the dead for the eclipse of his light;
mourn over the fool for the eclipse of his wits.
Mourn less bitterly for the dead, for he is at rest;
but the fool's life is worse than death.

12 Mourning for the dead lasts seven days,
but for a godless fool it lasts all his life.

13 Do not talk long with a fool
or visit a stupid man.
Beware of him, or you may be in trouble

[a] *Some witnesses add* (9) Children well brought up reveal no trace of any humble origin. (10) But those who run riot, haughty and undisciplined, sully the nobility of their parentage.

and find yourself bespattered when he shakes himself.
Avoid him, if you are looking for peace,
and you will not be worn out by his folly.
What is heavier than lead? 14
What is its name but 'Fool'?
Sand, salt, and a lump of iron 15
are less of a burden than a stupid man.

A tie-beam fixed firmly into a building 16
is not shaken loose by an earthquake;
so a mind kept firm by intelligent advice
will not be daunted in a crisis.
A mind solidly backed by intelligent thought 17
is like the stucco that decorates a smooth wall.
As a fence set on a hill-top 18
cannot stand against the wind,
so a mind made timid by foolish fancies
is not proof against any terror.

☆ We now return to the theme of 21: 12–26 – the contrast between wisdom and lack of intelligence, here illustrated, in the style of ancient proverbs, by many similes from everyday life: walls, fences and buildings symbolizing security (verses 16–18), various heavy natural substances symbolizing lifelessness (verses 14–15), mourning customs (verses 6, 11–12) and mending broken pots (verse 7) which easily break again and symbolize inability to retain teaching in the mind – an unintelligent mind leaks knowledge like 'a leaky bucket' (21: 14).

9–10 (in the footnote), added at the side of a few manuscripts, were intended to expand on children's ingratitude, discussed in verses 3–5.

12. *seven days* of *Mourning* was the usual period, as observed by Joseph for his father (Gen. 50: 10), by the Jews for Judith (Judith 16: 24) and by orthodox Jews today.

16. *A tie-beam* was placed in the middle of the structure of *a building* between the walls to strengthen them.

17. *intelligent thought* lies behind a wise person's *mind* giving it secure backing, just as a smoothly hewn stone *wall* lies behind plaster *stucco* decoration. ✶

ON FRIENDSHIP

19 Hurt the eye and tears will flow;
hurt the mind and you will find it sensitive.

20 Throw a stone at the birds and you scare them away;
abuse a friend and you break off your friendship.

21 If you have drawn your sword on a friend,
do not give up hope, there is still a way back.

22 If you have quarrelled with your friend,
never fear, there can still be a reconciliation.
But abuse, scorn, a secret betrayed, a stab in the back –
these will make any friend keep his distance.

23 Win your neighbour's confidence while he is poor,
and you will share the joy of his prosperity;
stand by him in time of trouble,
and you will be his partner when he comes into a
fortune.

24 As furnace-fumes and smoke come before the flame,
so insults come before bloodshed.

25 I will not be afraid to protect my friend
nor will I turn my back on him.

26 If harm should befall me on his account,
everyone who hears of it will beware of him.

✹ In 6: 5–17 Ben Sira has described the faithfulness of true friendship; here he shows how *abuse*, *scorn* and deceitfulness can damage and destroy a friendship much more than an open fight or quarrel. Damage to friendship is discussed in verses 19-22 and 24, positive allegiance in friendship in verse 23, and the section concludes with a personal testimony of loyalty in the first person (verses 25–6). ✹

A PRAYER FOR SELF-DISCIPLINE

Oh for a sentry to guard my mouth 　　　　　　27
and a seal of discretion to close my lips,
to keep them from being my downfall,
and to keep my tongue from causing my ruin!
Lord, Father, and Ruler of my life, 　　　　　　**23**
do not abandon me to the tongue's control
or allow me to fall on its account.
Oh for wisdom's lash to curb my thoughts 　　　2
and to discipline my mind,
without overlooking my mistakes
or condoning my sins!
Then my mistakes would not multiply 　　　　　3
nor my sins increase,
humiliating me before my opponents
and giving my enemy cause to gloat.
Lord, Father, and God of my life, 　　　　　　4
do not let me have a supercilious eye.
Protect me from the onslaught of desire; 　　　5
let neither gluttony nor lust take hold of me, 　　6
nor give me over to the power of shameless passion.

✹ After a series of secular proverbs the author returns to a more obviously religious theme, as in 19: 20 and 21: 1–11.

More particularly Jewish subjects are discussed through to the end of this major section – oaths by the sacred name of God (23: 9–11), scurrilous talk and parental respect (23: 12–15) and sin and disobedience to the law (23: 16–27). This recurring return to religious themes shows the theological background to all Ben Sira's apparently secular advice. Wishes for *discretion* (22: 27) and for self-discipline (23: 2–3) are followed by prayers asking God to grant these requests (23: 1 and 4–6). *

MORE ON DISCIPLINE IN SPEECH

7 Hear, my sons, how to discipline the mouth,
take warning, and you will never be caught out.

8 It is by his own words that the sinner is ensnared;
he is tripped up by his own scurrility and pride.

9 Do not inure your mouths to oaths
or make a habit of naming the Holy One.

10 As a slave constantly under the lash
is never free from weals,
so the man who has oaths and the sacred name for ever
on his lips
will never be clear of guilt.

11 A man given to swearing is lawless to the core;
the scourge will never be far from his house.
If he goes back on his word, he must bear the blame;
if he wilfully neglects it, he sins twice over;
if his oath itself was insincere, he cannot be acquitted;
his house will be filled with trouble.

12 There is a kind of speech that is the counterpart of death;
may it never be found among Jacob's descendants!
The pious keep clear of such conduct
and do not wallow in sin.

Do not make a habit of coarse, vulgar talk,   13
or you will be bound to say something sinful.
Remember your father and mother   14
when you take your seat among the great,
or you may forget yourself in their presence
and make a fool of yourself through bad habit;
then you will wish you had never been born,
and curse the day of your birth.
A man addicted to scurrilous talk   15
will never learn better as long as he lives.

* Discipline in speech, already discussed in 20: 1-8, is taken up again with special reference to scurrilous gossip (verses 8, 12-15) and to sacred oaths (verses 9-11).

8. Scurrilous talk is linked with *pride* because desire to gossip arises from a person's feeling of self-importance at knowing so much.

9. By *naming the Holy One* Ben Sira means not pronouncing the personal name of God (probably *Yahweh*) which in those days was uttered only by the high priest in the temple on the Day of Atonement, but using more general words for God. If you mention God cheaply in everyday speech, you will mention him cheaply in *oaths*. Swearing today has lost its religious significance and indicates either poor use of language and inability to say what one wants or desire to shock, but in Ben Sira's day to use a divine name in an oath was a serious religious act and to practise it without serious religious intention was sin. Criticism of cheap oaths appears also in the New Testament where it is said to be better not to swear at all but just to use 'yes' and 'no' (Matt. 5: 33-7; Jas. 5: 12).

11. Risks incurred by habitual *swearing* are here three: an oath sincerely intended, but unfulfilled; an oath lightly sworn; and an oath consciously *insincere*. The *scourge* is that of divine punishment which takes the form of *trouble* and disaster.

12. *a kind of speech that is the counterpart of death:* probably refers to the scurrilous talk of the next few verses rather than to sacred oaths. *Jacob's descendants* refer to Jews as distinct from Gentiles.

14. The obligation to respect one's parents, basic in Judaism from the Ten Commandments (Exod. 20: 12) onwards and stressed by Ben Sira in 3: 2–16, is here almost an inbred quality which stops you making *a fool of yourself.* ✶

ON THE SIN OF ADULTERY

16 Two kinds of men add sin to sin,
and a third brings retribution on himself.
Hot lust that blazes like a fire
can never be quenched till life is destroyed.
A man whose whole body is given to sensuality
never stops till the fire consumes him.

17 To a seducer every loaf is as sweet as the last,
and he does not weary until he dies.

18 The man who strays from his own bed
says to himself, 'Who can see me?
All around is dark and the walls hide me;
nobody can see me, why need I worry?
The Most High will not take note of my sins.'

19 The eyes of men are all he fears;
he forgets that the eyes of the Lord
are ten thousand times brighter than the sun,
observing every step men take
and penetrating every secret.

20 Before the universe was created, it was known to him,
and so it is since its completion.

21 This man will pay the penalty in the public street,

caught where he least expected it.

So too with the woman who is unfaithful to her husband, 22
presenting him with an heir by a different father:

first, she disobeys the law of the Most High; 23
secondly, she commits an offence against her husband;
thirdly, she has prostituted herself
by bearing bastard children.

She shall be disgraced before the assembly, 24
and the consequences will fall on her children.

Her children will not take root, 25
nor will fruit grow on her branches.

A curse will rest on her memory, 26
and her shame will never be blotted out.

All who survive her will learn 27
that nothing is better than the fear of the Lord
or sweeter than obeying his commandments.[a]

* A new literary form is introduced here – the numerical proverb, which was very popular in the ancient Near East where most learning was transmitted by oral repetition. Thus whole collections of numerical proverbs are found in the biblical Proverbs (especially in ch. 30) and in the Mishnah and Talmud. Ben Sira has included some numerical proverbs (23: 16; 25: 1–2, 7; 26: 5, 28) but, instead of grouping them closely together, has interposed discussions of the subjects of one of the proverbs – here the results of sexual sin for both man (23: 16–21) and woman (verses 22–7) – as well as the hymn in ch. 24. Adultery was regarded by Jewish law as a very serious crime: it was prohibited in the Ten Commandments (Exod. 20: 14), and was, theoretically, punishable by death until A.D. 40.

[a] *Some witnesses add* (28) To follow God brings great honour; to win his approval means long life.

16. *Two kinds of men. . .and a third:* the first two lines are to be taken together – there are three *kinds of men* who *add sin to sin* and bring *retribution* on themselves. According to the pattern of numerical proverbs we should expect three specific *kinds of men* to be listed as are the 'three kinds of men who arouse' hatred in 25: 2; but Ben Sira's feelings against the adulterer (presumably the first of the three *kinds*) are so strong that he spends the rest of the section condemning adultery in both sexes without ever reaching the second kind of man. By a play on words *the fire* that *consumes him* probably refers both to strong sexual passion and to fire as a figure for sudden destruction.

18–21 echo earlier doctrinal passages on God's control of the universe: verse 18 recalls objections that man can conceal his deeds from God's notice (16: 17–22); verses 19–20 summarize the answers given to those objections (16: 24 – 17: 20); verse 21 repeats the warning of sudden disaster as punishment in the call to repentance of 5: 4-7. But no repentance is here envisaged for a serious crime like adultery.

24-6. As Ben Sira did not believe in life after death, man's only hope for survival lay in continuance of family and good reputation.

27. *fear of the Lord* and *obeying his commandments* together represent the devotional and practical sides of religion for Ben Sira – themes which recur again and again. It is fitting that this summary should conclude the first third of the book. The verse in the footnote was added in some manuscripts to emphasize the reward of following God. *

The praise of wisdom

WISDOM ROOTED IN ISRAEL

Hear the praise of wisdom from her own mouth, **24**
as she speaks with pride among her people,
before the assembly of the Most High   2
and in the presence of the heavenly host:
'I am the word which was spoken by the Most   3
    High;
it was I who covered the earth like a mist.
My dwelling-place was in high heaven;   4
my throne was in a pillar of cloud.
Alone I made a circuit of the sky   5
and traversed the depth of the abyss.
The waves of the sea, the whole earth,   6
every people and nation were under my sway.
Among them all I looked for a home: 7
in whose territory was I to settle?
Then the Creator of the universe laid a command upon   8
    me;
my Creator decreed where I should dwell.
He said, "Make your home in Jacob;
find your heritage in Israel."
Before time began he created me,   9
and I shall remain for ever.
In the sacred tent I ministered in his presence,   10
and so I came to be established in Zion.
Thus he settled me in the city he loved   11
and gave me authority in Jerusalem.

12 I took root among the people whom the Lord had
    honoured
  by choosing them to be his special possession.

* The series of numerical proverbs is interrupted by ch. 24
which concludes the first part of the book with a passage
expounding Ben Sira's doctrine of wisdom more explicitly.
The second part of the book is similarly closed by a hymn
expounding the doctrine of creation (42: 15 – 43: 33), and
the third by another passage on wisdom (51: 13–30). That
Ben Sira intended this to be the plan of the work is shown by
the many links in vocabulary between, for example, 24: 1–22
and the introductory passage to the whole book (1: 1–20):
thus 'the depth of the abyss' is referred to in both 1: 3 and
24: 5, and both 1: 20 and 24: 16 speak of wisdom as a tree
spreading its branches.

As in Prov. 8: 4–6 wisdom is personified and makes a
speech commending herself to men. This chapter, like
Proverbs 8, describes wisdom as of cosmic significance,
created 'Before time' (24: 9, see Prov. 8: 22–31), and shows
other similarities, often echoing the language of the Proverbs
passage. But Ben Sira takes the doctrine further by making
this cosmic wisdom the special possession of Israel: wisdom
is now localized in Jerusalem (verses 10 and 11). As 1: 10 says,
the Lord 'has given her...in plenty to those who love him':
these are now identified as the Jews. This prepares the reader
for the explicit identification of wisdom with the Jewish
law (hinted at in passages like 19: 20) in Ben Sira's later com-
ments on wisdom's hymn (24: 23).

After an introduction (verses 1 and 2) wisdom is described as
cosmic in power (verses 3–6) yet with particular links with the
Jews in Jerusalem (verses 7–12). After a series of images drawn
from nature (verses 13–17) wisdom's speech ends with a
personal appeal to men to follow her, as in Prov. 8: 32–6.

1–2. *her people* probably refers to Israel, anticipating

verses 8–12. These introductory verses thus cover both themes of the first section of wisdom's speech: cosmic significance, by reference to the ancient concept of the heavenly court (verse 2), and the Jews' special share in it (verse 1).

3. '*I am the word. . .spoken by the Most High*': today we think of words as weak things which we can apologize for: the ancient Hebrews thought that a word, once spoken, had a power which could not be reversed, although no doubt some tried to reverse it by spells. So authors spoke in the Old Testament of God's word which created the universe, which would 'not return to me fruitless without accomplishing my purpose' (Isa. 55: 11). Ben Sira here refers to the opening chapters of Genesis where God's creation of the universe is described as happening through a series of creative words. By *mist* he means the 'flood' (or 'mist') which in Gen. 2: 6 watered the ground.

4. The *pillar of cloud* symbolized the presence of the Lord during the wanderings in the Sinai desert between Egypt and Palestine (Exod. 33: 9). Later Jews coined the word *shekinah* ('dwelling', or 'resting presence') to describe God's presence on the basis of the passage in Exodus.

5. Wisdom belongs to God's cosmic sphere, and does the same things as God, who 'walks to and fro on the vault of heaven' (Job 22: 14) and measures 'the depth of the abyss' (Ecclus. 1: 3). The *circuit of the sky* probably means the arched metal firmament which the Hebrews believed separated the upper waters from the lower waters in ancient cosmology; God is pictured as walking round it.

7. '*Among them all I looked for a home*' provides the link between wisdom's place in the universe and her localization on earth. Ben Sira is here in marked opposition to other writers: for in other books of the time wisdom seeks for a place on earth, but does not find any and returns to heaven.

10. It is claimed that wisdom finds perfect expression in the worship *In the sacred tent* and in the Jerusalem temple as the law prescribes. This seems inconsistent with the emphasis

on ethical conduct in the book, but Ben Sira had a strong
interest in such worship, as shown in the note on 7: 31.

11. The importance of *Jerusalem* as the holy city increased
rather than decreased as the Jews spread throughout the world,
and has culminated in the Zionist movement of the present
day. In these verses Ben Sira sums up both sides of the doctrine of God's special choice of the Jews: his choice of the
Jews as his people (by deliverance from Egypt and guidance
through the Sinai desert) and his choice of Jerusalem as his
holy city (as chosen and preserved by the Davidic line of
kings). ✳

WISDOM'S FRUIT

13 'There I grew like a cedar of Lebanon,
   like a cypress on the slopes of Hermon,
14 like a date-palm at Engedi,
   like roses at Jericho.
   I grew like a fair olive-tree in the vale,
   or like a plane-tree planted beside the water.
15 Like cassia or camel-thorn I was redolent of spices;
   I spread my fragrance like choice myrrh,
   like galban, aromatic shell, and gum resin;
   I was like the smoke of incense in the sacred tent.
16 Like a terebinth I spread out my branches,
   laden with honour and grace.
17 I put forth lovely shoots like the vine,
   and my blossoms were a harvest of wealth and honour.[a]

19 'Come to me, you who desire me,
   and eat your fill of my fruit.
20 The memory of me is sweeter than syrup,

[a] *Some witnesses add* (18) I give birth to noble love, reverence, knowledge, and holy hope; and I give all these my eternal progeny to God's
elect (*probable meaning; Gk. obscure*).

the possession of me sweeter than honey dripping from
    the comb.
Whoever feeds on me will be hungry for more,   21
and whoever drinks from me will thirst for more.
To obey me is to be safe from disgrace;   22
those who work in wisdom will not go astray.'

* After various images drawn from nature (verses 13–17) – of
uncertain significance – wisdom, still personified, closes her
speech with an appeal to men to receive and use what she
offers, using images of food and drink familiar from many
biblical passages and taken up in, for example, John 4: 14.

13–14. *Lebanon* and *Hermon* are high mountain ranges in
the extreme north of Palestine, and *Jericho* and *Engedi* are
near the Dead Sea in the south, well below sea level. These
place names may be intended to show that wisdom's appeal
is to the whole of Israel, both north and south, high ground
and low. Further, the cedars *of Lebanon*, compared to the
righteous in Ps. 92: 12, were famous as durable wood; the
Jewish historian Josephus and the Roman author Pliny praise
the date-palms of *Engedi* for their beauty on the arid shores of
the Dead Sea.

15. Many of these *spices* are mentioned as constituents in the
recipe for 'sacred anointing oil' to be used by Moses 'in the
sacred tent' (Exod. 30: 23–4). The verse recalls the liturgical
reference of verse 10.

18 (in the footnote) was added in some manuscripts to
stress certain religious virtues given to the Jews only – probably to guard against the universalistic view that all men
could enjoy the gifts of wisdom.

19–20. Wisdom's *fruit* is a commonplace metaphor in wisdom literature. 'The LORD's decrees' are said in Ps. 19: 10 to be
'sweeter than syrup or honey from the comb'; Ben Sira may
be quoting this passage deliberately to foreshadow the identification of wisdom with the law to be made in verse 23. *

IDENTIFICATION OF WISDOM AS THE LAW

23 All this is the covenant-book of God Most High,
    the law which Moses enacted to be the heritage of the
        assemblies of Jacob.*

25 He sends out wisdom in full flood like the river Pishon
    or like the Tigris at the time of firstfruits;

26 he overflows with understanding like the Euphrates
    or like Jordan at the time of harvest.

27 He pours forth instruction like the Nile,*
    like the Gihon at the time of vintage.

28 No man has ever fully known wisdom;
    from first to last no one has fathomed her;

29 for her thoughts are vaster than the ocean
    and her purpose deeper than the great abyss.

✳ After the end of wisdom's speech Ben Sira develops his
own thesis on the common identity of wisdom and the Jewish
law, of which verse 23 is the clearest statement. By his time
study and reinterpretation of the law had already become the
way to understand more of God's revelation of himself, as
shown by verses 28–9.

23. *All this*, that is, all the praise given to wisdom in the
speech, is to be interpreted as true of *the law* also. The personification of wisdom does not mean any semi-independent
heavenly being but is merely a manner of speaking poetically
about the law which already dominated the life of the pious
Jew. To follow wisdom and the fear of God is to practise *the
law which Moses enacted to be the heritage of the assemblies of
Jacob*, in the Greek an exact quotation of Deut. 33: 4, though

[a] *Some witnesses add* (24) Never fail to be strong in the Lord; hold fast
to him, so that he may strengthen you; the Lord Almighty is God
alone; beside him there is no saviour.
[b] *So one Vs.; Gk.* He makes instruction shine like light.

the words differ in the N.E.B. *the assemblies of Jacob* probably denote Jewish communities throughout the world which the original Greek translator wished to serve, as stated in the Preface.

24, inserted in some manuscripts by a copyist as a pious exhortation, consists of various liturgical phrases from the Old Testament.

25-7. Man is dependent on the law for spiritual life as the ancient farmers in river valleys were dependent on floods for irrigation to maintain physical life. The prophets had described a future golden age for the Jews in terms of the renewal of the fertility of paradise (= the garden of Eden); Ben Sira uses the four rivers which in Gen. 2: 11-14 flow from Eden throughout the world, to describe knowledge of the law flowing inexhaustibly from God through the Jews to renew the spiritual life of the world. The *Pishon* may be the Indus, and *the Gihon* the Nile; but identification was unimportant to the author (who appears to mention the Nile twice) compared with the theological vision of a world restored to God's will. To the four rivers of Genesis Ben Sira adds the *Jordan*, the major river of Palestine. The *Jordan*, *Tigris* and *Euphrates* flooded in the spring (*the time of firstfruits*), *the Nile* in the autumn (*the time of vintage*). In verse 27 the Greek translator misread the Hebrew *kay'eōr* ('as the Nile') for *kā'ōr* ('as the light'), as noted in the footnote. ✶

BEN SIRA'S VOCATION

As for me, I was like a canal leading from a river,   30
a watercourse into a pleasure-garden.
I said, 'I will water my garden,   31
drenching its flower-beds';
and at once my canal became a river
and my river a sea.
I will again make discipline shine like the dawn,   32

so that its light may be seen from afar.

33 I will again pour out doctrine like prophecy
and bequeath it to future generations.

34 Truly, my labour has not been for myself alone
but for all seekers of wisdom.

✶ Ben Sira now reveals his view of his own contribution in
spreading knowledge of wisdom and the law: he is making
the *discipline* of study *shine* so that Jews far from Palestine may
learn their heritage and religion (verse 32). He continues to
use the irrigation metaphors of the previous section, likening
himself to an irrigation *canal leading from a* large *river* (verse
30); just as a *canal* overflows because of too much water, so
through private study he realized that all his increasing knowledge should be made available *not . . . for myself alone, but for
all seekers of wisdom* (verse 34). Hence the book he wrote.

33. *like prophecy:* he feels that his inspiration is as compelling
as that of the prophets before him. ✶

MORE NUMERICAL PROVERBS

25 There are three sights which warm my heart[a]
and are beautiful in the eyes of the Lord and of men:
concord among brothers, friendship among neighbours,
and a man and wife who are inseparable.

2 There are three kinds of men who arouse my hatred,
who disgust me by their manner of life:
a poor man who boasts, a rich man who lies,
and an old fool who commits adultery.

3 If you have not gathered wisdom in your youth,
how will you find it when you are old?

[a] *So Vss.; Gk.* which make me beautiful.

Sound judgement sits well on grey hairs　　　　4
and wise advice comes well from older men.
Wisdom is fitting in the aged,　　　　5
and ripe counsel in men of eminence.
Long experience is the old man's crown,　　　　6
and his pride is the fear of the Lord.

✻ The series of numerical proverbs which started in 23 : 16 and
was interrupted by ch. 24 is now resumed. Verses 1 and 2
contrast three good relationships between people living
together with three men whose bad conduct isolates them from
society. This contrast relates to social behaviour and the next
major section on *Counsels upon social behaviour* (25: 13 – 34:
12) ought probably to begin here. As in ch. 23, the following
verses develop a subject arising from the numerical proverb –
behaviour in old age.

　　3. *If you have not gathered wisdom in your youth. . .* was
quoted by later Jewish scholars in discussions about old age. ✻

TEN HAPPY PEOPLE

I can think of nine men I count happy,　　　　7
and I can tell you of a tenth:
a man who can take delight in his children,
and one who lives to see his enemy's downfall;
happy the husband of a sensible wife,　　　　8
the farmer who does not plough with ox and ass together,[a]
the man whose tongue never betrays him,
and the servant who has never worked for an inferior!
Happy the man who has found a friend,[b]　　　　9
and the speaker who has an attentive audience!

[a] the farmer. . .together: *so Heb.; Gk. omits.*
[b] *So Vss.; Gk.* found good sense.

10 How great is the man who finds wisdom!
   But no greater than he who fears the Lord.
11 The fear of the Lord excels all other gifts;
   to what can we compare the man who has it?*a*

✴ Here we find the classic pattern of numerical proverb where the highest grade comes last – 'he who fears the Lord' (verse 10). Ben Sira then completes the section in verse 11 by declaring the incomparable worth of the fear of God, one of the recurring themes of the book.

7. When men believe that judgement falls on the wicked in this life, as did Ben Sira and many Old Testament writers, they naturally expect to live *to see* an *enemy's downfall*. Thus the writer of a psalm listens 'for the downfall of my cruel foes' (Ps. 92: 11). Even in the Old Testament this view is condemned: 'he who gloats over another's ruin will answer for it' (Prov. 17: 5), and the New Testament directs men to love their enemies (Matt. 5: 43-4).

8. The Greek text lists only nine different people instead of ten. The N.E.B. has supplied the missing person, *the farmer*, from the Hebrew text which has the full number. The phrase *plough with ox and ass together* comes originally from Deut. 22: 10 where this practice is prohibited. Ben Sira uses the phrase metaphorically, as did the later Syriac author Bar Hebraeus, to mean unequal partnership in marriage – here a sensible husband married to a stupid wife. ✴

[a] *Some witnesses add* (12) The fear of the Lord is the source of love for him, and faith is the source of loyalty to him.

Counsels upon social behaviour

ON BAD WIVES

ANY WOUND BUT a wound in the heart!   13
Any spite but a woman's!
Any disaster but one caused by hate!   14
Any vengeance but the vengeance of an enemy!
There is no venom*a* worse than a snake's,   15
and no anger worse than an enemy's.

I would sooner share a home with a lion or a snake   16
than keep house with a spiteful wife.
Her spite changes her expression,   17
making her look as surly as a bear.
Her husband goes to a neighbour for his meals   18
and cannot repress a bitter sigh.

There is nothing so bad as a bad wife;   19
may the fate of the wicked overtake her!*b*
It is as easy for an old man to climb a sand-dune   20
as for a quiet husband to live with a nagging wife.
Do not be enticed by a woman's beauty   21
or set your heart on possessing her.
If a man is supported by his wife   22
he must expect tantrums, shamelessness, and outrage.
A bad wife brings humiliation,   23
downcast looks, and a wounded heart.

[a] *Probable meaning, based on one Vs.; Gk.* head.
[b] *Or* may it fall to her lot to marry a scoundrel!

Slack of hand and weak of knee
is the man whose wife fails to make him happy.

24 Woman is the origin of sin,
and it is through her that we all die.

25 Do not leave a leaky cistern to drip
or allow a bad wife to say what she likes.

26 If she does not accept your control,
divorce her and send her away.

* Ben Sira now compares bad wives (25: 13–26) with good wives (26: 1–4); the length of the section on bad wives reflects his personal prejudice against women. Earlier wisdom literature had criticized, for example, 'nagging and ill-tempered' wives (Prov. 21: 19) but had also praised dutiful wives at length (Prov. 31: 10–31). Ben Sira regarded daughters as a source of continual anxiety (42: 9) and even stated that 'a man's wickedness' was better than 'a woman's goodness' (42: 14). Fortunately such prejudice was not typical of Judaism.

20. Climbing *a sand-dune* when your feet fall back in soft sand is extremely hard work requiring patience – especially *for an old man*.

24. Rabbinic theology traced the historical origin of sin to the account of Adam and Eve eating the forbidden fruit in the garden of Eden (Gen. 3: 1–19), when, they considered, mankind was punished by being made subject to death. 'Dust you are, to dust you shall return' (Gen. 3: 19). Rabbinic tradition usually regarded Adam as primarily responsible, but Ben Sira here, together with some early Palestinian exegesis in Aramaic translations, regards Eve as *the origin of sin . . . through* whom *we all die*. The New Testament sometimes seems to regard Adam (Rom. 5: 12–14), sometimes Eve (1 Tim. 2: 14) as responsible for sin and death. Death is elsewhere regarded by Ben Sira not as punishment for sin but as 'the Lord's decree for all living men' (41: 4) – part of the natural order.

26. *divorce her:* the right of divorce is assumed in Mosaic law. If a wife 'does not win' her husband's 'favour', he may write her 'a note of divorce', give it to her and dismiss her (Deut. 24: 1). Two centuries after Ben Sira divorce was the subject of fierce debate in Judaism: rigorists admitted only adultery and sexual misconduct as grounds for divorce, whereas liberals allowed even the charge that a wife had cooked a meal badly. Ben Sira seems remarkably liberal – perhaps because of his prejudice! ✶

ON GOOD WIVES

A good wife makes a happy husband;   **26**
she doubles the length of his life.
A staunch wife is her husband's joy;   2
he will live out his days in peace.
A good wife means a good life;   3
she is one of the Lord's gifts to those who fear him.
Rich or poor, they are light-hearted,   4
and always have a smile on their faces.

✶ The virtuous wife, here contrasted with the bad wife, was a universal theme of proverbs. Verses 1 and 3 were quoted by later Jewish teachers in discussions on the place of women.

3. *A good wife...is one of the Lord's gifts:* Ben Sira again relates a sphere of social life to his 'background' theme of the fear of the Lord, as discussed in notes on 3: 1–16. ✶

MORE ON GOOD AND BAD WOMEN

Three things there are that alarm me,   5
and a fourth I am afraid to face:
the scandal of the town, the gathering of a mob,

and calumny – all harder to bear than death;

6 but it is heart-ache and grief when a wife is jealous of a
    rival,
and everyone alike feels the lash of her tongue.

7 A bad wife is a chafing yoke;
controlling her is like clutching a scorpion.

8 A drunken wife is a great provocation;
she cannot keep her excesses secret.

9 A loose woman betrays herself by her bold looks;
you can tell her by her glance.

10 Keep close watch over a headstrong daughter;
if she finds you off your guard, she will take her
    chance.

11 Beware of her impudent looks
and do not be surprised if she disobeys you.

12 As a parched traveller with his tongue hanging out
drinks from any spring that offers,
she will open her arms to every embrace,
and her quiver to the arrow.

13 A wife's charm is the delight of her husband,
and her womanly skill puts flesh on his bones.

14 A silent wife is a gift from the Lord;
her restraint is more than money can buy.

15 A modest wife has charm upon charm;
no scales can weigh the worth of her chastity.

16 As beautiful as the sunrise in the Lord's heaven
is a good wife in a well-ordered home.

17 As bright as the light on the sacred lamp-stand
is a beautiful face in the settled prime of life.

Like a golden pillar on a silver base   18
is a shapely leg with a firm foot.[a][b]

＊ Starting with another numerical proverb (verses 5–6) Ben
Sira renews his description of bad women (verses 7–12),
closing the section with more similes describing the good wife.
     5–6. Another classic numerical proverb like 25: 7–10
stressing the last item as the most important – here a *jealous*
wife. The *rival* referred to could be the second wife of a
polygamous household, but may simply refer to two women
competing for a man's affections.
     7–8 refer to the pain suffered by the husband: his wife's
reaction to attempts to control her is like the sting of a
scorpion and her drunkenness provokes him to anger.
     10–12. Women did not often go out in public alone. If your
headstrong daughter wandered outside on her own, she would
make you 'the talk of the town' by displaying her beauty to

[a] is. . .foot: *probable meaning; Gk. obscure.*   [b] *Some witnesses add*

My son, guard your health in the bloom of your youth,	19
and do not waste your vigour on what belongs to others.	
Search the whole plain for a fertile plot;	20
sow your own seed, trusting in your pedigree.	
Then the children you leave behind	21
will prosper, confident in their parentage.	
A woman of the streets counts as mere spittle,	22
a married woman as a mortuary for her lovers.	
A godless woman is a good match for a lawless husband,	23
a pious one for a man who fears the Lord.	
A brazen woman courts disgrace,	24
but a virtuous one is modest even before her husband.	
A wilful woman is a shameless bitch,	25
but a modest one fears the Lord.	
A woman who honours her husband is accounted wise by all,	26
but if she despises him, all know her as proud and godless.	
A good wife makes a happy husband;	
she doubles the length of his life.	
A strident, garrulous wife is like a trumpet sounding the charge;	27
in a home like hers a man lives in the tumult of war.	

men (42: 11–12); an over-anxious father might well imagine her opening *her quiver to* every *arrow* – a phrase probably intended to be taken obscenely.

17–18. Both *golden pillar* and *sacred lamp-stand* refer to furniture in the Temple at Jerusalem, the *lamp-stand* being the seven-branched lamp-stand (*menōrāh*) associated with the festival of rededication after the Maccabean revolt (*Ḥanukkāh*) and featured on coins and in art. Although Ben Sira praises the virtuous wife's face and legs, he means not only physical beauty but also spiritual worth.

19–27 appear only in the Syriac version and a few Greek manuscripts. The verses (in the footnote) contain more proverbs on good and bad wives, drawn mainly from other passages in Proverbs and Ecclesiasticus. ✴

ON TESTING THE QUALITIES OF MEN

28 Two things grieve my heart,
and a third excites my anger:
a soldier in distress through poverty,
wise men treated with contempt,
and a man deserting right conduct for wrong –
the Lord will bring him to the scaffold.

29 How hard it is for a merchant to keep clear of wrong
or for a shopkeeper to be innocent of dishonesty!
27 Many have cheated for gain;[a]
a money-grubber will always turn a blind eye.
2 As a peg is held fast in the joint between stones,
so dishonesty squeezes in between selling and buying.
3 Unless a man holds resolutely to the fear of the Lord,
his house will soon be in ruins.

[a] *Some witnesses read* for a trifle.

Shake a sieve, and the rubbish remains;   4
start an argument, and discover a man's faults.
As the work of a potter is tested in the furnace,   5
so a man is tried in debate.
As the fruit of the tree reveals the skill of its grower,   6
so the expression of a man's thought reveals his character.
Do not praise a man till you hear him in discussion,   7
for this is the test.

If justice is what you seek, you will succeed,   8
and wear it like a splendid robe.
Birds of a feather roost together,   9
and honesty comes home to those who practise it.
A lion lies in wait for its prey,   10
and so do sins for those who do wrong.

✽ A numerical proverb of the classic type (like 25: 7–10 and
26: 5–6) leads to a general discussion. In the proverb (26: 28)
the condition of each person is the reverse of what it should be.
The last item of the proverb, the 'man deserting right conduct for wrong', leads first to a brief discussion of trade
(26: 29 – 27: 3), anticipating lengthier treatment of money
matters in 29: 1–10; secondly to various ways in which a
person's character is tested in debate and argument (27: 4–7)
and thirdly to factors in character that affect the result of
testing, 'justice' and 'honesty' for good and 'sins' for bad
(27: 8–10).

29. The increasingly international character of Judaism
meant a wide network of acquaintance for trade, many Jews
becoming merchants. The travelling connected with trade
left little time for study and orthodox Jewish teachers dis-
approved of it. Although Ben Sira advises people not to be
ashamed of 'making a profit out of trade' (42: 5), clearly he
believed some dishonesty to be inescapable.

27: 2. *dishonesty* is involved in trade as surely as *a peg* jammed *between stones* is difficult to remove.

3. Another 'background' reference to *the fear of the Lord* as the only guide to life.

4. As *a sieve* is shaken, the grain falls through leaving the husks.

5. As flaws in a pot show up when it is fired, so a man's stupidity shows when he reasons.

9. If a man is honest to others, he will attract other honest men to himself; they will *roost together*. The N.E.B. uses a famous English proverb to translate a famous Hebrew proverb quoted by later Jewish teachers. This is *not* the origin of the English proverb. *

INTRODUCING THE EVILS OF BAD SPEECH

11 The conversation of the pious is constantly wise,
   but a fool is as changeable as the moon.
12 Grudge every minute spent among fools,
   but linger among the thoughtful.
13 The conversation of fools is repulsive;
   they make a joke of unbridled vice.
14 Their cursing and swearing make the hair stand on end;
   when such men quarrel, others stop their ears.
15 The quarrels of the proud lead to bloodshed;
   their abuse offends the ear.

* Debate as a method of testing people leads to a series of sections on different kinds of evil speech (27: 16 – 28: 26), preceded by this general introduction on conversation. The poor conversation of an unintelligent person (*a fool*) is a recurrent theme: he speaks before he thinks (21: 26), is not worth listening to (21: 16) and is coarse and vulgar (23: 13) – all paralleled in this passage. *

ON DECEITFUL SPEECH

The betrayer of secrets loses his credit   16
and can never find an intimate friend.
Love your friend and keep faith with him,   17
but if you betray his secrets, keep out of his way;
as a man kills his enemy,   18
so you have killed your neighbour's friendship.
As a bird that is allowed to escape your hand,   19
your neighbour, once lost, will not be caught again.
He has gone too far for you to pursue him,   20
and escaped like a gazelle from a trap.
A wound may be bandaged, an insult pardoned,   21
but the betrayer of secrets has nothing to hope for.

A man who winks is plotting mischief;   22
those who know him will keep their distance.
He speaks sweetly enough to your face   23
and admires whatever you say,
but later he will change his tune
and use your own words to trip you.
There are many things I hate, but him above all;   24
the Lord will hate him too.

Whoever throws a stone up in the air is throwing it at 25
    his own head,
and a treacherous blow means wounds all round.
Dig a pit and you will fall into it;   26
set a trap and you will be caught by it.
The wrong a man does recoils on him,   27
and he does not know where it has come from.

28 An arrogant man deals in mockery and insults,
  but retribution lies in wait for him like a lion.

29 Those who rejoice at the downfall of good men will be
    trapped
  and consumed with pain before they die.

* Various kinds of deceitful speech are now listed: betrayal of
secrets (27: 16–21), insincerity (27: 22–4), contentiousness
(28: 8–12) and gossip (28: 13–26). The series is broken by
warnings against the arrogance that causes such deceitful
speech (27: 25–9) which Ben Sira then relates to various
theological doctrines (27: 30 – 28: 7).

16–21. Betrayal *of secrets* was frequently criticized in
proverbial literature as, for example, in Prov. 25: 9. 'A secret
betrayed...will make any friend keep his distance' (22: 22)
and kills *friendship* irredeemably – hence the metaphors of
birds flying away.

22–4. A wink of an eye is associated with 'crooked talk' in
Prov. 6: 12–13. Ben Sira clearly viewed it as a sure sign of
insincerity, meaning deliberate shiftiness of glance rather than
a nervous twitch.

25–9. As in Prov. 26: 22–7 description of the gossip and
hypocrite leads directly to warnings that *The wrong a man does
recoils on him* (verse 27). In the next section Ben Sira passes
from this 'natural' retribution observable in life to theological
doctrines of forgiveness and divine punishment from the
standpoint of faith.

25. *a stone* thrown *up in the air* falls upon the *head* of the
thrower. The context implies that the man who deals *a
treacherous blow* should suffer for it.

29. *consumed with pain before they die:* punishment for sin
before death according to Ben Sira's belief. *

DIVINE PUNISHMENT AND FORGIVENESS

Rage and anger, these also I abhor,   30
but a sinner has them ready at hand.

The vengeful man will face the vengeance of the Lord,   **28**
who keeps strict account of his sins.

Forgive your neighbour his wrongdoing;   2
then, when you pray, your sins will be forgiven.

If a man harbours a grudge against another,   3
is he to expect healing from the Lord?

If he has no mercy on his fellow-man,   4
is he still to ask forgiveness for his own sins?

If a mere mortal cherishes rage,   5
where is he to look for pardon?

Think of the end that awaits you, and have done with hate;   6

think of mortality and death, and be true to the
    commandments;

think of the commandments, and do not be enraged at   7
    your neighbour;

think of the covenant of the Most High, and overlook
    faults.

* From observable punishment in social life Ben Sira turns to
the theology of divine retribution and how to avoid it –
forgiveness of others. Christians have sometimes thought that
the words on forgiveness in the Lord's Prayer ('Forgive us the
wrong we have done, as we have forgiven those who have
wronged us' Matt. 6: 12) were peculiarly Christian and that
the later frequent encouragement to forgive others in Jewish
writings was due to Christian influence. 'So long as we are
merciful, God is merciful to us; if we are not merciful to
others, God is not merciful to us' (Babylonian Talmud,
Megillah 28a) is very similar to 'if you forgive others the

wrongs they have done, your heavenly Father will also forgive you; but if you do not forgive others, then the wrongs you have done will not be forgiven by your Father' (Matt. 6: 14–15). However, Ben Sira's words in 28: 2–4 (especially verse 2) show that this relation between human and divine forgiveness existed in Jewish teaching two centuries before Christ was born. Verses 6 and 7 stress more traditional Jewish concepts: 'death' as punishment for sin (as in 25: 24), obedience to 'the commandments' of the law and loyalty to 'the covenant' which here means faithfully following the law. This section illustrates well the theological background of all Ben Sira's practical advice.

30 adds *Rage and anger* to the attitudes mentioned in the previous section, and with the word *sinner* introduces the theological atmosphere of the section.

28: 3. By *healing* is meant forgiveness for sin. ✻

MORE ON EVIL SPEECH

8 To avoid a quarrel is a setback for sin,
   for it is a hot temper that kindles quarrels.
9 A sinner sows trouble between friends
   and spreads scandal where before there was peace.
10 A fire is kept hot by stoking
   and a quarrel by persistence.
   A man's rage is in proportion to his strength,
   and his anger in proportion to his wealth.
11 A hasty argument kindles a fire,
   and a hasty quarrel leads to bloodshed.
12 Blow on a spark to make it glow, or spit on it to put it out;
   both results come from the one mouth.

13 Curses on the gossip and the tale-bearer!
   For they have been the ruin of many peaceable men.

The talk of a third party has wrecked the lives of many 14
and driven them from country to country;
it has destroyed fortified towns
and demolished the houses of the great.
The talk of a third party has brought divorce on staunch 15
    wives
and deprived them of all they have laboured for.
Whoever pays heed to it will never again find rest 16
or live in peace of mind.
The lash of a whip raises weals, 17
but the lash of a tongue breaks bones.
Many have been killed by the sword, 18
but not so many as by the tongue.
Happy the man who is sheltered from its onslaught, 19
who has not been exposed to its fury,
who has not borne its yoke,
or been chained with its fetters!
For its yoke is of iron, 20
its fetters of bronze.
The death it brings is an evil death; 21
better the grave than the tongue!
But it has no power over the godfearing; 22
they cannot be burned in its flames.
Those who desert the Lord fall victim to it; 23
among them it will burn like fire and not be quenched.
It will launch itself against them like a lion
and tear them like a leopard.
As you enclose your garden with a thorn hedge, 24
and lock up your silver and gold,
so weigh your words and measure them, 25
and make a door and a bolt for your mouth.

26 Beware of being tripped by your tongue
   and falling into the power of a lurking enemy.

✻ The author resumes the series of sections on evil speech
which began in 27: 16 by deploring quarrels (verses 8–12) and
closes the series by condemning gossip (verses 13–26).

8–12. Quarrels arise from hastiness, and *strength* and *wealth*
increase a man's *persistence* in anger (verse 10), yet everyone
can halt a quarrel if he wishes (verse 12).

14. *a third party:* the literal translation is 'a third tongue' –
in later Jewish literature a technical term for a slanderer. The
author is thinking of relations between two people ruined by
malicious tales told by another person; this can happen
particularly in marriage.

15. *divorce* was not infrequent, as shown by further references
in 7: 26 and 25: 26.

17. *the lash of a tongue breaks bones* probably developed
from 'a soft tongue may break down solid bone' (Prov. 25:
15), altered to indicate the psychological and social damage
caused by gossiping tongues as more harmful than the
physical damage of *a whip* or even a *sword* (verse 18).

21. Gossip *brings an evil death* because of the misery caused
before death.

26 closes the series on evil speech with fitting references
back to other sections: *a lurking enemy* betrays secrets (27:
16–18) and 'spreads scandal' (28: 9); 'He speaks sweetly
enough to your face. . .but later he will change his tune and
use your own words to trip you' (27: 23) unless you are
careful. ✻

ON LENDING MONEY

29 A devout man lends to his neighbour;
   by supporting him he keeps the commandments.
2 Lend to your neighbour in his time of need;
   repay your neighbour punctually.

Be as good as your word and keep faith with him,   3
and your needs will always be met.

Many treat a loan as a windfall   4
and bring trouble on those who helped them.

Until he gets a loan, a man kisses his neighbour's hand   5
and talks with bated breath about his money;
but when it is time to repay, he postpones it,
pays back only perfunctory promises,
and alleges that the time is too short.[a]

If he can pay, his creditor will scarcely get back half,   6
and will count himself lucky at that;
if he cannot pay, he has defrauded the other of his money,
and gratuitously made an enemy of him;[b]
he will pay him back in curses and insults
and with shame instead of honour.

Because of such dishonesty many refuse to lend,   7
for fear of being needlessly defrauded.

Nevertheless be patient with the penniless,   8
and do not keep him waiting for your charity;
for the commandment's sake help the poor,   9
and in his need do not send him away empty-handed.

Be ready to lose money for a brother or a friend;   10
do not leave it to rust away under a stone.

Store up for yourself the treasure which the Most High   11
     has commanded,
and it will benefit you more than gold.

Let almsgiving be the treasure in your strong-room,   12
and it will rescue you from every misfortune.

[a] *Or* that times are hard.   [b] and. . .him: *some witnesses read* and the
other has won himself an enemy at his own expense.

13 It will arm you against the enemy
better than stout shield or strong spear.

✻ Jewish participation in trade started with the spread of Jews
throughout the Roman Empire, as noted on 26: 29. The
traders famous in Ben Sira's days were the Greeks, and any
offensive caricature of the Jews as Shylock-like money-
lenders with mid-European accents should be forgotten.
Whereas Babylonian law allowed for interest charges on
loans at 20%, Jewish law forbade any interest charges on
loans to fellow-Jews, and encouraged people to be generous
in their help of others: 'When one of your fellow-countrymen
...becomes poor,...Be open-handed towards him and
lend him on pledge as much as he needs' (Deut. 15: 7–8) and
'If you advance money to any poor man amongst my people,
you shall not act like a money-lender: you must not exact
interest in advance from him' (Exod. 22: 25). Later Jewish
teaching continued to condemn money-lending for profit.
Helping the poor ('almsgiving') was regarded in the early
centuries A.D. as a good deed of such value that it could secure
eternal life for the giver, and the Hebrew word used in the
Old Testament for 'righteousness' (*tsedāqāh*) came to be used
for 'almsgiving' as in verse 12 here. The teaching of Jesus
in the New Testament takes up the duty of lending (Matt.
5: 42), but lays emphasis on doing these things without
expecting any reward; the worldly wisdom of Ben Sira (who
always has an eye to the future) is totally lacking.

3–7. Prompt repayment of loans was considered of great
importance by Jewish teachers for moral reasons rather than
because one's *needs will always be met*. In the Mishnah (*Aboth*
2: 9) Rabbi Simeon chooses as 'the evil way which a man
should shun' 'he that borrows and does not repay', quoting
'The wicked man borrows and does not pay back, but the
righteous is a generous giver' (Ps. 37: 21). A *windfall* is a
surprise gift, like a legacy, which you feel justified in keeping.

8. With genuinely poor people you should *be patient* and

help without assessing too exactly their ability to repay, being prepared to lose money if necessary.

9–12. Orthodox Judaism so pervades Ben Sira's outlook that, as in 17: 14; 28: 7 and 29: 1, keeping the commandments is the norm of all moral and social life. Money is for use and not for miserly storage: Ben Sira anticipates the advice of the New Testament: 'Do not store up for yourselves treasure on earth, where it grows rusty...Store up treasure in heaven, where there is ... no rust' (Matt. 6: 19–20). ✵

ON GIVING GUARANTEES FOR DEBTORS

A good man will stand surety for his neighbour;   14
only a man who has lost all sense of shame will fail him.
If a man stands surety for you, do not forget his kindness, 15
for he has staked his very self for you.
A sinner wastes the property of his surety,   16
and an ungrateful man fails his rescuer.   17
Suretyship has ruined the prosperity of many   18
and wrecked them like a storm at sea;
it has driven men of influence into exile,
and set them wandering in foreign countries.
When a sinner commits himself to suretyship,   19
his pursuit of gain will involve him in lawsuits.
Help your neighbour to the best of your ability,   20
but beware of becoming too deeply involved.

✵ When a debtor could not repay his debt, another person could 'stand surety' for him, that is, guarantee repayment, by intervening on his behalf and assuming responsibility for repayment, either by obtaining the money from the debtor or by substituting himself so that if the debtor is not trustworthy the patron's own person could be seized by the creditor. Ben Sira's advice on this is much more charitable

than that in Proverbs where a man 'who gives a guarantee and
surrenders himself to another as surety' is said to be 'without
sense' (Prov. 17: 18 – advice given five times in Proverbs in
different places). This change of attitude is probably due to
changing economic conditions and to Ben Sira's own deep
sense of piety. But he is careful to warn of the dangers
(verses 16–18) and of 'becoming too deeply involved' beyond
one's means (verse 20).

18–19. *suretyship:* whereas verse 18 describes the suffering
of some good men who stand surety for others, verse 19
condemns evil men who pose as benefactors to make profits
by extorting the debtors. ✳

ON BEING POOR BUT INDEPENDENT

21 The necessities of life are water, bread, and clothes,
   and a home with its decent privacy;
22 better the life of a poor man in his own hut
   than a sumptuous banquet in another man's house.
23 Be content with whatever you have,
   and do not get a name for living on hospitality.[a]
24 It is a poor life going from house to house,
   keeping your mouth shut because you are a visitor.
25 You receive the guests and hand the drinks without being
        thanked for it,
   and into the bargain must listen to words that rankle:
26 'Come here, stranger, and lay the table;
   whatever you have there, hand it to me.'
27 'Be off, stranger! Make way for a more important guest;
   my brother has come to stay, and I need the guest-room.'
28 How hard it is for a sensible man to bear
   criticism from the household or abuse from his creditor!

[a] *Reading based on one Vs.; Gk.* and do not hear reproaches from your
family.

✻ Ben Sira, closing the section on money matters (ch. 29), emphasizes the virtues of independence, however humble, by vividly describing the life of those who live on other people's hospitality (verses 22–7). Like the 'parasites' of rich Roman houses attacked by Latin satirists like Juvenal, such 'visitors' were expected to perform certain menial duties at table and keep quiet in return for their board and lodging. It is better to keep one's self-respect.

27. When *a more important guest* arrives the 'visitor' is sent away to wander 'from house to house' again (verse 24).

28. As 28: 26 summed up the sections on evil speech, so this verse sums up the sections on money matters. ✻

ON CORPORAL PUNISHMENT FOR CHILDREN

A man who loves his son will whip him often **30**
so that when he grows up he may be a joy to him.
He who disciplines his son will find profit in him   2
and take pride in him among his acquaintances.
He who gives his son a good education will make his   3
    enemy jealous
and will boast of him among his friends.
When the father dies, it is as if he were still alive,   4
for he has left a copy of himself behind him.
While he lived he saw and rejoiced,   5
and when he died he had no regrets.
He has left an heir to take vengeance on his enemies   6
and to repay the kindness of his friends.

A man who spoils his son will bandage every wound   7
and will be on tenterhooks at every cry.
An unbroken horse turns out stubborn,   8
and an unchecked son turns out headstrong.

9 Pamper a boy and he will shock you;
play with him and he will grieve you.
10 Do not share his laughter, for fear of sharing his pain;
you will only end by grinding your teeth.
11 Do not give him freedom while he is young
or overlook his errors.
12 Break him in while he is young,
beat him soundly while he is still a child,
or he may grow stubborn and disobey you
and cause you vexation.
13 Discipline your son and take pains with him
or he may offend you by some disgraceful act.

✡ Ben Sira agrees with most ancients that corporal punishment is necessary for bringing up children properly. Egyptian proverbial literature, much used in formal education, likened training children to rearing beasts (like the 'unbroken horse' and 'unchecked son' of verse 8), and claimed that if a father struck his own son he saved him from death (*Aḥikar* 81) – presumably the result of bad discipline. Israelite wisdom copied this pattern: 'take the stick to him, and save him from death' (Prov. 23: 13). The best family life existed where parents kept themselves remote: any father who was over-familiar or played with his children was thought to lose their respect (verses 9 and 10). Family life today is very different, and recognizes the independent personality of the child much more; many oppose corporal punishment, trusting rather in rational persuasion within a closer relationship.

4. *it is as if he were still alive:* as Ben Sira did not believe in any life after death, immortality was possible only through the memory of other people (as noted on 10: 17 and expounded in 44: 7–15) or through the continuity of parental likeness in children.

7. Children at play must learn to stand up for themselves.

Parents who imagine *every cry* comes from their own child coddle them too much and halt the development of their independence.

10. In Ezek. 18: 2 it was 'the children's teeth' that were 'set on edge' because of their fathers' sins. That proverb is here reversed: fathers grind their *teeth* as they see in their children the results of weak discipline. ✶

ON HEALTH AND HAPPINESS

Better a poor man who is healthy and fit   14
than a rich man racked by disease.

Health and fitness are better than any gold,   15
and bodily vigour than boundless prosperity.

There is no wealth to compare with health of body,   16
no festivity to equal a joyful heart.

Better death than a life of misery,   17
eternal rest than a long illness.

Good things spread before a man without appetite   18
are like offerings of food placed on a tomb.

What use is a sacrifice to an idol   19
which can neither taste nor smell?

So it is with the man afflicted by the Lord.
He gazes at the food before him and sighs   20
as a eunuch sighs when he embraces a girl.

Do not give yourself over to sorrow   21
or distress yourself deliberately.

A merry heart keeps a man alive,   22
and joy lengthens his span of days.

Indulge yourself, take comfort,   23
and banish sorrow;

for sorrow has been the death of many,
and no advantage ever came of it.

24 Envy and anger shorten a man's life,
and anxiety brings premature old age.

25 A man with a gay heart has a good appetite
and relishes the food he eats.

* A rich man who is ill cannot enjoy the results of wealth and when he dies he must 'leave his wealth to others' (11: 19). True happiness thus lies in prolonging physical life: good 'health' is preferable to 'wealth' (verses 14-16), a shorter, healthier life to a longer life full of 'illness' (verses 17-20) and reasonable self-indulgence to self-motivated 'sorrow' and 'anxiety' (verses 21-4). Verse 25 ends the section by drawing together the themes of health ('appetite') and happiness.

17-20 describe the feelings of a sick man who cannot enjoy any pleasures. *death* is described as *eternal rest* in accordance with Ben Sira's belief in no life after death. Verse 18 is probably linked with verse 17 rather than with verse 19, and refers to an ancient practice, taken over from the Canaanites but probably disused in Ben Sira's time, of placing *food* on tombs for the dead. The practice is deplored in Deut. 26: 14, but is approved in a later addition to Tobit (4: 17) where it is re-interpreted as giving alms at funerals. Ben Sira emphasizes the uselessness of *Good things* when they cannot be enjoyed through illness or death. Verse 19, wrongly interpreting verse 18 as offerings to idols, is probably a later addition using familiar passages like 'gods that can neither see nor hear' (Deut. 4: 28, see also Ps. 115: 4-7).

23. *Indulge yourself. . .banish sorrow. . .*: although the Babylonian Talmud quotes this verse, the theme is more characteristic of Ecclesiastes than of Ben Sira: 'Banish discontent from your mind, and shake off the troubles of the body' (Eccles. 11: 10). *

ON THE DISADVANTAGES OF WEALTH

A rich man loses weight by wakeful nights,   **31**
when the cares of wealth drive sleep away;
sleepless worry keeps him wide awake,   2
just as serious illness banishes[a] sleep.
A rich man toils to amass a fortune,   3
and when he relaxes he enjoys every luxury.
A poor man toils to make a slender living,   4
and when he relaxes he finds himself in need.

Passion for gold can never be right;   5
the pursuit of money leads a man astray.[b]
Many a man has come to ruin for the sake of gold   6
and found disaster staring him in the face.
Gold is a pitfall to those who are infatuated with it,   7
and every fool is caught by it.
Happy the rich man who has remained free of its taint   8
and has not made gold his aim!
Show us that man, and we will congratulate him;   9
he has performed a miracle among his people.
Has anyone ever come through this test unscathed?   10
Then he has good cause to be proud.
Has anyone ever had it in his power to sin and refrained,
or to do wrong and has not done it?
Then he shall be confirmed in his prosperity,   11
and the whole people will hail him as a benefactor.

✶ Ben Sira expands on the theme of 30: 14–15: wealth is not
only inferior to bodily health but also brings anxiety (verses

[a] banishes: *probable meaning, based on Heb.; Gk. obscure.*
[b] the pursuit. . .astray: *so Heb.; Gk.* the man who pursues destruction
shall have his fill of it.

1–2) and temptation to sin (verses 6–7). Verses 8–11 show how hard he considered it for a rich man to remain 'free of its taint' – no less than 'a miracle'! Similarly early Christians thought it hard for a rich man 'to enter the kingdom of Heaven' (Matt. 19: 23). Ben Sira approved the good things of life if they could be enjoyed without undue anxiety, pride or oppression; the rhetorical questions of verse 10 show how rarely he expected a rich man to remain untainted.

3–4 do not fit the context: in 30: 14 'a poor man who is healthy and fit' was preferred to 'a rich man racked by disease', and this passage is generally critical of the rich. But proverbs are often arranged by subject rather than by logical argument and were originally directed to different situations. These verses recall the man who 'slaves and strains and hurries and is all the farther behind' in an earlier passage on wealth (11: 11).

5. *the pursuit of money leads a man astray:* since verse 6 describes the destructive power of wealth, a Greek copyist wrote the Greek word for 'destruction' (*diaphthoran*) instead of that for *money*, 'gain' (*diaphora*). The verses refer to those who seek to 'get rich quick'.

11. *the whole people will hail him as benefactor:* both the Greek (*ekklesia*, used in the New Testament of 'church') and the Hebrew (*qāhāl*) words for *the whole people* are used for religious and national gatherings, and suggest a reference to the custom of inscribing the names of benefactors on the walls of synagogues. Many such inscriptions have been found, especially in Rome. ✳

ON BEHAVIOUR AT BANQUETS

12 If you are sitting at a grand table,
   do not lick your lips and exclaim, 'What a spread!'
13 Remember, it is a vice to have a greedy eye.
   There is no greater evil in creation than the eye;
   that is why it must shed tears at every turn.
14 Do not reach for everything you see,

or jostle your fellow-guest at the dish;
judge his feelings by your own   15
and always behave considerately.
Eat what is set before you like a gentleman;   16
do not munch and make yourself objectionable.
Be the first to stop for good manners' sake   17
and do not be insatiable, or you will give offence.
If you are dining in a large company,   18
do not reach out your hand before others.
A man of good upbringing is content with little,   19
and he is not short of breath when he goes to bed.
The moderate eater enjoys healthy sleep;   20
he rises early, feeling refreshed.
But sleeplessness, indigestion, and colic
are the lot of the glutton.
If you cannot avoid overeating at a feast,   21
leave the table and find relief by vomiting.

Listen to me, my son; do not disregard me,   22
and in the end my words will come home to you.
Whatever you do, do it shrewdly,
and no illness will come your way.
Everyone has a good word for a liberal host,   23
and the evidence of his generosity is convincing.
The whole town grumbles at a mean host,   24
and there is precise evidence of his meanness.

Do not try to prove your manhood by drinking,   25
for wine has been the ruin of many.
As the furnace tests iron when it is being tempered,   26
so wine tests character when boastful men are wrangling.
Wine puts life into a man,   27

if he drinks it in moderation.
What is life to a man deprived of wine?
Was it not created to warm men's hearts?

28 Wine brings gaiety and high spirits,
if a man knows when to drink and when to stop;

29 but wine in excess makes for bitter feelings
and leads to offence and retaliation.

30 Drunkenness inflames a fool's anger to his own hurt;
it saps his strength and exposes him to injury.

31 At a banquet do not rebuke your fellow-guest
or make him feel small while he is enjoying himself.
This is no time to take up a quarrel with him
or pester him to pay his debts.

32 If they choose you to preside at a feast, do not put on airs;
behave to them as one of themselves.
Look after the others before you sit down;

2 do not take your place until you have discharged all your
duties.
Let their enjoyment be your pleasure,
and you will win the prize for good manners.

3 Speak, if you are old – it is your privilege –
but come to the point and do not interrupt the music.

4 Where entertainment is provided, do not keep up a stream
of talk;
it is the wrong time to show off your wisdom.

5 Like a signet of ruby in a gold ring
is a concert of music at a banquet.

6 Like a signet of emerald in a gold setting
is tuneful music with good wine.

Speak, if you are young, when the need arises,   7
but twice at the most, and only when asked.

Be brief, say much in few words,   8
like a man who knows and can still hold his tongue.

Among the great do not act as their equal   9
or go on chattering when another is speaking.

As lightning travels ahead of thunder,   10
so popularity goes before a modest man.

Leave in good time and do not be the last to go;   11
go straight home without lingering.

There you may amuse yourself to your heart's content,   12
and run no risk of arrogant talk.

And one thing more: give praise to your Maker,   13
who has filled your cup with his blessings.

✳ In 31: 12 – 32: 13 Ben Sira gives advice on behaviour at important banquets under various topics: overeating (31: 12–21), guests' attitudes to hosts (31: 22–4), drunkenness (31: 25–31), presiding at table (32: 1–2), musical entertainment (32: 3–6) and conversation (32: 7–13). Egyptian proverbial literature, used for training future civil servants, was rich in such detailed advice on behaviour at social occasions, but Hebrew wise men had been content with warning against greed and drunkenness as in Prov. 23: 1–3, for example. Encouragement of moderate pleasure in eating and drinking occurs in the Old Testament only in Ecclesiastes: 'that a man should eat and drink and enjoy himself. . .is a gift of God' (Eccles. 3: 13). Ben Sira's exhortation in 32: 13 to praise God for these things shows a deeper position which has integrated a full part in public life with religious faith. Public life had now become influenced by Greek social behaviour; secular feasting appears little in the Old Testament, which mentions mainly religious feasts and feasts after military victory. The customs of having a president (32: 1–2) and of providing musical 'entertainment' (32: 3–6) were both Greek. The section on overeating follows well on the previous advice to the rich on self-restraint (31: 8–11).

13. *the eye* seems to be regarded as the bodily organ most likely to lead a man to sin, and Ben Sira naively judges it right that *the eye* should be the source of *tears* which flow as the results of sin.

21. If too much food has been provided and you cannot eat it all, the good manners of Ben Sira's day required you to eat what your host provided even if you had to retire and vomit part of the meal.

22–4. Concerning the behaviour of hosts one rabbinical saying states that 'three things make a man popular with his fellow-creatures – an open hand, a free table and a little gaiety' – echoing Ben Sira's positive attitude. The renewed appeal for the reader's attention in verse 22, coming strangely in a series of sections on related themes, probably emphasizes the importance of what follows.

25–31. 'moderation' is the key-word for Ben Sira's advice on drinking wine as on eating in verses 12–21.

26–30. *As the furnace* reveals the quality of the *iron* so drinking *wine* reveals a man's *character*, as explained in verses 27–30. The wise man *knows when...to stop* and retains his good humour when *men are wrangling*; the *fool* drinks too much, loses control and provokes quarrels, *to his own hurt*. Knowing the right moment, whether for stopping to drink, showing penitence (18: 21), anger (1: 23) or self-defence against accusations (4: 20) was a favourite theme for Ben Sira and represents an important aspect of his ideal person.

32: 1–2. The Jews seem to have taken over the Greek custom of having a president for a banquet whose duties included putting guests at ease with conversation, arranging seating, tasting wine (as in John 2: 8–9), saying grace, etc. – a difficult task in preparation and performance. The author of 2 Maccabees remarks on his difficulties in summarizing the work of Jason of Cyrene into one book: 'It means toil and late nights, just as it is no light task for the man who plans a dinner-party and aims to satisfy his guests' (2 Macc. 2: 27).

3–6. It was the *privilege* of an *old* man to speak without interruption, but it was bad manners for a long-winded but unmusical guest to *interrupt the music* provided by his host. Musical *entertainment*, another Greek custom, is mentioned again in 49: 1.

7–13. The sections on behaviour at banquets close with instructions not to talk too much – particularly for young people, who should allow older men to speak, as hinted in verse 3; the young man's place is to listen.

10. According to Ben Sira modesty leads to *popularity* as inevitably as *lightning* precedes *thunder* – a strangely inapt simile which is hardly true to life.

11. Etiquette demands that the host should invite guests to stay beyond the usual hour for departure and that guests should not linger and embarrass the host.

13. *give praise to your Maker* probably refers to the prayer of thanksgiving to be said at home after return from such a meal, but also conveniently rounds off the sections on behaviour at banquets with a reference to the religious background of the book as in other passages (4: 28; 19: 17; 23: 27; 25: 11). ✻

ON THE CORRECT PREPARATION FOR LIFE THROUGH RELIGION

The man who fears the Lord will accept his discipline,   14
and the diligent will receive his approval.

The genuine student will find satisfaction in the law,   15
but it will prove a stumbling-block to the insincere.

Those who fear the Lord will discover what is right,   16
and will make his decrees[a] shine out like a lamp.

A sinner will not accept criticism;   17
he will find precedents to justify his choice.

[a] *Or* their good conduct.

18 A sensible man can always take a hint;
   but an arrogant heathen does not know the meaning of
      diffidence.

19 Never do anything without deliberation,
   and afterwards you will have no regrets.[a]

20 Do not travel by a road full of obstacles
   and stumble along through its boulders.

21 Do not be careless on a clear road

22 but watch where you are going.[b]

23 Whatever you are doing, rely on yourself,
   for this too is a way of keeping the commandments.

24 To rely on the law is to heed its commandments,
   and to trust the Lord is to want for nothing.

* Ben Sira has several times declared that wisdom is best achieved through fearing God: wisdom 'will come out to meet' 'The man who fears the Lord' (15: 1–2). Fear of the Lord and keeping the commandments are the correct way to live as God wills – which is true wisdom for Ben Sira. Thus, together with 1: 11–20 and 24: 1–29, this passage constructs Ben Sira's threefold theological scheme: true wisdom equals personal devotion (fear of the Lord) and obedience to the law. In this section he stresses the need for approaching wisdom via fearing God and keeping the law by showing that correct preparation is necessary in all things: for a journey you must choose beforehand a route clear of 'obstacles' (verse 20); for making decisions you must be open to hints from others (verse 18); and even 'A sinner' prepares to justify his actions by finding 'precedents' (verse 17)! Those who fear the Lord and 'rely on the law' prepare for life correctly and will 'want for nothing' (verse 24).

[a] you. . .regrets: *or* do not change your mind.
[b] but. . .going: *so Heb.; Gk.* and keep an eye on your children.

16. *his decrees* and 'their good conduct' (in the footnote) are alternative translations of a Greek word meaning 'righteous deeds'.

18. *A sensible man* takes *a hint* by being receptive to other people's suggestions, whereas *an arrogant heathen* considers no thoughts but his own.

23 appears to contradict verse 18; but the 'sensible man', although he takes 'a hint', relies on himself to choose the right course. To *rely on yourself* means to be faithful to your religious commitment. ✱

ON THE RESULTS OF TRUST IN GOD

Disaster never comes the way of the man who fears the **33**
　　Lord:
in times of trial he will be rescued again and again.
A wise man never hates the law,　　　　　　　　　　　**2**
but the man who is insincere about it is like a boat in a
　　squall.
A sensible man trusts the law　　　　　　　　　　　　**3**
and finds it as reliable as the divine oracle.

Prepare what you have to say, if you want a hearing;　**4**
marshal your learning and then give your answer.
The feelings of a fool turn like a cart-wheel,　　　　**5**
and his thoughts spin like an axle.
A sarcastic friend is like a stallion　　　　　　　　　**6**
which neighs no matter who is on its back.

✱ Careful preparation for life through fearing God, expounded in the previous section, leads to the results now described. Obedience to the law is found to be entirely reliable and steady, unlike boats in squalls (verse 2), cart-wheels and axles which are always moving (verse 5; on ancient carts axle-trees sometimes revolved with the wheel). Similarly 'sarcastic' friends neigh out their sarcasm however close the ties of friendship (verse 6).

3. *the divine oracle:* the Greek text is uncertain, but probably the same word is used for *oracle* as in 45: 10 where 'the oracle of judgement' refers to the Urim and Thummim, specially re-served stones used by earlier Hebrews to determine God's will by sacred lot. In 1 Sam. 28: 6 Saul consults the Lord 'by Urim' as well as 'by prophets'. The use of this lot is described in 1 Sam. 14: 41–2. This practice had ceased long before Ben Sira's time but, just as he selects literary images from earlier books for illustration, so he selects earlier religious practices from Israel's history familiar to readers of the Old Testament. ✳

ON OPPOSITES IN THE NATURAL WORLD

7 Why is one day more important than another,
   when every day in the year has its light from the sun?
8 It was by the Lord's decision that they were distinguished;
   he appointed the various seasons and festivals:
9 some days he made high and holy,
   and others he assigned to the common run of days.
10 All men alike come from the ground;
   Adam was created out of earth.
11 Yet in his great wisdom the Lord distinguished them
   and made them go various ways;
12 some he blessed and lifted high,
   some he hallowed and brought near to himself,
   some he cursed and humbled
   and removed from their place.
13 As clay is in the potter's hands,
   to be moulded just as he chooses,
   so are men in the hands of their Maker,

to be dealt with as he decides.
Good is the opposite of evil, and life of death; 14
yes, and the sinner is the opposite of the godly.
Look at all the works of the Most High: 15
they go in pairs, one the opposite of the other.

✻ Ben Sira inserts a doctrinal passage discussing the contra-
dictory nature of God's world. As a devout Jew Ben Sira
believed in one God and the unity of his creation: God's
knowledge is perfect (42: 18–21), he can be seen in all his
works, and 'All that the Lord has made is very good' (39: 16).
Although modern problems of predestination had not yet
arisen (see note on 15: 11–20), the problem of the existence
of sin had caused him to insert a doctrinal passage together
with answers to objections in 15: 11 – 17: 24, where he
stressed God's control of the universe and his gift to men of
free choice between good and evil, 'life and death' (15: 17).
He now expounds his own doctrine that the world was
deliberately created full of opposites, carefully balanced: all
created things 'go in pairs, one the opposite of the other'
(verse 15), and illustrates this from the calendar and differing
status among men. The same examples occur in a story from
the Babylonian Talmud: a Roman officer asked Rabbi Akiba,
'Wherein does the Sabbath differ from any other day?' He
replied, 'Wherein does one man differ from another?' –
'Because my Lord (the Emperor) wishes it.' Rabbi Akiba
replied, 'The Sabbath too, then, is distinguished because the
Lord wishes it so' (*Sanhedrin* 65b).

7–9. Although *every day* is lit by the same sunshine, each is
different. The different length and weather of days would suit
verse 7, but verses 8–9 refer to the liturgical calendar – weekly
and annual *festivals*. The moon was regarded as 'a perpetual
sign to mark the divisions of time' for the reckoning
of 'feast-days' (43: 6–7). Divisions of time were widely
regarded by Jews of the last two centuries B.C. as directions

ordained by God for the correct ordering of the liturgical calendar.

10–13. The tension between good and evil was seen to threaten the doctrine of God's control. Although in one place (25: 24) woman is said to be 'the origin of sin', Ben Sira elsewhere states the orthodox Jewish position that when God 'made man in the beginning, he left him free to take his own decisions' (15: 14), possibly hinting at the doctrine of the two inclinations discussed in the note on 15: 11–20. The meaning here is not that God *moulded* man's character from the beginning but that God ordained that the results of man's free choice between good and evil should make *them go various ways* (verse 11). The resultant course of men's lives is therefore *in the hands of their Maker* (verse 13).

12. The good and the wicked are intended by those *lifted high* and those *cursed and humbled*. Those *hallowed and brought near* are priests, as the Greek word for *brought near* is used technically of priests in Lev. 8: 24, 'He then brought forward the sons of Aaron', and Ezek. 40: 46. ✶

A PERSONAL NOTE FROM THE AUTHOR

16 I was the last to wake up,
   I was like a gleaner following the grape-pickers;
   by the Lord's blessing I arrived in time
   to fill my winepress as full as any of them.
17 Remember that I did not toil for myself alone,
   but for all who seek learning.
18 Listen to me, you dignitaries;
   leaders of the assembly, give me your attention.

✶ Ben Sira includes a personal note to the reader as in 24: 30–4; 39: 12–13 and 50: 27. The three verses show his self-awareness as part of the Jewish community, with the past (verse 16), with his reading public (verse 17) and with the political and religious leaders (verse 18).

16. *I was like a gleaner:* Ben Sira gleans material from the whole of the Old Testament and not just the wisdom literature – his use of phrases and images from Israel's past literature has often been called 'anthological' in style. ✻

ON KEEPING ONE'S INDEPENDENCE

As long as you live, give no one power over yourself – 19
son or wife, brother or friend.
Do not give your property to another,
in case you change your mind and want it back.
As long as you have life and breath, 20
never change places with anyone.
It is better for your children to ask from you 21
than for you to be dependent on them.
Whatever you are doing, keep the upper hand, 22
and allow no blot on your reputation.
Let your life run its full course, 23
and then, at the hour of death, distribute your estate.

✻ Further advice on social life concerns looking after one's money and retaining control of it. Pious generosity can leave one in need (verse 19). Verses 20 and 22 stress the need for self-confidence and not forfeiting one's independence by copying other people, wishing to *change places with* them. ✻

ON TREATMENT OF SLAVES

Fodder, and stick, and burdens for the donkey; 24
bread, and discipline, and work for the servant!
Make your slave work, if you want rest for yourself; 25
if you leave him idle, he will be looking for his liberty.

26 The ox is tamed by yoke and harness,
the bad servant by racks and tortures.
27 Put him to work to keep him from being idle,
for idleness is a great teacher of mischief.
28 Set him to work, for that is what he is for,
and if he disobeys you, load him with fetters.

29 Do not be too exacting towards anyone
or do anything contrary to justice.
30 If you have a servant, treat him as an equal,
because you bought him with blood.
31 If you have a servant, treat him like a brother;
you will need him as much as you need yourself.
If you ill-treat him and he takes to his heels,
where will you go to look for him?

☆ In the ancient world slaves were regarded as personal property of the owner like money, and are mentioned on the same level as cattle in the Ten Commandments (Exod. 20: 10, 17). Verse 25 implies that, unless slaves were worked hard, desire for freedom came to the forefront of their minds. Verses 29–31, like 7: 20–1, show some awareness of humane treatment due to a slave but is based, unfortunately, not on any concept of human rights but on self-interest – in case your slave deserted: if a run-away slave escaped and took refuge with someone else the law did not force them to surrender the slave to his owner (Deut. 23: 15–16). The law contained some such provisions to protect slaves: freedom was granted in the seventh year (Exod. 21: 2; Deut. 15: 12–18) and also as compensation for loss of eye or tooth through the owner's brutality (Exod. 21: 26–7). But it is doubtful if the law was strictly kept. Some quote verses 26–8 as evidence for brutality, but Ben Sira was not a hard master, as shown by 7: 20–1, and probably intends the 'racks', 'tortures' and 'fetters' to be taken metaphorically.

30. *blood* here means 'life', 'substance', 'money for living'. If you bought a slave with part of your money, Ben Sira argues (obscurely) that you bought him with part of yourself. *

ON THE WORTHLESSNESS OF DREAMS

Vain hopes delude the senseless,   **34**
and dreams give wings to a fool's fancy.
It is like clutching a shadow, or chasing the wind,   2
to take notice of dreams.
What you see in a dream is nothing but a reflection,   3
like the image of a face in a mirror.
Purity cannot come out of filth;   4
how then can truth issue from falsehood?
Divination, omens, and dreams are all futile,   5
mere fantasies, like those of a woman in labour.
Unless they are sent by intervention from the Most High,   6
pay no attention to them.
Dreams have led many astray   7
and ruined those who built their hopes on them.
Such delusions can add nothing to the completeness of   8
     the law;
the wisdom spoken by the faithful is complete in itself.

* Dreams were used in early Israel as a major source of divine revelation, and occur side by side with Urim and prophets in 1 Sam. 28: 6 (see note on 33: 3); but dependence on them was censured by the law (Deut. 13: 1–5) and some prophets (Jer. 29: 8, where the citizens set wise women 'to dream dreams' in opposition to the prophets). Ben Sira strongly commends study of the written law, rightly interpreted by 'the faithful' (verse 8), as the reliable source of revelation, and condemns dreams, excepting only those 'sent by intervention from the Most High' (verse 6). We do not know whether he is

referring to a still current practice of dream interpretation or to the many occasions described in the Old Testament when God revealed his will through dreams – these he could hardly deny!

1. *hopes* created through *dreams* end in disappointment.

3. Just as reflections in mirrors are not real people, so *What you see in* dreams is not real. Ben Sira does not imply that 'puzzling reflections in a mirror' are glimpses of eternal truth like Paul in 1 Cor. 13: 12, but stresses the unreality of the image.

4. *filth* and *falsehood* refer to disreputable methods used by professional diviners, who had probably increased with Greek influence and whom he despised.

8. *the wisdom spoken by the faithful* (the law) *is complete in itself:* the Jews believed that *the* written *law,* together with the oral tradition (see note on 39: 2–3), contained the complete revelation of God's will. ✻

ON THE AUTHOR'S WIDE EXPERIENCE

9 An educated man knows many things,
　and a man of experience understands what he is talking about.

10 An inexperienced man knows little,
　but a man who travels grows in ability.

11 I have seen many things in the course of my travels,
　and understand more than I can tell.

12 I have often been in deadly danger
　and escaped, thanks to the experience I had gained.

✻ The wise man 'travels in foreign countries and learns at first hand the good or evil of man's lot' (39: 4). Wide travel increases *experience*, and Ben Sira adds another personal note like that in 33: 16–18 to show the reader his qualifications for writing. He did not value life in a closed religious ghetto, as shown by his description of the ideal wise man in 39: 1–11. ✻

True piety and the mercy of God

ON THE SECURITY OF THOSE WHO FEAR GOD

THOSE WHO FEAR the Lord shall live,   13
for their trust is in one who can keep them safe.
The man who fears the Lord will have nothing else to fear;   14
he will never be a coward, because his trust is in the Lord.
How blest is the man who fears the Lord!   15
He knows where to look for support.
The Lord keeps watch over those who love him,   16
their strong shield and firm support,
a shelter from scorching wind and midday heat,
a safeguard against stumbles and falls.
He raises the spirits and makes the eyes sparkle,   17
giving health, and life, and blessing.

✶ Before returning to social life in *Man in society* (36: 18 –
42: 14), the author includes a group of sections on specifically
religious topics. 34: 13–17 stress the security of *The man who
fears the Lord*, and both wrong (34: 18–26) and right (35: 1–11)
kinds of offerings are described; after an exposition of God's
mercy for the oppressed (35: 12–20) comes a prayer for national deliverance (36: 1–17).

As previously noted, the fear of the Lord implies for Ben
Sira a warm, personal trust and reverence (see note on 1:
11–20): these hints are now made explicit in this description
of the reliability of God. Many phrases from the psalms are
echoed in Ben Sira's religious poetry and illustrate the anthological style previously noted (on 33: 16–18). Compare, for
example, *How blest is the man who fears the Lord!*' (verse 15)
with 'Happy is the man who fears the LORD' (Ps. 112: 1)
where the original Hebrew was probably the same. ✶

ON SACRIFICES TO GOD: THE WRONG KIND

18 A sacrifice derived from ill-gotten gains is contaminated,
   a lawless mockery that cannot win approval.

19 The Most High is not pleased with the offering of the
      godless,
   nor do endless sacrifices win his forgiveness.

20 To offer a sacrifice from the possessions of the poor
   is like killing a son before his father's eyes.

21 Bread is life to the destitute,
   and it is murder to deprive them of it.

22 To rob your neighbour of his livelihood is to kill him,
   and the man who cheats a worker of his wages sheds blood.

23 When one builds and another pulls down,
   what have they gained except hard work?

24 When one prays and another curses,
   which is the Lord to listen to?

25 Wash after touching a corpse and then touch it again,
   and what have you gained by your washing?

26 So it is with the man who fasts for his sins
   and goes and does the same again;
   who will listen to his prayer?
   what has he gained by his penance?

✳ Although Ben Sira claimed that wisdom ministered 'In
the sacred tent' and in the temple 'in Zion' (24: 10) and loved
the liturgical traditions of Israel, as 45: 6–22 and 50: 1–21 show,
sacrificial worship without personal devotion was abhorrent
to him. Anyone who presumed on God's forgiveness through
sacrifices without turning from sin (7: 9) was wrong, especially
if they repeated the same sinful actions afterwards (34: 25–6).
'Turn to the Lord and have done with sin; make your prayer

in his presence' (17: 25). The repentance and prayer of the giver, not the sacrifice itself, were effective in obtaining God's forgiveness. Earlier wisdom literature stated that 'The wicked man's sacrifice is abominable to the LORD; the good man's prayer is his delight' (Prov. 15: 8) – a theme expanded here in both negative and positive aspects. Later rabbis appealed to the early prophets for this point of view: Joshua ben Hananiah, on seeing the ruins of the temple after it had been destroyed in A.D. 70, is said to have cried out, 'Woe to us, for the place where the sins of Israel were atoned for is destroyed'; Johanan ben Zakkai replied, 'Do not grieve, my son, for we have an atonement which is just as good, namely, deeds of mercy', and quoted 'loyalty is my desire, not sacrifice' (Hos. 6: 6). Judaism survived the destruction of the temple because it was recognized that the condition of God's forgiveness was moral, not ritual.

20. The sacrifices of the wealthy were often financed through oppression of *the poor* – 'conscience money'? – and were as heart-rending to God as the murder of *a son*.

22. The Babylonian Talmud states that 'everyone who withholds an employee's wages is as though he deprived him of his life' (*Baba Metzia* 112a). This kind of injustice was common, as the law forbids keeping back 'a hired man's wages till next morning' (Lev. 19: 13), and the practice is deplored in Jer. 22: 13 and Tobit 4: 14.

23–4 should be taken together: just as *one* man *pulls down* what *another* has built, so the curses of the poor reverse the rich man's prayer.

25–6 are often quoted to show the importance in Judaism of a radical change at repentance. Whoever 'touches a corpse' and purifies himself from ceremonial pollution (Num. 19: 11) and then pollutes himself again gains no advantage; so whoever *fasts for his sins* on the Day of Atonement and then performs *the same* sins cannot expect forgiveness. ✳

ON SACRIFICES TO GOD: THE RIGHT KIND

35 Keeping the law is worth many offerings;
   to heed the commandments is to sacrifice a thank-offering.
2 A kindness repaid is an offering of flour,
   and to give alms is a praise-offering.
3 The way to please the Lord is to renounce evil;
   and to renounce wrongdoing is to make atonement.
4 Yet do not appear before the Lord empty-handed;
5 perform these sacrifices because they are commanded.
6 When the just man brings his offering of fat to the altar,
   its fragrance rises to the presence of the Most High.
7 The just man's sacrifice is acceptable;
   it will never be forgotten.
8 Be generous in your worship of the Lord
   and present the firstfruits of your labour in full measure.
9 Give all your gifts cheerfully
   and be glad to dedicate your tithe.
10 Give to the Most High as he has given to you,
   as generously as you can afford.
11 For the Lord always repays;
   you will be repaid seven times over.

* Having condemned insincere sacrifices, Ben Sira now commends sacrifices as part of fulfilling the law. 'Keeping the law' is an effective, and more reliable, substitute for sacrifices (verse 1), but sacrifices should be performed 'because they are commanded' (verse 5). The law takes precedence over ritualistic ceremony for Ben Sira as shown in his description of Israel's response to God in 17: 10–14 where he lays stress on the law and morality without mentioning ritualistic sacrifice.
   2 mentions two non-obligatory private sacrifices: the

offering of flour described in Lev. 2: 1–3 and the *praise-offering*
in thanks for deliverance from danger.

3. *to make atonement*, that is, to restore the relationship
with God broken by sin, lies in decisive renunciation of
wrongdoing rather than in a liturgical act.

8. A general reference to the offerings of *firstfruits* required
by Deut. 26: 2.

9. The full load of contributions upon the pious are listed
in Tobit 1: 6–8, where Tobit pays 'the firstfruits of crops and
herds, the tithes of the cattle, and the first shearings of the
sheep. . .to the priests of Aaron's line for the altar, and the
tithe of wine, corn, olive oil, pomegranates and other fruits
to the Levites'; he converted 'The second tithe (Deut.
14: 22–6). . .into money, and . . .distributed it in Jerusalem
year by year among the orphans and widows'.

11. The number *seven* is used to denote a large amount as in
7: 3 and 20: 12. ✳

ON GOD'S MERCY FOR THE OPPRESSED

Do not offer him a bribe, for he will not accept it,   12
and do not rely on a dishonest sacrifice;
for the Lord is a judge
who knows no partiality.
He has no favourites at the poor man's expense,   13
but listens to his prayer when he is wronged.
He never ignores the appeal of the orphan   14
or the widow when she pours out her complaint.
How the tears run down the widow's cheeks,   15
and her cries accuse the man who caused them!
To be accepted a man must serve the Lord as he requires,   16
and then his prayer will reach the clouds.
The prayer of the humble pierces the clouds,   17
but he is not consoled until it reaches its destination.

He does not desist until the Most High intervenes,
gives the just their rights, and sees justice done.

18 The Lord will not be slow,
neither will he be patient with the wicked,
until he crushes the sinews of the merciless
and sends retribution on the heathen;
until he blots out the insolent, one and all,
and breaks the power of the unjust;

19 until he gives all men their deserts,
judging their actions by their intentions;
until he gives his people their rights
and gladdens them with his mercy.

20 His mercy is as timely in days of trouble
as rain-clouds in days of drought.

✣ Discussion on human generosity in the previous section
leads Ben Sira to describe God's generosity to man; he 'knows
no partiality' for the rich (verse 12) and cares especially for
the poor (verse 13). In verses 19 and 20 the objects of God's
mercy change from the poor to Israel, 'his people', prepara-
tory to the prayer for help in 36: 1–17.

12. *a dishonest sacrifice* is one offered from money dishonestly
acquired as in 34: 20.

14. The Old Testament frequently commends care of *the
orphan* and *the widow* who had none to provide for them. The
law forbids one to 'ill-treat any widow or fatherless child'
(Exod. 22: 22) and in Ps. 68: 5 God is called 'father of the
fatherless, the widow's champion'. ✣

A PRAYER FOR ISRAEL'S DELIVERANCE

36 Have pity on us, O Lord, thou God of all; look down,
2 and send thy terror upon all nations.
3 Raise thy hand against the heathen,

and let them see thy power.

As they have seen thy holiness displayed among us,   4
so let us see thy greatness displayed among them.

Let them learn, as we also have learned,   5
that there is no God but only thou, O Lord.

Renew thy signs, repeat thy miracles,   6
win glory for thy hand, for thy right arm.

Rouse thy wrath, pour out thy fury,   7
destroy the adversary, wipe out the enemy.

Remember the day thou hast appointed and hasten it,[a]   8
and give men cause to recount thy wonders.

Let fiery anger devour the survivors,   9
and let the oppressors of thy people meet their doom.

Crush the heads of hostile princes,   10
who say, 'There is no one to match us.'

Gather all the tribes of Jacob,   11
and grant them their inheritance,[b] as thou didst long ago.

Have pity, O Lord, on the people called by thy name,   12
Israel, whom thou hast named thy first-born.

Show mercy to the city of thy sanctuary,   13
Jerusalem, the city of thy rest.

Fill Zion with the praise of thy triumph;   14
fill thy people with thy glory.

Thou didst create them at the beginning; acknowledge   15
     them now
and fulfil the prophecies spoken in thy name.

Reward those who wait for thee;   16
prove thy prophets trustworthy.

[a] Remember . . . it: *some witnesses read* Hasten the day and remember
thy oath.
[b] *Or* and take them to be thy own.

17 Listen, O Lord, to the prayer of thy servants,
who claim Aaron's blessing upon thy people.
Let all who live on earth acknowledge
that thou art the Lord, the eternal God.

✳ Ben Sira inserts as a prayer for national deliverence a psalm
filled with echoes of many Old Testament passages, both
prose and poetry, describing Israel's deliverence both past and
future. He may either have selected the passages himself or have
used a liturgical source; but such anthological style lacks life
and the poem lacks the variety of tone and mood familiar
in the Old Testament psalms: it is all request and no thanksgiving. Many think the poem presupposes the political ten-
sions in the early second century B.C. before the Maccabean
revolt when Palestine was still under foreign rule; if so, the
dullness of this poem compared with Ben Sira's descriptions
of dinner-parties and social life show that, in spite of foreign
travel, he cannot have felt the political crisis acutely. Ben Sira
is more concerned with the religious than the political triumph
of the Jews, and the tone of his survey of past history in chs.
44–50 shows this. This poem starts with a reference to
'thou God of all' (verse 1) and closes with the wish that 'all
who live on earth' should 'acknowledge that thou art the
Lord, the eternal God' (verse 17).

3. *the heathen* are identified by some as the Greek rulers of
Palestine, but probably refer to non-Jews generally like 'all
nations' in verse 2.

4–5. God's *holiness* had been shown to Israel in punishment
for her sins, and the theme of the books of Kings as well as
many of the prophetical books is that through the destruction
of the temple and the exile in Babylon as punishment for
apostasy the Jews had *learned that there* was *no God but* Yahweh.
God would now display his *greatness* among the heathen by
humbling them as punishment for oppressing God's people.

6. *Renew thy signs:* during captivity in Egypt God had said,
'Then will I show sign after sign and portent after portent'

174

to force Pharaoh to release the Hebrews (Exod. 7: 3). *win glory for thy hand, for thy right arm:* in Ps. 98: 1–2 God is said to display 'his righteousness to all the nations' with 'his right hand and holy arm'.

7. *pour out thy fury. . .* echoes 'Pour out thy fury on nations that have not acknowledged thee' (Jer. 10: 25). Such phrases seem bloodthirsty, but Ben Sira uses them merely as hallowed phrases from the past.

8. *the day thou hast appointed* was the day heathen rule would break. In much Jewish apocalyptic literature of the last two centuries B.C. this process was described in great detail with many references to armies, battles and the chosen prince, the Messiah – strangely absent in Ecclesiasticus. Here Ben Sira refers to God's triumph in general terms; that God should have ordained a 'right time' for his triumph was natural for an author who believed that God had organized everything as described in 33: 7–15.

9–10. Not *the. survivors* of a battle but those *oppressors* who still live at the time of God's triumph. The *hostile princes* may refer to the arrogance of such rulers as Antiochus III who controlled Palestine after the battle of Paneas in 19^ B.C.

11. The gathering of world-wide Jewry (the Diaspora) preceded God's triumph in passages like Isa. 11: 11. The phrase *tribes of Jacob* recalls Israel's task as God's servant 'to restore the tribes of Jacob, to bring back the descendents of Israel' (Isa. 49: 6).

12. *thy first-born:* during the Exodus narrative God instructs Moses to tell Pharaoh that Israel was his 'first-born son' (Exod. 4: 22).

15. *Thou didst create them at the beginning:* later Jews claimed that Israel was among seven things created by God before the creation of the world. The author awaits the fulfilment of many Old Testament *prophecies* foretelling the future triumph of God and his people.

17. *Aaron's blessing* may refer to the priestly blessing given to the sons of Aaron in Num. 6: 24–6, but some think the

author may mean the eight, more detailed, benedictions recited by the high priest according to the Mishnah (*Yoma* 7: 1): 'for the Law, for the Temple-Service, for the Thanksgiving, for the Forgiveness of Sin, and for the Temple separately, and for the Israelites separately, and for the priests separately; and for the rest a (general) prayer'; these subjects certainly cover Ben Sira's interests better. ✶

Man in society

ON CAREFUL DISCRIMINATION

18 ALL IS FOOD for the stomach,
   but one food is better than another.
19 As the palate identifies game by its taste,
   so the discerning mind detects lies.
20 A warped mind makes trouble,
   but a man of experience can pay it back.

✶ In 36: 21 Ben Sira starts to review various persons in society: wives (36: 21–6), friends (37: 1–6), counsellors (37: 7–18), teachers (37: 19–26), doctors (38: 1–15), the dead (38: 16–23) and various kinds of craftsmen (38: 24–34), culminating in the ideal wise man (39: 1–11). He introduces the series with this short section illustrating the need to discriminate between different people from the function of the palate in discriminating between various kinds of food. This theme of discrimination heads several of the later sections, as in 36: 21 and 37: 1, and he inserts another general warning on the need to test people in 37: 27–31.

20. *experience* brings ability to discriminate correctly and thus to escape danger, as Ben Sira had found out for himself (34: 11–12). ✶

MORE ON WIVES

A woman will take any man for husband,   21
but a man may prefer one girl to another.
A woman's beauty makes a man happy,   22
and there is nothing he desires more.
If she has a kind and gentle tongue,   23
then her husband is luckier than most men.
The man who wins a wife has the beginnings of a fortune,   24
a helper to match his needs and a pillar to support him.
Where there is no hedge, property is plundered;   25
and where there is no wife, the wanderer sighs for a home.
Does anyone trust a roving bandit   26
who swoops on town after town?
No more will they trust a homeless man
who lodges wherever night overtakes him.

✱ To start his series on different persons in society, Ben Sira
adds to his previous remarks about wives in 25: 19 – 26: 18,
here concentrating on good wives. Discrimination was
exercised by man in choosing a wife (verse 21), whereas the
woman, in a subordinate position, had to accept such offer of
marriage as she received.

22. *A woman's beauty makes a man happy:* good looks feature
in 26: 17–18, but Ben Sira seems to prefer silence, modesty
and a well-ordered home in 26: 14–16.

24. *a wife* is considered a good investment. A sum was paid
on marriage to the bride's family – a remnant of an ancient
custom of bride purchase. So a husband expends some
money to gain *the beginnings of a fortune*. Verses 24–6 then
describe the benefits.

25–6. The *roving bandit* probably refers to the Greek mercenary soldiers who wandered round the Mediterranean

world ready to fight for anyone who hired them as did the rulers of Egypt in the fifth to second centuries B.C. So an unmarried man has no base or security, and his reputation *is plundered*; a wife protects home base and reputation as a *hedge* protects *property*. ✳

MORE ON FRIENDS

37 Every friend says, 'I too am your friend';
   but some are friends in name only.
2 What a mortal grief it is
   when a dear friend turns into an enemy!
3 Oh this propensity to evil, how did it creep in
   to cover the earth with treachery?
4 A friend may be all smiles when you are happy,
   but turn against you when trouble comes.
5 Another shares your toil for the sake of a meal,
   and yet may protect you against an enemy.
6 Never forget a friend
   or neglect him when prosperity comes your way.

✳ Testing friends has already been advised in 6: 7–17. Discrimination among women in the previous section had led Ben Sira to redress the balance of earlier remarks on largely bad wives; here he balances earlier discussion of good friends in 22: 19–26 with warnings on false friends.

   1. Just as 'all is food for the stomach' (36: 18), so *Every friend* claims friendship; but just as 'one food is better than another', so *some* friends *are friends in name only*.

   3. The *propensity to evil* reflects the rabbinic doctrine of two (good and evil) inclinations in man discussed in the note on 15: 11–20. Ben Sira asks why man chose evil but gives no answer here. ✳

178

ON GOOD AND BAD COUNSELLORS

Every counsellor says his own advice is best,   7
but some have their own advantage in view.
Beware of the man who offers advice,   8
and find out beforehand where his interest lies.
His advice will be weighted in his own favour
and may tip the scales against you.
He may say, 'Your road is clear',   9
and stand aside to see what happens.
Do not consult a man who is suspicious of you   10
or reveal your intentions to those who envy you.
Never consult a woman about her rival   11
or a coward about war,
a merchant about a bargain
or a buyer about a sale,
a skinflint about gratitude
or a hard-hearted man about a kind action,
an idler about work of any sort,
a casual labourer about finishing the job,
or a lazy servant about an exacting task –
do not turn to them for any advice.
Rely rather on a godfearing man   12
whom you know to be a keeper of the commandments,
whose interests are like your own,
who will sympathize if you have a setback.
But also trust your own judgement,   13
for it is your most reliable counsellor.
A man's own mind has sometimes a way of telling him   14
    more
than seven watchmen posted high on a tower.

15 But above all pray to the Most High
   to keep you on the straight road of truth.

16 Every undertaking begins in discussion,
   and consultation precedes every action.

17 Here you can trace the mind's variety.

18 Four kinds of destiny are offered to men,
   good and evil, life and death;
   and always it is the tongue that decides the issue.

* Counsellors are to be tested for their trustworthiness, especially those who offer advice unasked (verse 8). Ben Sira then lists unreliable counsellors (verse 11), advises consultation with 'a godfearing man' (verse 12), but prefers people to trust their 'own judgement' under God's guidance (verses 13–15). The section ends with a brief reference to the power of 'the tongue' (verse 18), which 'has power of life and death' (Prov. 18: 21) in both counselling and teaching – the theme of the next section.

7 follows the pattern of 36: 18: *Every counsellor* commends *his own advice*, but *some* only through self-interest.

11. A woman's *rival* was the second wife. Polygamy was not forbidden in Judaism until the tenth century A.D., but was rarely practised in Ben Sira's time and this is the only reference to it in wisdom literature. Wherever polygamy is practised rivalry between wives is common – particularly with regard to barrenness, as related in the stories of Rachel and Leah in Gen. 30 and of Hannah and her rival in 1 Sam. 1: 6. *a coward*'s advice *about war* is coloured by his cowardice as that of merchants and buyers by their desire for profit. *a casual labourer* was employed only for a fixed period and one stage of a *job*, and had no interest in the result.

14. Possibly the *watchmen posted high on a tower* are astrologers watching for portents in the sky, although we should expect the author to say so more clearly; more likely they are

soldiers on the watch for danger. What Ben Sira finds better
than the advice of seven exterior experts may be either a
man's own intuition or perhaps that combination of observance of others and confidence in one's own judgement that
makes for maturity in life. ✻

ON TEACHERS

A man may be clever enough to teach others   19
and yet be useless to himself.

A brilliant speaker may make enemies   20
and end by dying of hunger,

if the Lord has withheld the gift of popular appeal,   21
because he is devoid of wisdom.

If a man is wise in the conduct of his own life,   22
his good sense can be trusted when he speaks.

If a man is wise and instructs his people,   23
then his good sense can be trusted.

A wise man will have praise heaped on him,   24
and all who see him will count him happy.

The days of a man's life can be numbered,   25
but the days of Israel are countless.

A wise man will possess the confidence of his people,   26
and his name will live for ever.

✻ The theme of discrimination underlies this section although
the pattern of a general introductory statement is not followed
as in 37: 1 and 7. Fluent teachers who do not follow their own
(good) advice (verse 19) or who are little employed through
lack of 'popular appeal' or tactlessness (verses 20–1) are distinguished from those whose conduct, consistent with their
advice, shows them trustworthy; they practise what they
preach. Verses 23–6 show that it was the wise man's responsi-

bility to gain practical experience and teach other people, as Ben Sira did in his school (51: 23) and in his book (33: 17 and 34: 9-12). These verses provide a summary of his description of the ideal wise man in 39: 1-11.

20-1. *wisdom* here means sound common-sense and tact concerning other people's feelings. The *brilliant speaker* may only offend people with sarcasm and thus may be unemployed.

25-6 should be taken together. Whereas the individual is soon forgotten but the nation is remembered for ever, so the *wise man* who teaches the community 'will live on' in the memory of the community: 'The memory of him will not die', but 'his praises will be sung in the assembly' (39: 9-10). *

MORE ON THE NEED FOR DISCRIMINATION

27 My son, test yourself all your life long;
   take note of what is bad for you and do not indulge in it.
28 For not everything is good for everyone;
   we do not all enjoy the same things.
29 Do not be greedy for every delicacy
   or eat without restraint.
30 For illness is a sure result of overeating,
   and gluttony is next door to colic.
31 Gluttony has been the death of many;
   be on your guard and prolong your life.

* This short reminder of the theme of discrimination echoes the introduction to the series (36: 18-20) by illustrating from choice of food: two general verses (verses 27-8) lead to three which depict the results on health of wrong choice and greed (verses 29-31). Mention of health leads naturally to the section on doctors and sickness (38: 1-15). *

ON DOCTORS AND MEDICINE

Honour the doctor for his services,   **38**
for the Lord created him.
His skill comes from the Most High,   2
and he is rewarded by kings.
The doctor's knowledge gives him high standing   3
and wins him the admiration of the great.
The Lord has created medicines from the earth,   4
and a sensible man will not disparage them.
Was it not a tree that sweetened water   5
and so disclosed its properties*a*?
The Lord has imparted knowledge to men,   6
that by their use of his marvels he may win praise;
by using them the doctor*b* relieves pain   7
and from them the pharmacist makes up his mixture.   8
There is no end to the works of the Lord,
who spreads health over the whole world.

My son, if you have an illness, do not neglect it,   9
but pray to the Lord, and he will heal you.
Renounce your faults, amend your ways,   10
and cleanse your heart from all sin.
Bring a savoury offering and bring flour for a token   11
and pour oil on the sacrifice; be as generous as you can.*c*
Then call in the doctor, for the Lord created him;   12
do not let him leave you, for you need him.
There may come a time when your recovery is in their   13
    hands;

[a] *Or* and revealed the power of the Lord.
[b] the doctor: *so Heb.; Gk.* he heals and...
[c] be...can: *so Heb.; Gk. obscure.*

14 then they too will pray to the Lord
   to give them success in relieving pain
   and finding a cure to save their patient's life.
15 When a man has sinned against his Maker,
   let him put himself in the doctor's hands.

✳ Ben Sira tries to integrate traditional Jewish belief with new Greek ways of thinking. Traditionally Jews held that illness came as punishment for sin: diseased skin was seen as 'the penalty of sin' (Num. 12: 10-11). The correct remedy was prayer, sacrifice and repentance, as stated in verses 9-11, not medicine, which was regarded as turning against God. King Asa is criticized for resorting to a doctor rather than seeking God's guidance for gangrene in the foot (2 Chron. 16: 12), and even in the Mishnah it is said that 'the best among physicians is destined for Gehenna (Hell)' (*Kiddushin* 4: 14). By Ben Sira's time the spread of Greek scientific knowledge had increased the high value already placed on medical skill in many areas, particularly Egypt, thus creating for Jews the tension between traditional faith and new scientific knowledge common to all religions today. Ben Sira states that 'The Lord has created medicines' and doctors (verses 1 and 4) and regards them as part of God's ordering of the world; the wise man, therefore, seeking to understand God's creation, will acknowledge and use the doctor as part of God's provision for man. The doctor is seen as God's way of curing illness; prayer and devotion are seen as important for the sufferer's behaviour and state of mind.

Ben Sira expounds his doctrine that doctors and medicines are part of God's creation in verses 1-8, states the traditional view in verses 9-11 and brings the two together in verses 12-15. Verse 15, however, seems to assume close connexion between sin and sickness, and rather spoils the argument of the section: Ben Sira has not dispensed completely with the traditional view, and has thus not followed his own argument through to the end.

3. *high standing:* outside Israel doctors often ranked high in ancient oriental courts.

5. When the refugee Hebrews reached Marah in the Sinai peninsula on their journey from Egypt, the *water* was too bitter to drink; at God's command Moses threw a log into the water which then became sweet (Exod. 15: 23–5). *and so disclosed its properties:* the Greek is ambiguous – if the translation in the footnote is adopted ('and revealed the power of the Lord'), the event remains miraculous but does not fit this context; if the text is correct, it fits the context of medicinal powers in nature, and Ben Sira re-interprets the sweetening of the waters as due to natural properties in the wood rather than to God's direct power. As God healed the water through the wood, so he heals humans through the doctor and his medicines. Verse 8 sees doctors as God's intermediaries, continuing his work of creation.

9–11 describe the sick man's duty to God in traditional terms: prayer, repentance and atonement through *sacrifice.* Verse 11 describes the meal-offering of Lev. 2: 1–3, part of which was mixed with *oil* and burnt on the altar making a pleasant smell. These verses reflect, not any legal prescription, but the traditional custom.

14. The doctor prays for correct diagnosis and skill to prescribe the correct remedy. ✳

ON MOURNING FOR THE DEAD

My son, shed tears for the dead; 16
raise a lament for your grievous loss.
Shroud his body with proper ceremony,
and do not neglect his burial.
With bitter weeping and passionate lament 17
make your mourning worthy of him.
Mourn for a few days as propriety demands,
and then take comfort for your grief.

18 For grief may lead to death,
and a sorrowful heart saps the strength.
19 When a man is taken away, suffering is over,
but to live on in poverty goes against the grain.
20 Do not abandon yourself to grief;
put it from you and think of your own end.
21 Never forget! there is no return;
you cannot help him and can only injure yourself.
22 Remember that his fate will also be yours:
'Mine today and yours tomorrow.'
23 When the dead is at rest, let his memory rest too;
take comfort as soon as he has breathed his last.

✲ Advice against too much mourning for the dead suits the present day, but seems ungenerous in Ben Sira's world where there were obligatory customs of public and private mourning. Jewish customs varied: some advised seven days' mourning as in 22: 12; but Greek and Hebrew here state literally 'one and two', meaning either the three days' mourning advised by other authorities or 'a few days' (as the N.E.B.), which could be up to seven. Ben Sira probably seeks to limit excessive emotional grief over something that cannot be reversed – whence his advice to 'take comfort for your grief' (verse 17) – hard-headed, practical advice echoed in the Babylonian Talmud: 'whoever indulges in grief to excess over his dead will weep for another', i.e. himself (*Moed Katan 27b*).

16. *proper ceremony* varied according to the deceased's station in life. Some relatives would shirk their duties either through dislike of incurring pollution (in the ceremonial, ritual sense) from contact with the corpse or through refusing to be in the same house as the corpse, there being no mortuaries or undertakers' chapels of rest.

21. *there is no return:* one of the clearest statements of Ben Sira's belief in no life after death.

22. '*Mine today and yours tomorrow*': a modern English proverb is used to translate the ancient one.

23. Elsewhere Ben Sira regards human *memory* as the only way a person can survive: some 'have left a name behind them to be commemorated in story' (44: 8), yet here he suggests one lets the *memory* of *the dead rest*. He should not be accused of inconsistency: contexts are different, and concentration on the present problem makes him emphatic. ✻

A LIST OF CRAFTSMEN

A scholar's wisdom comes of ample leisure;	24
if a man is to be wise he must be relieved of other tasks.	
How can a man become wise who guides the plough,	25
whose pride is in wielding his goad,	
who is absorbed in the task of driving oxen,	
and talks only about cattle?	
He concentrates on ploughing his furrows,	26
and works late to give the heifers their fodder.	
So it is with every craftsman or designer	27
who works by night as well as by day,	
such as those who make engravings on signets,	
and patiently vary the design;	
they concentrate on making an exact representation,	
and sit up late to finish their task.	
So it is with the smith, sitting by his anvil,	28
intent on his iron-work.	
The smoke of the fire shrivels his flesh,	
as he wrestles in the heat of the furnace.	
The hammer rings again and again in his ears,	
and his eyes are on the pattern he is copying.	
He concentrates on completing the task,	

and stays up late to give it a perfect finish.

29 So it is with the potter, sitting at his work,
turning the wheel with his feet,
always engrossed in the task
of making up his tally;
30 he moulds the clay with his arm,
crouching forward to apply his strength.
He concentrates on finishing the glazing,
and stays awake to clean out the furnace.

31 All these rely on their hands,
and each is skilful at his own craft.
32 Without them a city would have no inhabitants;
no settlers or travellers would come to it.
33 Yet they are not in demand at public discussions
or prominent in the assembly.
They do not sit on the judge's bench
or understand the decisions of the courts.
They cannot expound moral or legal principles
and are not ready with maxims.
34 But they maintain the fabric of this world,
and their prayers are about their daily work.[a]

✳ The series on discriminating among different people in
classes of society which started in 36: 18 but was diverted by
mention of the doctor to illness and death now reaches its
climax in 38: 24 – 39: 11, a section which contrasts various
craftsmen in manual trades (38: 24–34) with the ideal wise
man (39: 1–11). The passage on craftsmen is probably based
on a satirical account of manual workers contained in the
Maxims of Duauf, an Egyptian work popular in the thir-

[a] *Or* and their daily work is their prayer.

teenth century B.C. but probably in existence as early as 2000 B.C. It was composed by a civil servant in the administrative caste of ancient Egypt to ridicule people who worked with their hands. The parallels are quite close – even to the damage to the smith's skin from the heat of his fire in verse 28, but if Ben Sira used it he censored it of all ridicule. He is not ungenerous in praise of the crafts mentioned, and recognizes that craftsmen are skilful at their own crafts (though nothing else!) and provide the material things of civilization (verses 31–2). By repeating that each 'concentrates' on his 'task' and 'stays up late' (verses 26–30) he shows how preoccupation makes it impossible for them to study – that requires 'ample leisure' (verse 24). The craftsman cannot fulfil social tasks as described in verse 33. The praise of the wise man in 39: 1–11 completes the impression that craftsmen are far inferior to wise men.

24. A public figure, *scholar*, administrator or teacher could not follow any profession needing as much concentration as those Ben Sira goes on to describe. Later Jewish teachers differed on this point. Some agreed with Ben Sira: 'engage not overmuch in business but occupy thyself with the Law' (*Aboth* 4: 10). Others considered a trade a necessity for keeping in touch with life: 'excellent is study of the Law together with worldly occupation, for toil in them both puts sin out of mind. But all study of the Law without (worldly) labour comes to nought at the last' (*Aboth* 2: 2). Thus the custom grew for a rabbi to practise a trade (see note on 7: 15).

25–6. Ben Sira takes a tolerant attitude to farm-work in 7: 15, claiming that 'it was ordained by' God. The farmer is busy in the fields by day and in the cowhouse in the dark.

29. The *tally* of *the potter* is the fixed number of vessels he must produce by a certain time.

34. *they maintain the fabric of this world:* the craftsman, though inferior, is much more honourable in Ben Sira's view than the trader, for whom, he thought, it was difficult 'to keep clear of wrong' (26: 29) and who was almost certainly dishonest (27: 2). ✳

PORTRAIT OF AN IDEAL WISE MAN

39 How different it is with the man who devotes himself
to studying the law of the Most High,
who investigates all the wisdom of the past,
and spends his time studying the prophecies!

2 He preserves the sayings of famous men
and penetrates the intricacies of parables.

3 He investigates the hidden meaning of proverbs
and knows his way among riddles.

4 The great avail themselves of his services,
and he is seen in the presence of rulers.
He travels in foreign countries
and learns at first hand the good or evil of man's lot.

5 He makes a point of rising early
to pray to the Lord, his Maker,
and prays aloud to the Most High,
asking pardon for his sins.

6 If it is the will of the great Lord,
he will be filled with a spirit of intelligence;
then he will pour forth wise sayings of his own
and give thanks to the Lord in prayer.

7 He will have sound advice and knowledge to offer,
and his thoughts will dwell on the mysteries he has studied.

8 He will disclose what he has learnt from his own education,
and will take pride in the law of the Lord's covenant.

9 Many will praise his intelligence;
it will never sink into oblivion.
The memory of him will not die
but will live on from generation to generation;

10 the nations will talk of his wisdom,

and his praises will be sung in the assembly.
If he lives long, he will leave a name in a thousand,　　II
and if he goes to his rest, his reputation is secure.[a]

✻ Ben Sira contrasts the ideal wise man with the craftsmen of
38: 24–34. Instead of narrow concentration on one trade
(38: 27–30), the wise man reads and studies widely (39: 1–3);
whereas craftsmen 'are not in demand at public discussions'
or 'in the assembly' (38: 33), the wise man serves 'rulers' and
travels widely (39: 4); whereas they 'are not ready with
maxims' (38: 33), the wise man 'knows his way among
riddles' (39: 3); 'their prayers are about their daily work'
(38: 34), but the wise man's prayers, described at greater
length to show their importance, results in 'a spirit of'
creative 'intelligence' (39: 6) which enables him to serve
the community well. Emphasis on the wise man's attitude to
God shows how all his skill follows from this close relationship with God: 'Those who fear the Lord have their fill of
wisdom' (1: 16). Ben Sira also stresses the world-wide and
long-lasting fame of the wise man (39: 9–11), having assumed
in silence that the craftsmen's work perishes with them. Ben
Sira probably intends an ideal self-portrait, including his
highest aspirations for his own work and position, and the
passage should be read together with such passages as 1: 1–10;
4: 11–19; 6: 18–37; 14: 20 – 15: 10; 24 and 51: 13–30 to
make up Ben Sira's comprehensive picture of true wisdom and
its teachers; in no one place is it described fully.

1 describes the wise man's literary study of the Old Testament. The traditional divisions, mentioned in the grandson's
preface, were *the law*, the prophets and the writings: the
writings, here called *the wisdom of the past*, come second here
because of Ben Sira's emphasis on proverbial lore, but study of
the revealed law is basic, and the wise man takes pride in that
first (verse 8); as was said in 24: 23, 'All this (wisdom) is the

[a] his reputation is secure: *possible reading; Gk. obscure.*

covenant-book of God Most High' and 'the law which Moses
enacted.'

2–3 probably refer to the oral law (as opposed to the written
law) which was taught by oral repetition often as *the sayings of
famous men*, later to be written down in the Mishnah in the
late second century A.D. (see notes on pp. 4–5). *parables* and
riddles were particularly common, as in the Mishnaic tractate
Aboth, and interpretations were handed down also, as in the
parables of the New Testament.

4. Ben Sira mentions the experience gained from his own
travels in 34: 9–12 and 51: 13; the wide experience of travel is
here contrasted with the concentrated occupation of the
craftsman.

6 describes the literary activity of wise men in collecting and
editing the later books of the Old Testament and composing
works of their own, like Ben Sira.

11. The wise man's 'name will live for ever' (37: 26),
whereas 'sinners have no good name to survive them'
(41: 11). Immortality depended on fame for Ben Sira (44:
13–14) who hands on to future generations the fame of Jewish
heroes in 44–50. ✳

A DOCTRINAL HYMN ON CREATION

12 I have still more in my mind to express;
I am full like the moon at mid-month.

13 Listen to me, my devout sons, and blossom
like a rose planted by a stream.

14 Spread your fragrance like incense,
and bloom like a lily.
Scatter your fragrance; lift your voices in song,
praising the Lord for all his works.

15 Ascribe majesty to his name
and give thanks to him with praise,

with songs on your lips, and with harps;
let these be your words of thanksgiving:
'All that the Lord has made is very good;   16
all that he commands will happen in due time.'
No one should ask, 'What is this?' or 'Why is that?'   17
At the proper time all such questions will be answered.
When he spoke the water stood up like a heap,
and his word created reservoirs for it.
When he commands, his purpose is fulfilled,   18
and no one can thwart his saving power.
He sees the deeds of all mankind;   19
there is no hiding from his gaze.
From the beginning to the end of time he keeps watch,   20
and nothing is too marvellous for him.
No one should ask, 'What is this?' or 'Why is that?'   21
Everything has been created for its own purpose.
His blessing is like a river in flood   22
which inundates the parched ground.
But the doom he assigns the heathen is his wrath,   23
as when he turned a watered plain into a salt desert.
For the devout his paths are straight,   24
but full of pitfalls for the wicked.
From the beginning good things were created for the   25
    good,
and evil for sinners.
The chief necessities of human life   26
are water, fire, iron, and salt,
flour, honey, and milk,
the juice of the grape, oil, and clothing.
All these are good for the godfearing,   27
but turn to evil for sinners.

28 There are winds created to be agents of retribution,
    with great whips to give play to their fury;
    on the day of reckoning, they exert their force
    and give full vent to the anger of their Maker.

29 Fire and hail, famine and deadly disease,
    all these were created for retribution;

30 beasts of prey, scorpions and vipers,
    and the avenging sword that destroys the wicked.

31 They delight in carrying out his orders,
    always standing ready for his service on the earth;
    and when their time comes, they never disobey.

32 I have been convinced of all this from the beginning;
    I have thought it over and left it in writing:

33 all the works of the Lord are good,
    and he supplies every need as it occurs.

34 No one should say, 'This is less good than that',
    for all things prove good at their proper time.

35 Come then, sing with heart and voice,
    and praise the name of the Lord.

* Before a depressing account of man's hard life in 40: 1–11, Ben Sira includes a hymn, probably of his own composition, on God's ordering of creation, very similar to 16: 24 – 17: 14 in purpose and content. Both passages were written to answer questions and objections; here Ben Sira claims that to 'ask, "What is this?" or "Why is that?"' (verses 17, 21) is to doubt God's complete control over nature by implying there are things that have no purpose. His answer is that 'all things prove good at their proper time' (verse 34). This echoes his insistence that everything is ordered in detail by God (33: 7–15) even to the extent of being good or evil appropriately on different occasions: just as water may be given to create fertility or withheld to create a desert (verses 22–3), so most things 'are good for the godfearing, but turn to evil for sinners' (verse 27). But he spoils his argument with small inconsistencies: fire is 'created for retribution' (verse 29), yet is said to be 'good for the godfearing' and 'evil for sinners' (verses 26–7).

This learned discussion, typical of the lecture room, is sandwiched between an introduction (verse 15) and closure (verse 35) typical of the Old Testament psalms: it thus becomes a very academic hymn, with the doctrinal lesson that 'All that the Lord...commands will happen in due time' repeated almost like a refrain (verse 16, very similar to verses 21 and 34). The whole hymn (verses 15–35) is preceded by a brief exhortation in verses 12–14 expressing Ben Sira's insatiable desire to express knowledge and using images taken from the Old Testament psalms.

12. Ben Sira's *mind* is as full of material as the full *moon* of light.

16–18. Both answer (verse 16, *'All that the Lord has made is very good'*) and objector's question (verse 17, *' What is this?'* ...*'Why is that?'*) are re-echoed at various times in the hymn, the answer in verses 21 and 34. *the water stood up like a heap* at God's word when the Hebrews crossed the Red Sea dry-shod (Exod. 14: 21–2). This reference to God acting for his people's salvation in history leads to mention of *his saving power* in history in verse 18.

19 refers back to the argument of 17: 15–24 where nothing is 'hidden from his (God's) scrutiny' (17: 15).

23 recalls Ps. 107: 34: 'he turns fruitful land into salt waste, because the men who dwell there are so wicked' – a reference to God's destruction of Sodom narrated in Gen. 18: 16 – 19: 25.

28–31. As already noted, this passage is inconsistent with Ben Sira's doctrine that everything is good for the good but bad for the bad: all things mentioned in verses 28–30 seem to have been created for the evil only. Some have seen here poetic allusions to Babylonian demons and animals, but Ben Sira's allusions are always literary and orthodox. It is more likely that Ben Sira wants to warn sinners of *the anger of their Maker* (verse 28), and so emphasizes evil action; these verses should be viewed as emphasizing one side of the general statement in verse 27 which still holds good. *Fire and hail* were used to punish the Egyptians (Exod. 9: 23), and a pestilence punished David's subjects (2 Sam. 24: 15); *wild beasts* (Deut. 32: 24) and the Lord's *sword* (Isa. 34: 6) are frequently mentioned – more of Ben Sira's anthological style.

32. *I have been convinced...I have thought it over* recalls 33: 16–18 and 34: 9–12 with its personal note, coming oddly in the middle of a hymn. The hymnic style is taken up again to conclude the chapter. ✳

ON MAN'S COMMON LOT

40 Hard work is the lot of every man,
and a heavy yoke is laid on the sons of Adam,
from the day when they come from their mothers' womb
until the day of their return to the mother of all;
2 troubled thoughts and fears are theirs,
and anxious expectation of the day of their death.
3 Whether a man sits in royal splendour on a throne
or grovels in dust and ashes,
4 whether he wears the purple and a crown
or is clothed in sackcloth,
5 his life is nothing but anger and jealousy, worry and
perplexity,
fear of death, and guilt, and rivalry.
Even when he goes to bed at night,
sleep only brings to mind the same things in a new form.

His rest is little or nothing;   6
he begins to struggle as hard in his sleep as in the day.[a]
Disturbed by nightmares,
he fancies himself a fugitive from the battlefield;
and at the moment when he reaches safety, he wakes up,   7
astonished to find his fears groundless.

✻ Firmly convinced, as shown in the foregoing hymn, that
God controls all things, Ben Sira now describes the hard life
of mankind (40: 1 – 41: 13). In this series of sections he
emphasizes the extra suffering that sinners bring on themselves
(40: 8–17; 41: 5–13), includes discussions of a beggar's life
(40: 28–30) and of death (41: 1–4), and compiles a series of
comparisons to highlight 'the fear of the Lord' (40: 18–27).
In 40: 1–7 man's lot from God consists of 'hard work' and
anxiety experienced by all levels of society alike (verses 3–4);
this common lot can turn to good or evil as 39: 27 indicates,
but becomes much harder ('seven times over', 40: 8) for
sinners.

     1. *the mother of all* is the 'dust' of the ground to which all
must 'return' (Gen. 3: 19). Oddly the Hebrew phrase is not
used of the ground in Gen. 3: 19 but of Eve in Gen. 3: 20 –
has Ben Sira got his quotation wrong?

     4. *sackcloth* was worn by the poor because its coarseness was
durable.

     5–7. Anxiety leads to only a *little rest* in *sleep* followed by
restless tossing and *nightmares*. Verses 6–7 describe the contents
of the nightmare: *a fugitive from the battlefield* runs from danger,
always watching for the enemy to catch him up. *at the moment
when he reaches safety, he wakes up, astonished . . .*: in such
dreams one wakes up at crisis point, and the Greek should
probably be translated: '*at the moment when* deliverance is
urgently needed, *he wakes up*, satisfied *to find his fears groundless*'. ✻

     [a] he begins . . . day: *possible meaning; Gk. obscure.*

ON INCREASED SUFFERING FOR SINNERS

8 To all living creatures, man and beast –
and seven times over to sinners –

9 come death and bloodshed, quarrel and sword,
disaster, famine, ruin, and plague.

10 All these were created for the wicked,
and on their account the flood happened.

11 All that is of earth returns to earth again,
and all that is of water finds its way back to the sea.

12 Bribery and injustice will all vanish,
but good faith will last for ever.

13 The wealth of the wicked will dry up like a torrent
and die away like a great roll of thunder in a storm.

14 As a generous man will have cause for rejoicing,
so law-breakers will come to utter ruin.

15 The shoots of an impious stock put out few branches;
their tainted roots are planted on sheer rock.

16 The rush that grows on every river-bank
is pulled up before any other grass,

17 but kindness is like a luxuriant garden,
and almsgiving lasts for ever.

* The extra suffering of sinners is now described. As in
39: 29–30 the author includes a list of disasters (verse 9)
commonly regarded in the Old Testament as God's punishment for sinners; as in 39: 29 Ben Sira emphasizes their use
for evil rather than their double-edged neutrality. The complete ruin of the wicked is described in verses 12–17, sandwiched between the positive virtues of 'good faith' (verse 12)
and 'almsgiving' (verse 17) which 'lasts for ever'.

8. The number *seven*, used in 35: 11 to denote a large number, here denotes great frequency.

10. Gen. 6: 5 – 8: 22 tells the story of *the flood* sent by God to destroy all mankind because of their wickedness.

11 links the idea of the common origin and destination of all people with that of barren *earth* and the fertility of *water*, taken up in verses 13–17.

12. *Bribery and injustice will all vanish* in utter destruction, whereas reputation for *good faith* lasts *for ever*.

13. Streams in the mountains of Palestine are full and fierce in the wet season but *dry up* completely in the summer; thus Job's brothers are compared to 'a mountain stream' that runs dry (Job 6: 15). Similes using the fertility of water continue in verses 15–17.

15. *sheer rock* holds no water to enable a tree to grow; Ben Sira is possibly thinking of the man who meditates on the law and is compared in Ps. 1: 3 to 'a tree planted beside a water-course', which 'never withers'. ✶

A SERIES OF COMPARISONS

To be employed and to be one's own master, both are sweet, 18
but it is better still to find a treasure.

Offspring and the founding of a city perpetuate a man's 19
name,
but better still is a perfect wife.

Wine and music gladden the heart, 20
but better still is the love of wisdom.

Flute and harp make pleasant melody, 21
but better still is a pleasant voice.

A man likes to see grace and beauty, 22
but better still the green shoots in a cornfield.

A friend or companion is always welcome, 23
but better still to be man and wife.

24 Brothers and helpers are a stand-by in time of trouble,
but better still is almsgiving.

25 Gold and silver make a man stand firm,
but better still is good advice.

26 Wealth and strength make for confidence,
but better still is the fear of the Lord.
To fear the Lord is to lack nothing
and never to be in need of support.

27 The fear of the Lord is like a luxuriant garden;
it shelters a man better than any riches.

* Ben Sira inserts a list of riddles based on the formal pattern: one thing is good, 'but better still' something else. The pattern is followed strictly until the climax in verse 26 when 'the fear of the Lord' is shown to be best of all. The following two couplets then describe the results of this relationship with God. The series is included as contrast to the condemnation of the wicked in 40: 8–17 and 41: 5–13.

19. *the founding of a city:* many Greek cities were called after their founders, like Alexandria in Egypt, named after Alexander the Great.

24. *almsgiving* is preferred to help from *Brothers and helpers ...in time of trouble* because it arises from more particularly religious motives according to Ben Sira.

26–7 repeat one of the main themes of the book: *The fear of the Lord* 'brings cheerfulness and joy and long life' (1: 12); it 'excels all other gifts' (25: 11); one 'who fears the Lord will have nothing else to fear' (34: 14) etc. *

ON A BEGGAR'S LIFE

28 My son, do not live the life of a beggar;
it is better to die than to beg.

29 When a man starts looking to another man's table,

his existence is not worth calling life.
It is demoralizing to live on another man's food,
and a wise, well-disciplined man will guard against it.
When a man has lost all shame, he speaks as if begging 30
    were sweet,
but inside him there is a blazing fire.

✻ The mention of 'riches' in verse 27 leads Ben Sira to warn
readers against beggary. The evils of having to look 'to
another man's table' (verse 29) have been described in detail
in 29: 24–7; later Jewish teachers said that the life of one that
looks at the table of a friend is not (real) life. That riches and
wealth are not good (40: 13, 27) does not make poverty
good.

30 refers to the beggar's insincerity: he may pretend that he
likes *begging* (to keep his self-respect) but he suppresses resentment at the comfort of the rich and has *a blazing fire inside*
which carries its own destruction. ✻

ON DEATH

Death, how bitter is the thought of you   **41**
to a man living at ease among his possessions,
free from anxiety, prosperous in all things,
and still vigorous enough to enjoy a good meal!
Death, how welcome is your sentence   2
to a destitute man whose strength is failing,
worn down by age and endless anxiety,
resentful and at the end of his patience!
Do not be afraid of death's summons;   3
remember those who have gone before you, and those
    who will come after.
This is the Lord's decree for all living men;
                                                           4

why try to argue with the will of the Most High?
Whether life lasts ten years, or a hundred, or a thousand,
there will be no questions asked in the grave.

✻ 'Expectation of the day of...death' (40: 2) is one of the
worst parts of man's lot, even though death is certain for all
(41: 4, also 14: 17; 17: 2). Verses 1–2 show the different
significance the thought of death has for different people –
depressing for the rich and healthy, *welcome* to the poor and
sick. This accords with Ben Sira's doctrine of the two-sided
character of God's creation expounded in 33: 7–15. *no
questions* will be *asked in the grave* (verse 4) about wealth or
status in life, for 'All man's works decay and vanish' (14: 19)
at death, and there is no point in jealousy or envy over what is
finished. After death rich and poor, pious and wicked are
not distinguished for Ben Sira. Death is to be accepted as a
fact by all; mourners who over-mourn imply that death is
exceptional, and should 'Remember that his fate will also be'
theirs (38: 22). ✻

CURSES FOR THE SINNER

5 What a loathsome brood are the children of sinners,
   brought up in haunts of vice!
6 Their inheritance dwindles away,
   and their descendants suffer a lasting disgrace.
7 A godless father is blamed by his children
   for the disgrace they endure on his account.
8 Woe to you, godless men
   who have abandoned the law of God Most High!
9 When you are born, you are born to a curse,
   and when you die, a curse is your lot.
10 Whatever comes from earth returns to earth;
   so too the godless go from curse to ruin.

Men grieve over the death of the body,   11
but sinners have no good name to survive them.
Take thought for your name, for it will outlive you   12
longer than a thousand hoards of gold.
The days of a good life are numbered,   13
but a good name lasts for ever.

* Only family and reputation survive death. Sinners'
families 'suffer a lasting disgrace' (verse 6) because of the
reputation of their parents who 'have no good name to
survive them' (verse 11). Ben Sira tries to show in this section
how much worse is the death of a sinner than that of a good
man, but after his emphasis on the levelling nature of death
(41: 4) his argument for distinction seems weak.

10. *the godless go* from cursed birth to cursed death: the *ruin*
implied is interpreted as bad reputation but presumably also
includes evil descendants (verses 5–7). That the sinner's own
discomfort is not mentioned makes the passage ineffective.

13. The series on man's hardship ends on an encouraging
note: although, however *good* a life is, its *days . . . are numbered*
by the 'fixed span of life' set by God (17: 2); *a good name lasts
for ever* as already stated in 37: 26 and 39: 11. *

ON THINGS TO BE ASHAMED OF

My children, be true to your training and live in peace.   14
Wisdom concealed and treasure hidden –
what is the use of either?
Better a man who hides his folly   15
than one who hides his wisdom!

Show deference then to my teaching: 16
shame is not always to be encouraged,
or given unqualified approval in all circumstances.

17 Be ashamed to be found guilty of fornication by your
         parents,
     or of lies by a ruler or prince;
18 of crime by a judge or magistrate,
     or of a breach of the law by the assembly and people;
     of dishonesty by a partner or friend,
19 or of theft by the neighbourhood;
     be ashamed before the truth of God and his covenant.
     Be ashamed of bad manners at table,
     of giving or receiving with a sneer,
20 of refusing to return a greeting,
     or of ogling a prostitute.
21 Be ashamed of turning away a relative,
     or robbing someone of his rightful share,
     or of eyeing another man's wife.
22 Be ashamed of meddling with his slave-girl,
     and keep away from her bed.
     Be ashamed of reproaching your friends,
     or following up your charity with a lecture.
23 Be ashamed of repeating what you have heard
     and of betraying a secret.
24 Then you will be showing a proper shame
     and will be popular with everyone.

✧ Nearing the end of his advice on behaviour Ben Sira sums
up his teaching in two sections on one's sense of shame. After
an introduction (verses 14–15) he presents a list of things you
should be ashamed of (41: 16–24) followed by a list of things
not to be ashamed of (42: 1–8). Shame, a natural human
feeling, can be good or bad in differing circumstances – like
food (36: 18), friends (37: 1), advisers (37: 7), death (41: 1–2),
etc. – according to God's plan for the world (33: 7–15).

Man must learn to exercise control and show 'a proper shame' at all times. The details of both sections pick up many aspects of his teaching up to this point of the book.

14–16. The words from *Wisdom concealed... to... hides his wisdom* occur in more suitable context in 20: 30–1, and seem to have been repeated here to provide an introduction to the section on shame. The first line of verse 14 (*My children,... in peace*) does not seem to fit, and probably originally came before verse 16 as in the Hebrew text: being *true to* one's *training* and showing *deference to* Ben Sira's *teaching* go well together.

19. In the middle of things one should *be ashamed* of comes something to *be ashamed before*, i.e. *the truth of God and his covenant*. The Greek translation reminds the reader of the religious background of all the author's thought. But the Hebrew probably read '(be ashamed) of changing your oath and agreement'; the Greek translator mistook the Hebrew *'ālāh* ('oath') for *'elōah* ('God'), the consonantal text probably being the same, and then tried to make sense of the misreading. ✴

ON THINGS NOT TO BE ASHAMED OF

But at other times you must not be ashamed, **42**
or you will do wrong out of deference to others.
Do not be ashamed of the law and covenant of the Most 2
    High,
or of justice, for fear you acquit the guilty;
of settling accounts with a partner or a travelling- 3
    companion,
or of sharing an inheritance with the other heirs;
of using accurate weights and measures, 4
or of business dealings, large or small,
and making a profit out of trade; 5

of frequent disciplining of children,
or of drawing blood from the back of a worthless servant.

6 If your wife is untrustworthy, or where many hands are
    at work,
it is well to keep things under lock and key.

7 When you make a deposit, see that it is counted and
    weighed,
and when you give or receive, have it all in writing.

8 Do not be ashamed to correct the ignorant and foolish,
or a greybeard guilty of fornication.
Then you will be showing your sound upbringing
and will win everyone's approval.

* Ben Sira now turns to a list of things one should not be
ashamed of when ridiculed or criticized in public. 'deference to
others' (verse 1) is often correct, at banquets, for instance
(32: 7–9), but the temptation to defer to others against what
you know to be right must be avoided. 'sound upbringing'
counts most in the end (verse 8).

2. Gentile ridicule of Jewish observances had led many
Jews to be lax and remain popular. Similarly, bribes offered by
influential people had caused judges to *acquit the guilty*.

3–4, 7. Strict fairness in money matters is always best.
accounts with a business *partner* should be kept strictly with no
assumption that good will excuse slackness. The Mishnah
lays down the rule that 'the shopkeeper must clean out his
measures twice in the week and polish his weights once a
week and clean out his scales after every weighing' (*Baba
Bathra* 5: 10) to avoid dishonesty. In depositing or receiving
money, fairness lies in open counting, weighing and recording
in writing.

8. Proper respect for age should not be regarded as more important than condemning sin where *fornication* is concerned. *

ON THE DISCIPLINE OF DAUGHTERS

A daughter is a secret anxiety to her father, 9
and the worry of her keeps him awake at night;
when she is young, for fear she may grow too old to
    marry,
and when she is married, for fear she may lose her
    husband's love;
when she is a virgin, for fear she may be seduced 10
and become pregnant in her father's house,
when she has a husband, for fear she may misbehave,
and after marriage, for fear she may be barren.
Keep close watch over a headstrong daughter, 11
or she may give your enemies cause to gloat,
making you the talk of the town and a byword*a* among
    the people,
and shaming you in the eyes of the world.
Do not let her display her beauty to any man, 12
or gossip in the women's quarters.*b*
For out of clothes comes the moth, 13
and out of woman comes woman's wickedness.
Better a man's wickedness than a woman's goodness; 14
it is woman who brings shame and disgrace.

✳ Ben Sira, usually a balanced observer of human life, has
already revealed anti-feminine bias in, for example, his remarks
on wives in 25: 13–26 and on daughters in 26: 10–12. This
prejudice reaches its climax in 42: 14 where 'man's wickedness' is preferred to 'woman's goodness'. The statement that
'Woman is the origin of sin' (25: 24) is now capped by 'it

[a] a byword: *so Heb.; Gk. obscure.*
[b] Do not. . .quarters: *so Heb.; Gk. obscure.*

is woman who brings shame and disgrace' (verse 14). This
section on the anxiety of having daughters probably arises
from his previous remarks on not being ashamed of strict
discipline over children (verse 5) and wives (verse 6). Thus Ben
Sira adds greater emphasis to this advice before the hymns
on creation (42: 15 – 43: 33) and Israel's history (44: 1 –
50: 21), and lets himself down badly to modern readers –
although verses 9 and 10 were much admired and quoted by
some later Jewish teachers.

13. Either a *woman* goes from man to man as a *moth*
goes from garment to garment, or, more probably, it is
the nature of cloth to nourish moths and of *woman* to
nourish *wickedness*. ✼

The wonders of creation

PRAISE OF CREATION – GOD'S POWER

15 NOW I WILL CALL to mind the works of the Lord
and describe what I have seen;
by the words of the Lord his works are made.
16 As the sun in its brilliance looks down on everything,
so the glory of the Lord fills his creation.
17 Even to his angels the Lord has not given the power
to tell the full story of his marvels,
which the Lord Almighty has established
so that the universe may stand firm in his glory.
18 He fathoms the abyss and the heart of man,
he is versed in their intricate secrets;
for the Lord possesses all knowledge
and observes the signs of all time.

He discloses the past and the future,   19
and uncovers the traces of the world's mysteries.
No thought escapes his notice,   20
and not a word is hidden from him.
He has set in order the masterpieces of his wisdom,   21
he who is from eternity to eternity;
nothing can be added, nothing taken away,
and he needs no one to give him advice.
How beautiful is all that he has made,   22
down to the smallest spark that can be seen!
His works endure, all of them active for ever   23
and all responsive to their various purposes.
All things go in pairs, one the opposite of the other;   24
he has made nothing incomplete.
One thing supplements the virtues of another.   25
Who could ever contemplate his glory enough?

* The third part of the book contains two hymns of praise –
one concerning God's power and wisdom in creation (42: 15
– 43: 33), the other describing his greatness as shown in the
past history of Israel (44: 1 – 50: 24). The hymn on creation
starts by describing God's creation in general doctrinal terms
familiar from other parts of the book (42: 15–25) before
surveying the natural universe in detail (43: 1–26) and con-
cluding with renewed statements of God's greatness and
inviting the reader to join in praise (43: 27–33). In this section
God's perfect knowledge is stressed by mention of the 'intricate secrets' (verse 18) unknown to man himself; the doctrinal
passage on God's detailed ordering of creation in 33: 7–15 is
picked up by the quotation of 33: 15, that 'All things go in
pairs, one the opposite of the other' (verse 24). So Ben Sira
sums up various aspects of his doctrine of God in this hymn.

15. The hymn speaks of God creating by his *words*, as also in
43: 5, 10 and, especially, 43: 26 ('by his word all things are

held together'), echoing the doctrine of creation by the word
based on God's speeches in Gen. 1 ('Let there be light',
Gen. 1: 3, etc.). Wisdom is now linked with the word of
God, as in 24: 3 where wisdom claims to be 'the word which
was spoken by the Most High'. This doctrine is fully developed
in Wisd. of Sol. 9: 1: 'God of our fathers... who hast made
all things by thy word, and in thy wisdom hast fashioned
man.' This forms the background of the statement in John
1: 2 that 'all things came to be' through God's word.

16. God's *glory* may be seen in *his creation* – the argument for
the existence of God from the design of creation.

18–19. God's knowledge covers *the abyss*, the subterranean
waters of ancient thought mentioned in 1: 3. The *intricate
secrets* and *the signs of all time* do not indicate secrets to be
revealed to members of a closed sect, as in many ancient
mystery religions, but rather things unknowable by any man,
thus stressing God's perfect knowledge.

22. *down to the smallest spark* means 'even to the smallest
detail'. ✳

PRAISE OF CREATION – THE WONDERS OF THE SKY

43 What a masterpiece is the clear vault of the sky!
How glorious is the spectacle of the heavens!

2 The sun comes into view proclaiming as it rises
how marvellous a thing it is, made by the Most High.

3 At noon it parches the earth,
and no one can endure its blazing heat.

4 The stoker of a furnace works in the heat,
but three times as hot is the sun scorching the hills.
It breathes out fiery vapours,
and its glare blinds the eyes.

5 Great is the Lord who made it,
whose word speeds it on its course.

He made the moon also to serve in its turn,   6
a perpetual sign to mark the divisions of time.
From the moon, feast-days are reckoned;   7
it is a light that wanes as it completes its course.
The moon gives its name to the month;   8
it waxes marvellously as its phases change,
a beacon to the armies of heaven,
shining in the vault of the sky.

The brilliant stars are the beauty of the sky,   9
a glittering array in the heights of the Lord.
At the command of the Holy One they stand in their   10
     appointed place;
they never default at their post.

Look at the rainbow and praise its Maker;   11
it shines with a supreme beauty,
rounding the sky with its gleaming arc,   12
a bow bent by the hands of the Most High.

His command speeds the snow-storm   13
and sends the swift lightning to execute his sentence.
To that end the storehouses are opened,   14
and the clouds fly out like birds.
By his mighty power the clouds are piled up   15
and the hailstones broken small.
The crash of his thunder makes the earth writhe,   16–17
and, when he appears, an earthquake shakes the hills.
At his will the south wind blows,
the squall from the north and the hurricane.
He scatters the snow-flakes like birds alighting;

they settle like a swarm of locusts.

18 The eye is dazzled by their beautiful whiteness,
   and as they fall the mind is entranced.

19 He spreads frost on the earth like salt,
   and icicles form like pointed stakes.

20 A cold blast from the north,
   and ice grows hard on the water,
   settling on every pool,
   as though the water were putting on a breastplate.

21 He consumes the hills, scorches the wilderness,
   and withers the grass like fire.

22 Cloudy weather quickly puts all to rights,
   and dew brings welcome relief after heat.

23 By the power of his thought he tamed the deep
   and planted it with islands.

24 Those who sail the sea tell stories of its dangers,
   which astonish all who hear them;

25 in it are strange and wonderful creatures,
   all kinds of living things and huge sea-monsters.

26 By his own action he achieves his end,
   and by his word all things are held together.

✷ In the second part of the hymn we read a detailed description of sun, moon, stars, rainbow and other natural phenomena, largely concerning the weather. As in Ps. 104 the mass of detailed description is intended to lead the reader to praise God. The author returns to his doctrinal message by summing up all the detail in the statement that 'by his word all things are held together' (verse 26).

   1. The *vault of the sky* refers to the arched metal firmament which was thought to hold up the upper waters in the sky, as described in the notes on 24: 5.

4. *fiery vapours* is an extension of the furnace metaphor.

6–7. *the moon* and stars were created by God to 'serve as signs both for festivals and for seasons and years' (Gen. 1: 14), a point already made by Ben Sira in 33: 7–9. Yet another reference to God's ordering of creation.

8. The Hebrew word *ḥōdesh* meant both 'month' and 'new moon'. The stars were often referred to as 'the host of heaven', and *The moon* is here *a beacon* to direct the movements of the stars with its light. The military metaphor is continued in verse 10.

14. Old Testament poets refer several times to God's 'storehouses' (Jer. 10: 13) or 'rich treasure house' (Deut. 28: 12) where he stores up rain, clouds, snow, etc.

16–17. *thunder* and lightning were often used to describe God's presence, as in Ps. 77: 18 and, notably, in the thunderstorm on Mount Sinai at the giving of the Ten Commandments (Exod. 19: 19). Swarms of *locusts* were frequent in the Near East and covered the ground more completely than western minds can imagine.

21. The imagery returns suddenly to heat again, as shown by verse 22. ✧

PRAISE OF CREATION – WONDERS BEYOND DESCRIPTION

However much we say, we cannot exhaust our theme;   27
to put it in a word: he is all.

Where can we find the skill to sing his praises?   28
For he is greater than all his works.

The Lord is terrible and very great,   29
and marvellous is his power.

Honour the Lord to the best of your ability,   30
and he will still be high above all praise.

Summon all your strength to declare his greatness,
and be untiring, for the most you can do will fall short.

31 Has anyone ever seen him, to be able to describe him?
   Can anyone praise him as he truly is?
32 We have seen but a small part of his works,
   and there remain many mysteries greater still.
33 The Lord has made everything
   and has given wisdom to the godly.

* The details described in verses 1–26 are but 'a small part of
his works' (verse 32); the theme of God's varied works in
nature is inexhaustible, and amazement leads to another
outburst of praise to end the hymn. God is in fact 'high above
all praise' (verse 30) and human understanding (verse 32).

27. Some have seen in the words *he is all* the influence of
the (Greek) Stoic doctrine that God exists in all created things,
that God is immanent, some even suggesting the words are
quoted from a Stoic hymn. But the address to God as 'thou
God of all' in 36: 1 is sufficiently close to discount Stoic
influence, and the belief that God is in sole charge of the creation and maintenance of the universe lies behind such passages
as 18: 1–7 and 33: 7–15. *

Heroes of Israel's past

PRAISE FOR ISRAEL'S PAST – THOSE REMEMBERED
AND THOSE FORGOTTEN

44 LET US NOW SING the praises of famous men,
    the heroes of our nation's history,
 2 through whom the Lord established his renown,
   and revealed his majesty in each succeeding age.
 3 Some held sway over kingdoms
   and made themselves a name by their exploits.

Others were sage counsellors,
who spoke out with prophetic power.

Some led the people by their counsels   4
and by their knowledge of the nation's law;
out of their fund of wisdom they gave instruction.

Some were composers of music or writers of poetry.   5

Others were endowed with wealth and strength,   6
living peacefully in their homes.

All these won fame in their own generation   7
and were the pride of their times.

Some there are who have left a name behind them   8
to be commemorated in story.

There are others who are unremembered;   9
they are dead, and it is as though they had never
    existed,
as though they had never been born
or left children to succeed them.

Not so our forefathers; they were men of loyalty,   10
whose good deeds have never been forgotten.

Their prosperity is handed on to their descendants,   11
and their inheritance to future generations.[a]

Thanks to them their children are within the covenants –   12
the whole race of their descendants.

Their line will endure for all time,   13
and their fame will never be blotted out.

Their bodies are buried in peace,   14
but their name lives for ever.

Nations will recount their wisdom,   15
and God's people will sing their praises.

[a] Their prosperity...generations: *probable meaning, based on other Vss.;
Gk. obscure.*

✻ A much longer hymn now follows praising God for Israel's past history, which is traced from Enoch (44: 16) to Simon the Just (50: 1–21). Some claim that this long list of famous men was influenced by popular Greek biographical works of the time, but similar surveys of God's acts in history appear in the Old Testament, for example in Ps. 78. Jews at the beginning of the second century B.C. found inspiration and encouragement in narrating the past glories of Israel, as shown by Mattathias' speech to his sons in 1 Macc. 2: 49–64. The length and position given to the hymn shows how far wisdom had found a 'heritage in Israel' (24: 8) in Ben Sira's thought, and we see how far Ben Sira must have studied 'the law', investigated 'all the wisdom of the past' and examined carefully 'the prophecies' like the ideal wise man (39: 1); much of verses 3–6 recalls that earlier description. Verses 1–15 form a general introduction to the hymn, describing mainly people whose good name has lasted for ever (41: 13). Verse 9, on those 'unremembered', has been thought to refer to the godless; but godlessness is not mentioned, and it is probably a recognition that there are some good people who have left neither name nor family behind, although this contradicts one of Ben Sira's favourite themes that the good leave a good name. Some claim that verses 3–9 concern great people of every nation, but more probably Ben Sira is thinking of Jews in general before turning in verse 10 to the 'forefathers... whose good deeds' have been remembered in the Old Testament. The reading of this passage in some countries in services of remembrance for those killed in war from one particular nation therefore misrepresents the original intention of the author.

3–5. prophetic power, knowledge of the nation's law, wisdom and *instruction*, and *composers of music* may refer to different parts of the Old Testament (prophetical books, Pentateuch, Proverbs and Psalms respectively), but Ben Sira is probably re-describing the ideal wise man of 39: 1–11 in more general terms. ✻

ISRAEL'S PAST – BEFORE THE FLOOD

Enoch pleased the Lord and was carried off to heaven,   16
an example of repentance to future generations.
Noah was found perfect and righteous,   17
and thus he made amends in the time of retribution;
therefore a remnant survived on the earth,
when the flood came.
A perpetual covenant was established with him,   18
that never again should all life be swept away by a flood.

✵ Ben Sira starts his survey of Israel's history with Enoch and
Noah. Most of what he narrates is drawn directly from the Old
Testament, as with Noah, but occasionally, as with Enoch,
later Jewish discussion is reflected. He does not start with
Adam because Adam figured prominently in the fantastic,
mystical speculation that appears in later apocalyptic books.
Ben Sira was opposed to such speculation and seems deliberately to have omitted Adam, Shem and Seth here, all subjects
of similar speculation, although 49: 14–16 seems to have been
inserted to fill the omission (see notes there).

16. Enoch also figured in such works. The statement that he
'walked with God' and 'was seen no more, because God had
taken him away' (Gen. 5: 22–4) was thought by many later
Jews to indicate that he shared much of God's secret knowledge, ascended into heaven, thus avoiding natural death, and
even became a heavenly intercessor for Israel's sins. Others
considered him a sinner who overreached himself and died
naturally. Ben Sira admits the ascension (49: 14) but, although
the Hebrew text here calls him a 'sign of knowledge to all
generations', the Greek translator wrote *an example of repentance*, interpreting the Hebrew's 'knowledge' of those
'mysteries' of God that men cannot, and should not, try to
understand (3: 21–4; 43: 32). Enoch thus appears as a converted sinner, which suits the grandson's evangelistic purpose.

17–18. Noah and his family survived *the flood* as *a remnant* because he was *righteous* and 'the one blameless man of his time' (Gen. 6: 9). The *covenant* is described in Gen. 9: 8–11. Although legends about Noah were frequent, this book contains no reference to them. ✶

ISRAEL'S PAST – OUR FATHER ABRAHAM AND HIS FAMILY

19 Great Abraham was the father of many nations;
no one has ever been found to equal him in fame.
20 He kept the law of the Most High;
he entered into covenant with him,
setting upon his body the mark of the covenant;
and, when he was tested, he proved faithful.
21 Therefore the Lord swore an oath to him,
that nations should find blessing through his descendants,
that his family should be countless as the dust of the earth
and be raised as high as the stars,
and that their possessions should reach from sea to sea,
from the Great River to the ends of the earth.

22 To Isaac he made the same promise
for the sake of his father Abraham,
a blessing for all mankind and a covenant;
23 and so he transmitted them to Jacob.
He confirmed him in the blessings he had received
and gave him the land he was to inherit,
dividing it into portions,
which he allotted to the twelve tribes.

✶ Ben Sira's selection of material on Abraham follows biblical tradition in emphasizing him as an ancestor of Israel

218

as well as of other semitic nations. The colourless Isaac and the all-too-colourful Jacob are given brief treatment.

19. *the father of many nations* is, in both Hebrew and Greek though not in the N.E.B., a direct quotation of Gen. 17: 4 ('father of a host of nations'). Abraham is a figure of great sanctity to Moslems as well as to Jews and Christians.

20. Ancient readers would probably understand by *the law of the Most High* the Mosaic law, although Abraham lived before the giving of the law to Moses on Mount Sinai. But God regarded Abraham as having kept his commandments, statutes and laws (Gen. 26: 5), and his 'faith was counted as righteousness' in the New Testament (Rom. 4: 9). Circumcision was practised by many other peoples, but for the Jews it became a special *mark* on the *body...of the covenant* with Abraham (Gen. 17: 13). Abraham was *tested* by his willingness to sacrifice Isaac his son (Gen. 22: 1–18) – an act revered by later Jews: Mattathias refers to Abraham as 'steadfast under trial' (1 Macc. 2: 52).

21. The theme of Abraham's descendants occurs frequently in the Old Testament, and many favourite phrases are here included. The boundaries of Palestine (the promised land) vary in the Old Testament, but Ben Sira, unworried by geographical exactness, merely quotes Ps. 72: 8 word for word. *from sea to sea* probably means 'from the Red Sea to the sea of the Philistines (i.e. the Mediterranean)' (Exod. 23: 31), and *the Great River* refers to the Euphrates.

22. *To Isaac he made the same promise* refers to God's promise to Abraham concerning Isaac in Gen. 17: 19.

23. The division of *the land* and allotment *to the twelve tribes* are based on the poetic Blessing of Jacob in Gen. 49: 1–27. ✳

ISRAEL'S PAST – MOSES THE HUMBLE

From Jacob's stock the Lord raised up a loyal servant,   **45**
who won the approval of all mankind,
beloved by God and men,

Moses of blessed memory.

2 The Lord made him equal in glory to the angels
and gave him power to strike terror into his enemies.

3 At his request he put an end to the portents,
and enhanced his reputation with kings.
He gave him commandments for his people
and showed him a vision of his own·glory.

4 For his loyalty and humility he consecrated him,
choosing him out of all mankind.

5 He let him hear his voice
and led him into the dark cloud.
Face to face, he gave him the commandments,
a law that brings life and knowledge,
so that he might teach Jacob the covenant
and Israel his decrees.

✱ After Jacob we should expect the 'loyal servant', 'From
Jacob's stock' (verse 1) to be Joseph; but he is omitted here,
possibly because he was not prominent in later legend and is
unimportant theologically – although he appears in 49: 15.

Moses' high status in Judaism rests on the giving of the law
and the escape from Egypt: five verses seem few for a person
of such great reputation, especially when compared with
Aaron (seventeen verses!). The law is mentioned in verses
3 and 5, and events in the escape are alluded to in verse 3
without explicit mention of Egypt or Pharaoh. Ben Sira
stresses Moses' 'loyalty and humility' (verse 4, also verse 1)
most, probably to illustrate God's choice of the humble
(3: 18) – a favourite theme in the book. Moses is honoured
with the phrase 'of blessed memory', in Hebrew the regular
formula used in later Jewish literature after the name of a famous person.

2. *equal in glory to the angels:* the Hebrew text compares
Moses to a god, echoing 'I have made you like a god for

Pharaoh' (Exod. 7: 1); the Greek translator misunderstood *'elōhīm* ('god') as *angels*, as happens sometimes in the Septuagint to avoid likening a human to the one God. *'elōhīm* could mean any (pagan) god or the one true God.

3. God removed the frogs, flies, hail and locusts (*the portents*), sent to plague the Egyptians, at Moses' *request* (Exod. 8: 12, 31; 9: 33; 10: 19). In Exod. 33: 18 Moses asked to be shown God's *glory*.

4. Consecration here denotes choice for special service rather than ordination as a priest.

5. Moses entered *the dark cloud* of God's presence on Mount Sinai (Exod. 20: 21) to receive the stone tablets with the Ten Commandments. The phrase *law that brings life and knowledge*, probably not a scriptural reminiscence, recalls a major theme of the book, that study of the law is part of life-giving wisdom: God gave his people 'knowledge', 'endowed them with the life-giving law' and 'revealed to them his decrees' (17: 11–12). ✻

ISRAEL'S PAST – AARON THE HIGH PRIEST

He raised to a like holy office   6
Moses' brother Aaron from the tribe of Levi.

He made a perpetual covenant with him,   7
conferring on him the priesthood of the nation.
He honoured him with splendid ornaments
and clothed him in gorgeous vestments.

He robed him in perfect splendour   8
and armed him with the emblems of power,
the breeches, the mantle, and the tunic.

Round his robe he placed pomegranates   9
and a circle of many golden bells,
to make music as he walked,
ringing aloud throughout the temple
as a reminder to his people.

10 He gave him the sacred vestment adorned by an
        embroiderer
    with gold and violet and purple;
    the oracle of judgement with the tokens of truth;[a]

11 the scarlet thread spun with a craftsman's art;
    the precious stones, engraved like seals,
    and placed by the jeweller in a gold setting,
    with inscriptions to serve as reminders,
    one for each of the tribes of Israel;

12 the gold crown upon his turban,
    engraved like a seal with 'Holy to the Lord'.[b]
    What rich adornments to feast the eyes!
    What a miracle of art! What a proud honour!

13 Before him no such splendour existed,
    and no one outside his family has ever put them on,
    no one except his sons
    and his descendants in perpetuity.

14 Twice every day without fail
    they present his sacrifice of a whole-offering.

15 It was Moses who ordained him
    and anointed him with sacred oil,
    in token of the perpetual covenant made with him
    and with his descendants as long as the heavens endure,
    that he should be the Lord's minister in the priestly office
    and bless his people in his name.

16 He chose him out of all mankind
    to bring offerings to the Lord,

[a] the oracle...truth: *or* the breast-piece of judgement with the Urim
and Thummim (*Exodus 28: 30*).
[b] *Compare Exodus 28: 36; literally* a seal of holiness.

incense and the fragrance of memorial sacrifice,
to make atonement for the people.
He entrusted to him his commandments,   17
with authority to pronounce legal decisions,
to teach Jacob his decrees
and enlighten Israel about his law.

Upstarts grew jealous of him   18
and conspired against him in the desert,
Dathan and Abiram with their supporters
and Korah's band in their violent anger.
The Lord saw and refused his sanction;   19
he destroyed them in the heat of his wrath,
and worked a miracle against them
by consuming them in a blazing fire.
But he added fresh honours to Aaron   20
and gave him a special privilege,
allotting to the priests the choicest firstfruits,
to ensure that they above all should have bread in plenty.
For they eat the sacrifices of the Lord,   21
which he gave to Aaron and his descendants.
But he was to have no inheritance in the land of his people,   22
no portion allotted to him among them;
for the Lord himself is his portion, his inheritance.

* This long treatment of Aaron and the high priest's vestments and duties, together with the description of Simon in
50: 1–21, is said to show Ben Sira's love of the traditions of
the Jerusalem temple. He even implies in 24: 8–11 that wisdom
ministered in Jerusalem. However, this feeling appears nostal-
gic, and is firmly subordinated to social and moral demands,
as in 7: 29–31 where the reason given for paying the priests'

dues is not to fulfil the traditional ritual but rather not to
leave God's ministers without support. Similarly sacrifice,
prayer and fasting for its own sake are of no value unless
accompanied by sincere intentions (34: 18–26). Most of this
section is composed of phrases quoted from the Pentateuch;
Ben Sira is describing the traditional high priesthood in
biblical terms rather than analysing the system of his own day.
However, although various priestly dues and duties are allotted in the Pentateuch to Aaron by rule 'for all time' (Exod.
29: 9), a covenant specifically with the priestly line of Aaron
is made only with Phinehas (Num. 25: 12–13) and never with
Aaron as here in verses 7 and 15; undoubtedly the Jews
regarded this as a covenant with Aaron, however, as the
succession started with him. Before the exile there had been
rivalry between the priestly lines of Aaron and Zadok, who
had ousted the Aaronites from the high priesthood in
David's time. By Ben Sira's time the rivalry had died and all
priests, Zadokites included, seem to have been called sons of
Aaron.

8–12. The Mishnah (*Yoma* 7: 5) lists eight vestments worn
by the high priest: four were normal priestly garments:
tunic, trousers, turban and girdle; four were worn only by
the high priest: breastplate, apron, the upper garment and the
frontlet. These are described in detail in Exod. 28–9. Ben Sira
echoes many phrases from the Exodus passage, but his description is not clear, and the girdle has been left out. Verse 8
lists *breeches* (trousers), *mantle* (probably the 'upper garment'
of the Mishnah) and *tunic*. The *pomegranates* and *bells* of verse 9
were attached to the 'mantle of the ephod' (Exod. 28: 31) or
'apron' (Mishnah), the *bells* reminding the congregation of
the high priest's presence in the Holy of Holies in the temple
where he could not be seen. The N.E.B. translation, *oracle of
judgement with the tokens of truth*, refers to the ephod itself with
the sacred lot (the Urim and Thummim discussed in the note
on 33: 3), in which case *the sacred vestment* is the breastplate
in which the ephod was fixed. But Ben Sira was probably

quoting Exod. 28: 30 (see footnote), 'the breast-piece of judgement with the Urim and the Thummim', mistaking the breast-piece for the ephod. *the scarlet thread* and *precious stones* (verse 11) refer to the ephod, and *the gold crown* was the 'frontlet' on the *turban* (verse 12), the inscription quoted from Exod. 28: 36. Modern scholars are unclear about the breast-plate and the ephod; Ben Sira's confusion is therefore not surprising.

14. According to Lev. 6: 19–23 the daily meal-offering was offered (or, later, paid for) by the high priest, half being offered in the morning, half in the evening.

15. *bless his people in his name:* the special priestly blessing is written out in Num. 6: 23–7.

16. The *memorial sacrifice* refers to the Hebrew *'azkārāh* – the part of certain sacrifices which was completely burnt on the altar; what it was a *memorial* of is uncertain. The *atonement* refers to the high priest's duties on the annual Day of Atonement (Lev. 16).

17. Although priests had been responsible for *legal decisions* and teaching in earlier Israel, it is thought that by Ben Sira's time these functions were performed by the growing number of lay 'scribes'. This passage concerns the past, and is not evidence that the ancient practice continued still; indeed Ben Sira's description of the ideal wise man in 39: 1–11 shows that *legal decisions* and teaching formed a large part of his life. *Jacob* is a synonym of *Israel*; according to Gen. 35: 10 Jacob was renamed 'Israel'.

18–19. The rebellion of *Korah*, and *Dathan and Abiram* is narrated in Num. 16: 1–30. God *refused his sanction* by burning up the people who offered incense to appease his wrath (Num. 16: 35).

20. The *fresh honours* of the *firstfruits* are described in Num. 18: 8–19.

21. Part of *the sacrifices* were eaten by the priests (whence Ben Sira's concern for their livelihood in 7: 29–31), part burnt on the altar. Doubtless sometimes money was given

instead of sacrificial material, part of which would be spent on the altar offering.

22 follows Num. 18: 20 closely. ✻

ISRAEL'S PAST – PHINEHAS AND THE TWO COVENANTS

23 Phinehas son of Eleazar ranks third in renown
for being zealous in his reverence for the Lord,
and for standing firm with noble courage,
when the people were in revolt;
by so doing he made atonement for Israel.

24 Therefore a covenant was established with him,
assuring him command of the sanctuary and of the nation,
conferring on him and his descendants
the high-priesthood for ever.

25 Just as a covenant was made with David son of Jesse of
the tribe of Judah, ·
that the royal succession should always pass from father
to son,
so the succession was to pass from Aaron to his descendants.

26 May the Lord grant you a wise mind
to judge his people with justice,
so that their prosperity may never vanish
and their glory may be handed on to future generations!

✻ According to Num. 25: 13 the priestly covenant was made with Phinehas, Aaron's grandson, for his zealousness and 'noble courage' in murdering an Israelite and a Midianite woman with one hurl of his spear, 'pinning them together' (Num. 25: 6–8). He thus stopped the plague which God had sent as punishment for the introduction of non-Israelite women. Both Ben Sira and the militant Mattathias (1 Macc. 2: 54) omit this when praising Phinehas, not considering it a good reason for being granted hereditary rights of priesthood.

25 cites the Davidic *covenant* first mentioned in Nathan's prophecy to David in 2 Sam. 7: 16: 'Your family shall be established and your kingdom shall stand for all time...and your throne shall be established for ever.' The Davidic dynasty ruled in Jerusalem from about 1000 to 586 B.C. – the second capture of Jerusalem by the Babylonians. After that, expectation of a future king of David's line (later called the 'Messiah') rose and fell. In the first century B.C. some Jews expected two 'Messiahs', one royal and of David's line, one priestly and of Aaron's line, both fulfilling their respective everlasting covenants. Ben Sira's careful balancing of the two covenants in this verse, together with Mattathias' mention of Phinehas' 'everlasting priesthood' and David's 'everlasting kingdom' (1 Macc. 2: 54, 57), shows how such expectation arose.

26. *judge his people with justice:* in Ben Sira's day the high priest had become a political figure. This verse may have been addressed to the high priest of his day. ✳

ISRAEL'S PAST – JOSHUA THE MIRACULOUS WARRIOR

Joshua son of Nun was a mighty warrior, **46**
who succeeded Moses in the prophetic office.
He lived up to his name
as a great liberator of the Lord's chosen people,
able to take reprisals on the enemies who attacked them,
and to put Israel in possession of their territory.
How glorious he was when he raised his hand 2
and brandished his sword against cities!
Never before had a man made such a stand, 3
for he was fighting the Lord's battles.

4 Was it not through him that the sun stood still
and made one day as long as two?
5 He called on the Most High, the Mighty One,
when the enemy was pressing him on every side,
and the great Lord answered his prayer
6 with a violent storm of hail.
He overwhelmed that nation in battle
and crushed his assailants as they fled down the pass,
to make the nations recognize his strength in arms
and teach them that he fought under the very eyes of the
Lord,
for he followed the lead of the Mighty One.

7 In the time of Moses he had proved his loyalty,
he and Caleb son of Jephunneh:
they stood their ground against the whole assembly,
restrained the people from sin,
and silenced their wicked grumbling.
8 Out of six hundred thousand warriors
these two alone escaped with their lives
to enter the land and take possession of it,
the land flowing with milk and honey.
9 The Lord gave Caleb strength,
which still remained with him in his old age,
so that he was able to invade the hill-country
and win possession of it for his descendants.
10 So all Israel could see
how good it is to be a loyal follower of the Lord.

✶ Although Ben Sira has just described royal and priestly
successions, he now mentions Joshua as succeeding Moses

'in the prophetic office'. Early prophets were revered for their miraculous deeds rather than for their words, and so verses 1–6 select the more miraculous successes in Joshua's conquest of Palestine, the promised land. Verses 7–10 then revert to the journey through the Sinai desert and show how Joshua and Caleb were preserved to complete Moses' work and conquer Palestine.

1. *He lived up to his name as a great liberator* contains a pun on Joshua's name which means in Hebrew 'Yahweh (God) saves'.

2. When Joshua took the city of Ai, he 'pointed with his dagger towards Ai' as a signal for the ambush party (Josh. 8: 18) and 'did not draw back his hand until he had put to death all who lived in Ai' (Josh. 8: 26). What started as a signal finished as a miraculous sign.

4–6. Joshua's campaign against the Midianites was assisted by 'great hailstones' (Josh. 10: 11) and by the halting, at Joshua's request, of both *sun* and moon (Josh. 10: 13). Ben Sira connects Joshua's prayer wrongly with the hailstorm, whereas it was the halting of the sun that led the author of Joshua to write: 'Never before or since has there been such a day...on which the LORD listened to the voice of a man' (Josh. 10: 14).

7. When the disgruntled Hebrews wished to return to Egypt from the Sinai desert, Joshua and Caleb tried to stem the revolt by describing the fertility of southern Palestine which they had explored. They tried to restrain *the people from sin*, but the people 'threatened to stone them', and it was Moses' prayer and God's forgiveness that averted revolt (Num. 14: 6–25).

8. Moses claimed to have *six hundred thousand* men with him in the desert (Num. 11: 21), of whom only Joshua and Caleb were thought to have survived to enter Palestine (Num. 14: 38; 26: 65). Ben Sira's linking of these statements, together with his reference to the same number in 16: 10, suggests he may have taken his information from another, non-biblical account.

9. *The Lord gave Caleb strength...in his old age:* Josh. 14: 6–15 relates how Caleb was given the Hebron district to settle at the age of eighty-five. ✻

ISRAEL'S PAST – THE JUDGES

11 Then there are the judges, name after famous name,
all of them men who rejected idolatry
and never rebelled against the Lord:
blessings be on their memory!
12 May their bones send forth new life from the ground
    where they lie!
May the fame of the honoured dead be matched by their
    sons!

✻ Before extended treatment of Samuel (verses 13–20), Ben Sira praises the judges, the leaders of the loosely federated Hebrew tribes in Palestine before the monarchy. General praise of this heroic stage of Israel's history is appropriate because he has to exclude the two leaders most prominent in the book of Judges: Gideon and his family (Judg. 6–9), because Gideon made an idol which 'became a trap' for him 'and his household' (Judg. 8: 27), and Samson (Judg. 13–16), whom he probably considered to have 'rebelled against the Lord'.

12. *May their bones send forth new life:* Ben Sira did not believe in the resurrection of the body like later Pharisees, and hardly refers to later semitic practices of watering graves. In 49: 10 he says: 'May the bones of the twelve prophets also send forth new life from the ground where they lie!' The use of identical words in both passages probably shows his desire that Jews of his time should show the same heroic qualities and be worthy of their ancestors. ✻

ISRAEL'S PAST – SAMUEL THE KINGMAKER

Samuel was beloved by his Lord; 13
as prophet of the Lord he established the monarchy
and anointed rulers over his people.
As long as he dispensed justice according to the law of the 14
  Lord,
the Lord kept watch over Jacob.
Because of his fidelity he proved to be an accurate prophet; 15
the truth of his vision was shown by his utterances.
He called on the Mighty Lord, 16
when enemies were pressing him on every side,
and offered a sucking-lamb in sacrifice;
then the Lord thundered from heaven, 17
making his voice heard in a mighty crash,
and routed the leaders of the enemy,[a] 18
all the rulers of the Philistines.
Before the time came for his eternal sleep, 19
Samuel called the Lord and his anointed to witness:
'I never took any man's property,
not so much as a pair of shoes';
and no man accused him.
Even after he had gone to his rest he prophesied 20
and foretold to the king his death,
lifting up his voice in prophecy from the ground
to wipe out the people's guilt.

✳ With Samuel, another prophet, the miraculous is again
prominent (verses 15–20) as with Joshua (46: 1–6), although
Ben Sira also stresses his kingmaking and judicial activity:
Samuel 'established the monarchy' by anointing Saul king

[a] the enemy: *so Heb.; Gk.* Tyre.

(verse 13, 1 Sam. 10: 1), and acted as judge of the confederation of tribes (verse 14), going 'on circuit' to different centres (1 Sam. 7: 15).

15. Saul was recommended to consult Samuel about his father's lost asses as a man of 'great reputation, because everything he says comes true' (1 Sam. 9: 6).

16–18. Defeat by the Philistines near Mizpah was averted by Samuel's *sacrifice* of *a sucking-lamb* (1 Sam. 7: 9–10). 'Tyre' (N.E.B. footnote): the Greek translator mistook the Hebrew *tsār* ('enemy') for *tsōr* ('Tyre').

19. '*I never took . . . so much as a pair of shoes*': according to one tradition Samuel regarded the people's request for a king as rebellion against the Lord and a slight on himself: in 1 Sam. 12: 1–3 he asks whom he has 'wronged' and from whom he has 'taken a bribe'. Ben Sira echoes the Greek translation (Septuagint) of that passage (which may well represent the original Hebrew): 'From whose hand have I taken . . . shoes?' (1 Sam. 12: 3). This may merely indicate a bribe, but more probably refers to the symbolic use of shoes in certain legal transactions in Israel and the Near East. 'when property was redeemed or exchanged, it was the custom for a man to pull off his sandal and give it to the other party. This was the form of attestation in Israel' (Ruth 4: 7) in early times. To 'sell . . . the destitute for a pair of shoes' (Amos 2: 6) may have been a legal trick, and Samuel may be claiming that he has not twisted the law to trick anyone and make unfair profit.

20. *Even after he had gone to his rest*: after Samuel's death Saul, hard pressed by the Philistines, consulted Samuel's ghost through a medium for advice (1 Sam. 28: 3–20). Samuel foretold Saul's death, which seems to be interpreted by Ben Sira as wiping out *the people's guilt* – probably meaning the demand for a king for which Samuel had earlier threatened punishment from God (1 Sam. 12: 17). Ben Sira's view of Saul is most unfavourable – far from praising him, he never even mentions him by name, continuing the tendency to underrate Saul at David's expense already seen in 1 Chron. 10–29

where the narratives about Saul are shortened, and the narratives about David altered to omit unpleasant things and highlight the pleasant. ✷

ISRAEL'S PAST – DAVID, GOD'S CHOSEN KING

After him Nathan came forward   **47**
to be prophet in the reign of David.
As the fat is separated from the sacrifice,   2
so David was chosen out of all Israel.
He played with lions as though they were kids,   3
with bears as though they were lambs.
In his youth did he not kill a giant   4
and restore the honour of his people,
when he whirled his sling with its stone
and brought down boastful Goliath?
For he called on the Lord Most High,   5
who gave strength to his right arm
to strike down that mighty warrior
and win victory for his people.
So they hailed him as conqueror of tens of thousands,   6
they sang his praises for the blessings bestowed by the Lord,
when he was offered the royal diadem.
For he subdued their enemies on every side   7
and crushed the resistance of the Philistines,
whose power remains broken to this day.
In all he did he gave thanks,   8
ascribing glory to the Holy One, the Most High.
With his whole heart he sang hymns of praise,
to show his love for his Maker.
He appointed musicians to stand before the altar   9
and sing sweet music to the harp.

10 So he gave splendour to the festivals
and fixed for all time the round of sacred seasons,
when men praise the holy name of the Lord
and the sanctuary resounds from morning to night.

11 The Lord pardoned his sins
and endowed him with great power for ever:
he gave him a covenant of kingship
and the glorious throne of Israel.

✶ Ben Sira shares the approach of the author of 1 Chronicles
to David (see notes above on 46: 20), but with less lengthy
enthusiasm, selecting and adapting David's heroic fight against
the Philistine giant Goliath from 1 Sam. 17: 1 – 18: 9 and his
organization of religious festivals and music from 1 Chron.
16 and 23. The concept of a 'prophetic succession' starting
with Moses through Joshua and Samuel stops with Nathan
as the Davidic line of kings starts. With the virtual exclusion
of Saul, Nathan links Samuel and David.

2. David was *separated* from *all Israel* as particularly precious
to God as *the fat*, the choice part, was *separated from a sacrifice*
(Lev. 4: 8).

3–7. When David, still an unknown youth, asks Saul to
allow him to fight Goliath he boasts that, as a shepherd's
boy, he has killed *lions* and *bears* (1 Sam. 17: 32–7). Verse 6
quotes the song with which Saul was greeted on his home-
coming after victory:

'Saul made havoc among thousands
but David among tens of thousands' (1 Sam. 18: 7).

But *the royal diadem* was not *offered* to David as a result of this.
Due to Saul's jealousy he acted as a local Philistine governor
for some time before returning to be king of Judah on Saul's
death; only then did he permanently crush *the resistance of
the Philistines* (verse 7).

8–10. Ben Sira follows the tradition of 1 Chronicles in

attributing the organization of temple services and music to David even though the temple was not built until after his death; but whereas 1 Chronicles attributes as much credit for planning the building to David as possible, Ben Sira mentions only Solomon in relation to the building (verse 13). Thus the treatment of David illustrates Ben Sira's uncritical use of biblical material.

11. *he gave him a covenant of kingship:* takes up the Davidic covenant already discussed on 45: 25. ✶

ISRAEL'S PAST – SOLOMON, WISE MAN AND SINNER

He was succeeded by a wise son, Solomon,	12
who, thanks to his father David, lived in spacious days.	
He reigned in an age of peace,	13
because God made all his frontiers quiet,	
and so he was able to build a house in God's honour,	
a sanctuary founded to last for ever.	
How wise you were, Solomon, in your youth!	14
Your mind was like a brimming river;	
your influence spread throughout the world,	15
which you filled with your proverbs and riddles.	
Your fame reached to distant islands,	16
and you were beloved for your peaceful reign.	
Your songs, your proverbs, your parables,	17
and the answers you gave were the admiration of the world.	
In the name of the Lord God,	18
who is known as the God of Israel,	
you amassed gold and silver	
as though they were tin and lead.	

19 But you took women to lie at your side
and gave yourself up to their control.

20 You stained your reputation
and tainted your line.
You brought retribution on your children
and made them grieve over your folly,

21 because it divided the sovereignty
and produced out of Ephraim a rebel kingdom.

22 But the Lord never ceases to be merciful;
he does not destroy what he himself has made;
he will not wipe out the children of his chosen servant
or cut short the line of the man who has loved him.
So he granted a remnant to Jacob
and let one scion of David survive.

✶ As in the Old Testament Solomon has a two-sided character. On the one hand he built the temple in Jerusalem (verse 13
and 1 Kings 6), and was famous for his encouragement of wise
men and collectors of 'proverbs and riddles' and for his clever
judgements (verses 14–17; 1 Kings 3: 16–28; 4: 29–34).
Similarly his amassing of 'gold and silver' (verse 18) is here
approved, although legislation forbade the king to 'acquire
great quantities of silver and gold for himself' with Solomon's
example in mind (Deut. 17: 17). On the other hand the final
judgement on Solomon in 1 Kings 11: 1–3 is hostile because
he had allowed his foreign wives and concubines to introduce
idolatry. Ben Sira also condemns him, mentioning how he
gave himself up to his women's control (verse 19), but idolatry
is not mentioned and, in view of what Ben Sira has said
concerning women's influence on men (25: 13–26; 42: 13),
that 'Woman is the origin of sin' (25: 24), lack of self-discipline with women seems to be Solomon's chief sin! But
Ben Sira may be quoting biblical material without mentioning
the key-word, as when writing of Saul without mentioning

his name. As in 1 Kings 11: 12–13, the Davidic line is spared
because of David's excellence, and Solomon's sin is seen to
cause the division of the kingdom (verse 21), although this
is attributed to Rehoboam's policies in verse 23.

14. *in your youth:* when Solomon 'grew old, his wives
turned his heart to follow other gods, and he did not remain
wholly loyal to the LORD his God as his father David had
been' (1 Kings 11: 4). Riddles and proverbs teemed in his
mind as water in *a brimming river.*

21. The *rebel kingdom* was that of the northern ten tribes,
known as the kingdom of Israel and ruled over first by Jeroboam I, as opposed to the kingdom of Judah, ruled over by
the Davidic line of kings in Jerusalem. *Ephraim* was one of the
major northern tribes, and its name was used often for the
northern kingdom itself; the name is used here probably to
reserve 'Israel' for the Jewish community of Ben Sira's day.

22. The Davidic covenant, discussed on 45:25 and mentioned
in 47: 11, now carries the dynasty over its first test. ✶

ISRAEL'S PAST – THE DIVISION OF THE KINGDOM

So Solomon died like his forefathers   23
and left one of his sons to succeed him,
a man of weak intelligence, the fool of the nation,
Rehoboam, whose policy drove the people to revolt.
Then Jeroboam son of Nebat led Israel into sin
and started Ephraim on its wicked course.
Their sins increased beyond measure,   24
until they were driven into exile from their native land;
for they had explored every kind of wickedness,   25
until retribution came upon them.

✶ Soon after Solomon's death in about 922 B.C. the ten
northern tribes (all except Judah and Benjamin) set up an
independent kingdom ruled by Jeroboam I; according to

1 Kings 12: 1–20 this was due to Rehoboam's oppressive policies. As a deliberate substitute for the Jerusalem temple Jeroboam set up two calves for worship at Bethel and Dan; thus any supporter of the Jerusalem temple like the author of 1 and 2 Kings and of 1 and 2 Chronicles and Ben Sira himself condemned the northern kingdom automatically. 2 Chronicles ignores it virtually completely, but Ben Sira gives further attention to it in 48: 1–15. According to 2 Kings 17: 7–41 the Assyrian conquest and exile of the kingdom of Israel was due to idolatrous worship. ✲

ISRAEL'S PAST – ELIJAH: THE FIERY PROPHET

48 Then Elijah appeared, a prophet like fire,
whose word flamed like a torch.

2 He brought famine upon them,
and his zeal made their numbers small.

3 By the word of the Lord he shut up the sky
and three times called down fire.

4 How glorious you were, Elijah, in your miracles!
Who else can boast such deeds?

5 You raised a corpse from death
and from the grave, by the word of the Most High.

6 You sent kings and famous men
from their sick-beds down to their deaths.

7 You heard a denunciation at Sinai,
a sentence of doom at Horeb.

8 So you anointed kings for vengeance,
and prophets to succeed you.

9 You were taken up to heaven in a fiery whirlwind,
in a chariot drawn by horses of fire.

10 It is written that you are to come at the appointed time
with warnings,

to allay the divine wrath before its final fury,
to reconcile father and son,
and to restore the tribes of Jacob.
Happy are those who saw you   11
and were honoured with your love!*a*

✻ Ben Sira mentions many incidents in Elijah's prophetic career concerned with his struggle against the apostasy of the northern kingdom, and seems to have viewed the healing of the breach between the two kingdoms as Elijah's task, for he refers to the prophecies concerning Elijah in Malachi (verse 10). As with Joshua and Samuel, miraculous acts are noted rather than prophetic speeches.

2. Persecuted by Ahab for opposing apostasy, Elijah went to God's mountain, called Horeb in Kings, and heard God's 'sentence of doom' (verse 7) upon the kingdom. As a result of Elijah's pleading, seven thousand were spared from the punishment of death (1 Kings 19: 18). But Ben Sira's words read as if it was *his zeal* rather than God's will that *made their numbers small*.

3. In 1 Kings 17: 1 it is told how Elijah pronounced a drought from God on Israel as punishment for apostasy. He *called down fire* upon the altar on Mount Carmel (1 Kings 18: 38) and twice destroyed groups of messengers from Ahaziah by fire (2 Kings 1: 10–12).

5. The *corpse* raised *from death* was the son of a widow at Zarephath with whom Elijah had stayed (1 Kings 17: 17–24).

6–8. Elijah prophesied Ahab's death (1 Kings 21: 19–22) as well as that of Ahaziah (2 Kings 1: 4). *prophets to succeed you:* he appointed Elisha as his successor (1 Kings 19: 19–21). *you anointed kings for vengeance:* although Elijah was instructed to anoint Jehu and Hazael as kings in the knowledge that they would kill the reigning kings of Israel and Aram respectively

[a] honoured. . .love: *probable meaning; Gk. adds* for we also shall certainly live.

(1 Kings 19: 15–18), it was Elisha who was finally responsible for these events (2 Kings 8: 7–15; 9: 1–13). *at Sinai...at Horeb:* the sacred mountain is called variously Sinai and Horeb in the Old Testament. Originally these names referred to separate mountains of different and uncertain location, but later, as here, the two names were used for the same place with no regard to its geographical position.

9 refers to the story of Elijah's departure from the earth in 2 Kings 2: 1–18.

10. At the end of the last book of the Old Testament prophets *it is written* 'I will send you the prophet Elijah before the great and terrible day of the LORD comes. He will reconcile fathers to sons and sons to fathers' (Mal. 4: 5–6). In the Mishnah this verse from Malachi was interpreted as restoring *the tribes of Jacob*, i.e. gathering together refugees and exiles: 'Elijah will not come to declare unclean or clean, to remove far or to bring nigh, but to remove afar those (families) that were brought nigh by violence and to bring nigh those (families) that were removed afar by violence' (*Eduyoth* 8: 7). Thus Ben Sira adds to his selected biblical references some information which reappears in later rabbinical exegesis. Some later scholars said that Elijah would return as the forerunner of the Messiah, but Ben Sira shows no knowledge of this. What Ben Sira really thought *the divine wrath* in *its final fury* was, as he looks to the future so little, we do not know; in this context the emphasis is probably on reconciliation between northern and southern kingdoms, and the reference to *the divine wrath* comes with the quotation from Malachi.

11. The text of this verse is uncertain; the N.E.B. has omitted the phrase 'for we also shall certainly live', occurring only in the Greek, as a later reference to resurrection, agreeing with later exegesis of the Malachi passage but contradicting Ben Sira's frequently expressed disbelief in any future life. ✡

ISRAEL'S PAST – ELISHA: ELIJAH'S SUCCESSOR

When Elijah had vanished in a whirlwind,   12
Elisha was filled with his spirit.
Throughout his life no ruler made him tremble;
no one could make him subservient.
Nothing was too difficult for him;   13
even in the grave his body kept its prophetic power.
In life he worked miracles,   14
and in death his deeds were marvellous.

✻ This short section seems to sum up the miraculous activity
that Ben Sira thought typical of the prophets, at least before
Isaiah; indeed, the later prophets whose words are recorded –
usually more revered today than the earlier prophets – are
little mentioned.

12 refers to Elijah's departure already mentioned in verse 9.

13. In 2 Kings 13: 21 it is told how some men were once
'burying a dead man' when they saw some Moabite raiders.
'They threw the body into the grave of Elisha and made off;
when the body touched the prophet's bones, the man came to
life and rose to his feet.' ✻

ISRAEL'S PAST – PUNISHMENT OF THE NORTHERN
KINGDOM

In spite of all this the people did not repent   15
or renounce their sins,
until they were carried off as plunder from their land
and scattered over the whole earth.
Only a tiny nation was left,
with a ruler from the house of David;
and of these some did what was pleasing to the Lord,   16
but others heaped sin upon sin.

✳ The miracles of Elijah and Elisha should have brought the northern kingdom to repentance, Ben Sira implies; he suggests that the destruction, plunder and exile of the northern kingdom in 721 B.C. was due to the rejection of prophets who lived about 860–840 B.C., thus telescoping over a hundred years of history and ignoring the prophets Amos and Hosea who lived about 760–740 B.C.; this omission is probably because they are not mentioned in the books of Kings which Ben Sira used as a textbook. The ten tribes of the northern kingdom were reputedly *scattered* all over the Near East (whence the 'lost ten tribes'), but it is likely that the Assyrians deported only a section of the population. The *tiny nation* of verse 15 is Judah, continuing with its Davidic ruler; only two rulers of Judah *did what was pleasing to the Lord* (a favourite phrase in 1 and 2 Kings) – Hezekiah and Josiah, the only remaining kings Ben Sira mentions. ✳

ISRAEL'S PAST – HEZEKIAH: THE OBEDIENT

17 Hezekiah fortified his city,
bringing water within its walls;
he drilled through the rock with tools of iron
and made cisterns for the water.

18 In his reign Sennacherib invaded the country.
He sent Rab-shakeh from Lachish,[a]
who made threats against Zion
and grew arrogant in his boasting.

19 Then they were unnerved in heart and hand;
they suffered the anguish of a woman in labour.

20 So they called on the merciful Lord,
spreading out their hands in supplication to him.
The Holy One quickly answered their prayer from heaven
by sending Isaiah to the rescue;

[a] from Lachish: *other witnesses read* and went away.

he struck down the Assyrian camp,   21
and his angel wiped them out.

For Hezekiah did what was pleasing to the Lord,   22
and kept firmly to the ways of his ancestor David,
as he was instructed by Isaiah,
the great prophet whose vision could be trusted.

In his time the sun went back,   23
and he added many years to the king's life.

With inspired power he saw the future   24
and comforted the mourners in Zion.

He revealed things to come before they happened,   25
the secrets of the future to the end of time.

* The first of the remaining two 'good' kings of Judah,
Hezekiah (715–687 B.C.) is characterized by his obedience to
God as mediated by Isaiah, the first of the great prophets
whom Ben Sira mentions. Note that he stresses Isaiah's
miraculous acts with the Assyrian army and the sundial
rather than the contents of his prophecy (verses 21, 23–5).

17. Hezekiah *drilled* a tunnel *through the rock* to give Jerusalem a water-supply in time of siege. The tunnel was discovered
in 1880 and contained an inscription (the Siloam inscription)
carved by the workmen describing how they had done it.
(A translation may be found in *Documents from Old Testament
Times*; see a Note on Further Reading.) The Old Testament
mentions tunnel and pool only briefly in 2 Kings 20: 20 and
2 Chron. 32: 30.

18–21 describe the Assyrian siege of Jerusalem in 701 or
688 B.C., narrated in 2 Kings 18: 17 - 19: 37, where *Rab-
shakeh* is translated as an Assyrian administrative title, 'chief
officer'. Historians are uncertain of the date of the siege and
the reasons for Assyrian withdrawal, but Ben Sira accepts
the account in 2 Kings without question, and attributes it to
God's power through the prophet Isaiah.

23. In response to Hezekiah's request for a sign to prove Isaiah's prophecy of his cure reliable, God caused the shadow cast by the sun on the 'stairway of Ahaz' (probably a kind of sundial) to go back three steps (2 Kings 20: 8–11). Ben Sira, inaccurately, says *the sun went back* rather than the shadow.

24–5 for the first time refer to the contents of a prophetic book. Ben Sira assumed that Isaiah of Jerusalem wrote the whole book, and the comfort given to *mourners* probably refers to such passages as Isa. 40: 1: 'Comfort, comfort my people'. *the secrets of the future* may refer to 'messianic' passages like Isa. 9: 2–7, or passages describing the coming judgement like Isa. 24–7. ✷

ISRAEL'S PAST – JOSIAH, THE REFORMER

49 The memory of Josiah is fragrant as incense
blended by the skill of the perfumer,
sweet as honey to every palate
or as music at a banquet.
2 He did what was right: he reformed the nation
and rooted out their loathsome and lawless practices.
3 He was whole-heartedly loyal to the Lord
and in lawless times made godliness prevail.

✷ Josiah (640–609 B.C.), third of the three 'good' kings of Judah according to 49: 4, was famous for his renovation of the temple and religious reformation, usually dated 621 B.C., following the idolatrous practices of Manasseh and Amon, his predecessors (2 Kings 22: 3 – 23: 27).

1. *incense* was said in Exod. 30: 35 to be 'made by the perfumer's craft...a holy thing'. Ben Sira quotes the Exodus passage to emphasize Josiah's piety: the fragrance of his *memory* reminded one of God just as the *incense* in the temple. ✷

ISRAEL'S PAST – THE DESTRUCTION OF JERUSALEM

Except David, Hezekiah, and Josiah,　　　　　　　4
all were guilty of wrongdoing,
for they deserted the law of the Most High;
and so the royal line of Judah came to an end.
They surrendered their power to others　　　　　5
and their glory to a foreign nation,
who set fire to the chosen city, the city of the sanctuary, 6
and left its streets deserted, as Jeremiah prophesied;
for they had ill-treated him,　　　　　　　　　7
a prophet consecrated even before his birth
to uproot, to destroy, and to demolish,
but also to build and to plant.

✻ Ben Sira makes the evil kings of Judah responsible for the destruction of Jerusalem in 586 B.C. For him only two kings followed David's example in obedience to God: Hezekiah and Josiah (verse 4); Asa and Jehoshaphat are ignored, although approved by 2 Kings and 2 Chronicles.

4–5. *the royal line of Judah* ended, practically speaking, with Zedekiah's death in 586 B.C., although Jehoiachin, his predecessor, seems to have been recognized as a king-in-exile in Babylon (the *foreign nation* mentioned here).

6–7. The destruction of Jerusalem, narrated in 2 Kings 25: 9–10, was so frequently foretold by the prophet Jeremiah (as in Jer. 36: 30–1) that the citizens of Jerusalem thought he worked for the enemy, and *ill-treated him*. Verse 7 quotes the account of Jeremiah's call as *a prophet* (Jer. 1: 5, 10). ✻

ISRAEL'S PAST – EZEKIEL AND THE OTHER PROPHETS

8 Ezekiel had a vision of the Glory,
  which was revealed enthroned on the chariot of the
          cherubim.
9 The Lord remembered his enemies and sent a storm,
  but he did good to those who kept to the straight path.
10 May the bones of the twelve prophets also
  send forth new life from the ground where they lie!
  For they put new heart into Jacob,
  and rescued the people by their confident hope.

✲ Ben Sira now deals with the remaining prophetical books:
Ezekiel and the twelve minor prophets. Just as the original
words of Isaiah, Jeremiah and Ezekiel had formed the basis for
larger compilations, so the shorter prophetical books, from
Hosea to Malachi, had been collected into a fourth prophetic
compilation, 'the twelve prophets'. These prophets speak
judgement more frequently than comfort and 'confident
hope', but the author probably means passages like Joel 3:
17–21 and Zech. 9: 9–16 where the Jews are encouraged to
look for political and religious renewal.

8. Later Jews disliked referring directly to God, and
substituted various words such as 'the Presence' or (as here)
the Glory. The prophet Ezekiel saw a strange 'vision of God'
(Ezek. 1: 1) consisting of a fantastic, fiery chariot carried by
'four living creatures in human form' (Ezek. 1: 5) here interpreted as *cherubim*, which had animal bodies, human heads and
wings. The interpretation of Ezekiel's vision of the chariot
led to much obscure speculation in later Judaism.

9. The reference and text are uncertain: the prophecies
against Gog and Magog (Ezek. 38–9) may be intended. ✲

ISRAEL'S PAST – JERUSALEM REBUILT

How can we tell the greatness of Zerubbabel,   11
who was like a signet-ring on the Lord's right hand?
With him was Joshua son of Jehozadak;   12
in their days they built the house,
raising a holy temple to the Lord,
destined for eternal glory.
Great is the memory of Nehemiah,   13
who raised our fallen walls,
constructed gates and bars,
and rebuilt our ruined homes.

* These verses praise those who restored Jerusalem after the Babylonian exile to its position in Ben Sira's time: the temple was rebuilt by Zerubbabel and Joshua in 520–515 B.C. (Ezra 3: 2–13; Haggai; Zech. 1–8), and the walls by Nehemiah in 445–437 B.C. (Neh. 2: 11 – 4: 23). We need not be surprised at the omission of Ezra from Ben Sira's list of heroes: the only post-exilic persons mentioned, apart from the high priest Simon of his own time, are those involved in restoring the buildings of Jerusalem.

11. The Lord promises to take Zerubbabel and 'wear you as a signet-ring; for you it is that I have chosen' (Hag. 2: 23) – he was probably of Davidic descent and expected to lead a movement for political independence from Persian rule.

12. Joshua was high priest in Zerubbabel's time. He and Zerubbabel are *destined for eternal glory* through fame for rebuilding the *temple*.

13. Nehemiah was appointed governor of the province of Judah in 445 B.C., and, in addition to rebuilding the city *walls*, revived many Jewish customs and increased the population of the city. *

ISRAEL'S PAST – SOME IMPORTANT OMISSIONS

14 No one on earth has been created to equal Enoch,
for he was taken up from the earth.

15 No man has been born to be Joseph's peer,
the ruler of his brothers and the strength of his people;
and the Lord kept watch over his body.

16 Shem and Seth were given distinction among men,
but Adam holds pre-eminence over all creation.

* These verses were probably added to do justice to certain early heroes whose reputations grew in later teaching outside the Bible: none but Enoch has been mentioned before. Although Enoch was favourably treated (44: 16), he is here given the loftier position he occupied in later Judaism as described in the notes on 44: 16. The Joseph legends add little to a recital of God's acts in Israel's history, but the imagination of later teachers was caught by the care taken over the transfer of his bones from Egypt to Palestine by Moses (Gen. 50: 24–6; Exod. 13: 19). The Mishnah states: 'Whom have we greater than Joseph, for none other than Moses occupied himself with him. Moses was reckoned worthy to take the bones of Joseph (to Canaan)' (*Sotah* 1: 9).

15. *the Lord kept watch over his body:* the Greek text, literally translated, runs: 'and they cared for his bones', copying words used in Gen. 50: 25. Adam, the first man, was later honoured as an Israelite hero and acquires much importance in apocryphal legend and theological discussion. Shem, one of Noah's sons, gained importance later as Israel's ancestor after the flood, and Seth, Adam's third son, featured in later messianic expectation. *

FULFILLING ISRAEL'S PAST – SIMON, THE HIGH PRIEST

It was the high priest Simon son of Onias   **50**
in whose lifetime the house was repaired,
in whose days the temple was fortified.
He laid the foundation for the high double wall,   2
the high retaining wall of the temple precinct.
In his day they dug[a] the reservoir,   3
a cistern broad as the sea.
He applied his mind to protecting his people from ruin 4
and strengthened the city against siege.
How glorious he was, surrounded by the people,   5
when he came from behind the temple curtain!
He was like the morning star appearing through the clouds 6
or the moon at the full;
like the sun shining on the temple of the Most High   7
or the light of the rainbow on the gleaming clouds;
like a rose in spring   8
or lilies by a fountain of water;
like a green shoot upon Lebanon on a summer's day
or burning incense in the censer;   9
like a cup of beaten gold,
decorated with every kind of precious stone;
like an olive-tree laden with fruit   10
or a cypress with its top in the clouds.
When he put on his gorgeous vestments,   11
robed himself in perfect splendour,
and went up to the holy altar,
he added lustre to the court of the sanctuary.

[a] they dug: *so Heb.; Gk. obscure.*

12 When the priests were handing him the portions of the
    sacrifice,
   as he stood by the altar hearth
   with his brothers round him like a garland,
   he was like a young cedar of Lebanon
   in the midst of a circle of palms.

13 All the sons of Aaron in their magnificence
   stood with the Lord's offering in their hands
   before the whole congregation of Israel.

14 To complete the ceremonies at the altar
   and adorn the offering of the Most High, the Almighty,

15 he held out his hand for the libation cup
   and poured out the blood of the grape,
   poured its fragrance at the foot of the altar
   to the Most High, the King of all.

16 Then the sons of Aaron shouted
   and blew their trumpets of beaten silver;
   they sounded a mighty fanfare
   as a reminder before the Lord.

17 Instantly the people as one man fell on their faces
   to worship the Lord their God, the Almighty, the Most
    High.

18 Then the choir broke into praise,
   in the full sweet strains of resounding song,

19 while the people of the Most High
   were making their petitions to the merciful Lord,
   until the liturgy of the Lord was finished
   and the ritual complete.

20 Then Simon came down and raised his hands
   over the whole congregation of Israel,
   to pronounce the Lord's blessing,

proud to take his name on his lips;
and a second time they bowed in worship   21
to receive the blessing from the Most High.

✻ As climax of the list of Israel's heroes comes Simon, son
of Onias II, high priest at the beginning of the second century
B.C., clearly much admired by Ben Sira. Verses 1–4 describe
his building operations on the temple and defences of Jerusalem. That Simon, rather than the local governor, should have
carried these out, shows that the high priest at this time had
some political responsibility under the Syrian king. Verses
5–21 then describe some high-priestly duties in the temple
ritual – a subject dealt with at length by Ben Sira as shown by
his treatment of Aaron in 45: 6–22. He describes first the
high priest's duties on the annual Day of Atonement (verses
5–10), then the daily morning and evening offerings (verses
11–16), and seems to return to the Day of Atonement again
in verses 20–1. This is the only passage in which he seems
to describe contemporary practice in the temple rather than
to depend on biblical sources.

1–4. Similar restorations to buildings are mentioned in a
letter written by Antiochus III to the governor of the Palestine area after he had won Palestine from Egypt at the battle
of Paneas in 199 B.C. The letter, quoted by the historian
Josephus (*Antiquities* XII. 3. 3), is probably genuine, as Ben
Sira's account confirms the building details, and describes
various financial provisions for restoring the temple and other
buildings in Jerusalem. The date of this work lay between
199 B.C. and Simon's death about 195 B.C. No further details
are known.

5 describes the high priest on the Day of Atonement (*Yōm
Kippūr* in Hebrew). On that day, after a bath of purification,
he put on specially gorgeous vestments for the ritual which
involved entering the Holy of Holies, the innermost room of
the temple representing God's presence, entered only by the
high priest and only on that day. The bath and change of

clothes are described in Lev. 16: 23–5 and in the Mishnah (*Yoma* 3: 6–7). As the Holy of Holies was separated from the inner court of the temple by a curtain, the verse may refer to his return from the sacred room to the inner court.

6–10. A series of similes from the beauties of nature, similar to those in 24: 13–17, emphasizes the high priest's glory.

11–13. The morning and evening sacrifices offered by the high priest have already been mentioned in 45: 14 where Aaron's descendants offer them 'Twice every day without fail'. The regulations for this offering, known as the *tāmīd* ('perpetual offering'), are in Exod. 29: 38–42; but Ben Sira describes current post-biblical practice as detailed in the Mishnah (*Tamid* 7: 2–3), where the ordinary priests stand round the high priest at the altar handing him the different parts of the animal to be sacrificed together with the necessary instruments, rather like students and nurses round a surgeon at the operating table, slender *palms* round a strong Lebanon *cedar*.

14–15 describe libations of wine which the Mishnaic tractate *Tamid* (7: 3) includes as part of the daily rite together with the blasts on the trumpets. Ben Sira seems to describe contemporary temple practice which was later codified in the Mishnah, thus showing awareness of the oral tradition which the Pharisees regarded as authoritative but which the Sadducees rejected. Elsewhere he depends on biblical passages for descriptions of ritual practice.

16. The priests blew the *trumpets* 'On your festal days and at your appointed seasons and on the first day of every month' over certain offerings in the day to be 'a reminder' (Num. 10: 10).

20–1. *his name:* the personal name of God was always written YHWH in the consonantal text of the Old Testament. The vowels used were those of *'adōnay* ('my lord'), which the Jews substituted for the divine name in speech as God's name was considered too holy to be pronounced. 'Yahweh' is a modern attempt to reconstruct it. Only the high priest on the

Day of Atonement was allowed to utter the sacred name in his declaration of God's forgiveness as he recited Lev. 16: 30: 'on this day expiation shall be made...' (the ritual is described in Mishnah *Yoma* 3 : 8). According to the Mishnah (*Yoma* 6 : 2) 'when the priests and the people...heard the Expressed Name come forth from the mouth of the high priest, they used to kneel and bow themselves and fall on their faces'. *the Lord's blessing* is thus to be interpreted as the high priest's declaration of forgiveness in the words of Lev. 16: 30 rather than the normal priestly blessing. ✶

A PRAYER FOR ISRAEL'S PEACE

Come then, praise the God of the universe,   22
who everywhere works great wonders,
who from our birth ennobles our life[a]
and deals with us in mercy.
May he grant us a joyful heart,   23
and in our time send Israel lasting peace.
May he confirm his mercy towards us,   24
and in his own good time grant us deliverance.

✶ The Hebrew text of this section forms a prayer specifically for Simon and his successors in the Aaronic high priesthood. Two additional lines existed originally at the beginning of verse 24: 'may his (God's) mercy be confirmed to Simon, and may he establish with him Phinehas' covenant', referring to the priestly covenant discussed in the note on 45: 25. The Greek translator omitted these lines, as the direct Aaronic line had been broken by political intrigue and bribery by the time of his translation, and turned the verses into a general prayer for the peace and prosperity of Israel as a whole, following the recital of God's previous acts for them. ✶

[a] ennobles our life: *or* brings us up.

THREE NATIONS TO BE DETESTED

25 Two nations I detest,
and a third is no nation at all:
26 the inhabitants of Mount Seir,[a] the Philistines,
and the senseless folk that live at Shechem.

* Before the author's closing note (verses 27–9) a numerical
proverb cites three nations excepted from the preceding
prayer for peace – all three often included with Jews by
foreigners: the Edomites, *the Philistines* and the Samaritans.
Mount Seir is the mountainous region south-east of the Dead
Sea, the ancient Edom; the Jews hated the Edomites because,
largely due to pressure from desert tribes, they had occupied
much former Judaean land after the Babylonian conquest
in the sixth century B.C. John Hyrcanus forcibly circumcised
them later in the second century. *the Philistines*, enemies of
David's time, had lost their separate identity by the second
century B.C. Ben Sira may be recalling the ancient hostility
or deploring the rapid adoption of Greek customs by the
current inhabitants of the coastal strip, the ancient Philistia.
As in other numerical proverbs (25: 7–11; 26: 5–8) the most
important comes last. The Samaritans lived in the territory
covered by the northern kingdom until its fall in 721 B.C.
Hatred between Jews and Samaritans, vicious in New Testament times, had grown since the Jews' return from exile
in Babylon. The Samaritans had built a rival temple to that in
Jerusalem on Mount Gerizim near *Shechem*, south of modern
Nablus, which was still standing in Ben Sira's day, although it
was destroyed by the Jews in 128 B.C. The Samaritans of
today still celebrate the Passover on the site of their temple
near Nablus. The Samaritans also claimed that the Jewish
line of Aaronite high priests had been corrupted and that they
alone possessed the unbroken line from Aaron through

[a] Mount Seir: *so Heb.; Gk.* the mountain of Samaria.

Phinehas – another reason for Ben Sira's hostility, considering his belief in the covenant with Phinehas (45: 24–5). The passage recalls remarks on the Samaritans in the *Testament of the Twelve Patriarchs* (written probably between 200 B.C. and A.D. 70, possibly by a contemporary of Ben Sira; it contains much apocalyptic writing): 'from this day forward shall Shechem be called a city of imbeciles, for as a man mocketh a fool, so did we mock them' (*Levi* 7: 2). Ben Sira's spiteful language is hardly typical of the calm international statesman pictured in 39: 1–11. ✵

AUTHOR'S POSTSCRIPT AND SIGNATURE

In this book I have written   27
lessons of good sense and understanding,
I, Jesus son of Sirach,[a] of Jerusalem,
whose mind was a fountain of wisdom.
Happy the man who occupies himself with these lessons,   28
who lays them to heart and grows wise!
If he lives by them, he will be equal to anything,   29
with the light of the Lord shining on his path.

✵ Ben Sira broke with the traditional anonymity of biblical writers by adding a personal note and his signature at the end of his work. These verses complete the first edition of his book and sum up some of the contents: to follow wisdom means a successful and happy life and guidance by God. Verse 29 links secular wisdom with religious belief at the end as often at the end of smaller sections, for example in 2: 6 and 3: 16, and unites the secular and religious sides of Ben Sira's work. The addition of a personal note and summary from the author seems to follow Egyptian models. The *Wisdom of Amen-em-opet* closes thus: 'See thou these thirty chapters: they entertain; they instruct; they are the foremost of all books;

[a] Sirach: *some witnesses read* Sirach Eleazar.

they make the ignorant to know. If they are read out before the ignorant, then he will be cleansed by them. Fill thyself with them; put them in thy heart, and be a man who can interpret them...It has come to an end – in the name of Senu.' ✸

Epilogue

A PERSONAL PSALM OF THANKSGIVING

51 I THANK THEE, my Lord and King,
I praise thee, my God and Saviour,
I give thee thanks,

2 because thou hast been my protector and helper,
rescuing me from death,
from the trap laid by a slanderous tongue
and from lips that utter lies.
In the face of my assailants thou didst come to my help;

3 in the fullness of thy mercy and glory thou didst rescue me
from grinding teeth which waited to devour me,
from hands that threatened my life,
from the many troubles I endured,

4 from the choking fire around me,
from the flames I had not kindled,

5 from the deep recesses of the grave,
from the foul tongue and its lies –

6 a wicked slander spoken in the king's presence.
I came near to death;
I was on the brink of the grave.

7 They surrounded me on every side,
and there was no one to help me.

I looked for human aid and there was none.

Then I remembered thy mercy, Lord,   8
thy deeds in bygone days;
thou dost deliver those who patiently trust thee
and free them from the power of their enemies.

So I sent up a prayer from the earth   9
and begged for rescue from death.

I cried, 'Lord, thou art my Father;*a*   10
do not desert me in time of trouble,
when I am helpless in the face of arrogance.

I will praise thee continually,   11
I will sing hymns of thanksgiving.'

And my prayer was granted;
for thou didst save me from death   12
and rescue me from my desperate plight.

Therefore I will thank thee and praise thee
and bless thee, O Lord.

✻ Ecclesiasticus was not arranged as carefully as a modern
book, as the insertion of such passages as 49: 14-16 has already
shown. Although 50: 27-9 were plainly intended to end the
book, ch. 51 was added later – probably by Ben Sira himself
because of the similarity of style with the rest of the book.
Verses 1-12 contain a psalm expressing an individual's thanks
to God (not a public hymn) and echoes many stylized figures
of speech from the Old Testament psalms, as indicated below.
It is doubtful how far the psalm reflects Ben Sira's own
experience. In 34: 12 he refers to his own escape from 'deadly
danger', and the 'wicked slander spoken in the king's
presence' (verse 6) has been interpreted as some unknown
reporting of Ben Sira to Antiochus III for disloyalty. But the
large number of echoes from the Old Testament psalms of

[a] thou . . . Father: *so Heb.; Gk.* Father of my lord.

thanksgiving makes it likely that the psalm is written in Ben Sira's anthological style based on biblical precedents, although the series of stylized dangers in verses 3–5 may lead to the climax of an event in Ben Sira's life in verse 6.

1–2. The 'individual psalm of thanksgiving' traditionally started with (i) a declaration of the individual's intention to praise God, and (ii) his reasons for doing so, i.e. God's help; Ps. 138: 1–2 runs: '(i) I will praise thee, O LORD, with all my heart . . .' (ii) for thou hast made thy promise wide as the heavens.' Thus here '(i) I thank thee, my Lord. . .(ii) because thou hast been my protector and helper'.

2–6. A large number of traditional images are used to describe the ways and occasions of God's help; the individual using the psalm would read his own experience into these stylized passages. Rescue *from death* (verse 2), for example, compares with 'He has rescued me from death' (Ps. 116: 8), *hands that threatened my life* (verse 3) with 'deadly foes who throng round me' (Ps. 17: 9), *the deep recesses of the grave* (verse 5; Hebrew 'the abyss', Greek literally 'Hades' – the underworld) with 'thou hast brought me up from Sheol and saved my life as I was sinking into the abyss' (Ps. 30: 3), *the foul tongue and its lies* (verse 5) with 'blasts of calumny' and 'my enemies' contentious tongues' (Ps. 55: 9).

6–12. As verses 2–6 described the circumstances in which God was wont to save, so verses 6–12 describe the circumstances in which the individual was saved in the past – for which he gives thanks. *death* and *the grave* in verse 6 pick up the references to 'death' and 'the grave' in verses 2 and 5, and the *They* of verse 7 refers to the 'assailants' of verse 2. In verses 10–11 a short song of lament is quoted amid the thanksgiving as in Ps. 30: 9–10. The psalm finishes in verse 12 with praise as it began, like Ps. 145. *

FINALLY – STUDY WISDOM!

When I was still young, before I set out on my travels,   13
I asked openly for wisdom in my prayers.
In the forecourt of the sanctuary I laid claim to her,   14
and I shall seek her out to the end.
From the first blossom to the ripening of the grape   15
she has been the delight of my heart.
From my youth my steps have followed her without
    swerving.
I had hardly begun to listen when I was rewarded,   16
and I gained for myself much instruction.
I made progress in my studies;   17
all honour to him who gives me wisdom!
I determined to practise what I had learnt;   18
I pursued goodness, and shall never regret it.
I strove for wisdom with all my might,   19
and was scrupulous in whatever I did.
I spread out my hands to heaven above,
deploring my ignorance;
I set my heart on possessing wisdom,   20
and by keeping myself pure I found her.
With her I gained understanding from the first;
therefore I shall never be at a loss.
Because I passionately yearned to discover her,   21
I won a noble prize.
The Lord gave me eloquence as my reward,   22
and with it I will praise him.

Come to me, you who need instruction,   23
and lodge in my house of learning.

24 Why do you admit to a lack of these things,
   yet leave your great thirst unslaked?

25 I have made my proclamation:
   'Buy for yourselves without money,

26 bend your neck to the yoke,
   be ready to accept discipline;
   you need not go far to find it.'

27 See for yourselves how little were my labours
   compared with the great peace I have found.

28 Your share of instruction may cost you a large sum of
      silver,
   but it will bring you a large return in gold.

29 May you take delight in the Lord's mercy
   and never be ashamed of praising him.

30 Do your duty in good time,
   and in his own time he will reward you.

---

* These verses form an alphabetical poem to close the book
like the alphabetical poem on the virtuous wife in Prov. 31.
Together with the psalm in verses 1–12 it forms the additions
of Ben Sira's 'second edition' of his work. Parts of a Hebrew
text of the poem have been discovered in a scroll of biblical
and non-biblical psalms and hymns found in a cave at
Qumran with other Dead Sea Scrolls. The scroll dates
probably from the first century A.D. and contains a text much
earlier and more reliable than that of the Cairo Genizah
(see p. 3). The Greek translation which the N.E.B. translates
appears to be an interpretative account of the Qumran
Hebrew.

The poem sums up many wisdom themes and echoes various
passages of the book: verses 13–21 describe Ben Sira's search
for wisdom, copying the motif of wisdom as a bride to be
sought (found more explicitly in 14: 20–7 and Wisd. of Sol.

8: 1–18). Verses 22–30 then follow with an appeal to his readers to search for and study wisdom. The emphasis on quick reward (verse 16), 'noble prize' (verse 21) and 'great peace' found after little labour (verse 27) seem directed against the disillusionment of Ecclesiastes where applying one's mind to 'wisdom and knowledge' is said to be 'chasing the wind' (Eccles. 1: 17). Ben Sira is careful to end his book on a positive note. Strangely the religious piety with which he often ends his sections (as in 2: 6 and 3: 16) is lacking at the end of the book, where wisdom has its traditional meaning of education and training for life.

13. Travel was considered important by Ben Sira in acquiring experience of life, as stated in 34: 9–12 and 39: 4.

14–15. *From the first blossom . . .*: in other words, Ben Sira sought for wisdom all his life, from beginning to end. *the forecourt of the sanctuary* does not imply any connexion between wisdom and the cult as in 24: 10 but rather describes the place where he prayed for wisdom as a young man.

17. Ben Sira ascribes *honour to* God *who gives* him *wisdom*.

22. The *eloquence* given to a successful teacher provides an easy link with the appeal which follows.

23 contains, in the Hebrew, the first recorded use of the phrase *bēth hammidrāsh, house of learning* or 'school', used later of the groups of students whom rabbis gathered round themselves rather like Jesus and his disciples in the New Testament. Education, particularly in the law, grew rapidly in Judaism, and schools were often associated with synagogues. By A.D. 63 some maintained that every village should have its school and that all children should attend from the age of six or seven.

25–8. Learning was traditionally free, rabbis earning their living some other way, sometimes later by trade. Verse 28 does not imply payment in cash, but is rather a proverb cited to show how the labour put into learning is to the resulting wisdom as silver is to gold; in other words, the effort you put in is repaid many times over. The Mishnah uses financial language figuratively in the same way: 'If thou hast studied much in the Law much reward will be given to thee, and faithful is thy taskmaster who shall pay thee the reward of thy labour' (*Aboth* 2: 16). *

NOTES ON FURTHER READING

There has been no comprehensive commentary on *Ecclesiasticus* in English for many years. The volume in the previous Cambridge series edited by W. O. E. Oesterley (1912) is out of date. There is a useful chapter in R. H. Pfeiffer, *A History of New Testament Times, with an Introduction to the Apocrypha* (Black, 1954). The political background of Palestine in Ben Sira's time is covered in V. Tcherikover, *Hellenistic Civilisation and the Jews* (Jewish Publication Society, 1966) and in D. S. Russell, *The Jews from Cyrus to Herod*, New Clarendon Bible (O.U.P., 1967), and the religious background of Judaism is dealt with by W. Förster, *Palestinian Judaism in New Testament Times* (Oliver and Boyd, 1964) and by G. F. Moore, *Judaism in the first centuries of the Christian Era* (3 vols., Harvard U.P., 1927–30). General literary background to the Apocrypha may be found in *The Making of the Old Testament* (ed. E. B. Mellor) in this series. Non-biblical evidence for the history of the Old Testament period surveyed by Ben Sira may be found in *Documents from Old Testament Times*, ed. D. W. Thomas (Nelson, 1958).

INDEX

Aaron 46, 77, 220–6, 251; his blessing 174–5; sons of (=priests) 171, 175, 222, 226–7, 250–5

Abraham 82, 218–19

Acts of the Apostles 43

Adam 74, 130, 160, 217, 248

additions in Greek manuscripts 1–2; alternatives 10, 23, 87; doctrinal and religious 10, 57, 62, 69, 83, 89–90, 92, 98, 100, 105, 118, 123; illustrative 24, 111, 134; link between sections 12

adultery 116–18, 126, 131

advice: accepting of 35–6, 52, 127, 179, 200; given by author 4, 14, 37, 59, 186, by wise men 107, 190; offered to God 209

Ahiqar, Story of 30, 148

Akiba, rabbi 26, 161

Alexander the Great 7, 23, 200

almsgiving 64, 93, 198; destroys effect of sin 20–1, 24; equals a sacrifice 170; rescues giver from trouble 143–4, 200

alphabetical poem 260

Amen-em-opet, Instruction of 3, 255–6

Amos, prophet 242; book 25, 232

anger: God's 81, 194, 196, *see also* wrath of God; human 12–13, 19, 54, 129, 139–42, 150, 154, 196

anonymity of biblical writers 255

anthological style 163, 167, 174, 258

Antiochus III, king 55, 175, 251, 257

apocalyptic works 5, 157, 217

arrogance 13, 22–4, 54–5, 66, 81, 138, 155, 158, 257

Asa, king 95, 184, 245

ashamed, being 29, 204–5; not being 29, 135, 205–6

assembly, public 25–6, 107–8, 188, 191, 204; lawcourt 76, 204; =public humiliation 13–14, 117

astrologers 180

atonement, means of 24–5, 170–1,

185, 223, 226, especially 19–21; Day of Atonement 32, 169, 225, 249–53

author, personal notes 80, 125, 162–3, 166, 192, 194, 255; belief in wisdom as obedience to law and fear of Lord 158; conservative in thought 5, 12, 23–4, 80, 93, 109–10, 184; purpose in writing 7

Babylon 15, 245; exile in 174, 247 rule in Palestine 7, 89, 227, 254

banquets 146, 152–7

beggars 200–1

Benedictions, the eight 176

borrowing 96–7, 105

bribery 42, 171, 198–9, 206, 232

bride purchase 177

business dealings 61, 205

Cairo Genizah *see* Genizah

Caleb 228–30

calendar, liturgical 161–2

Canaanites 82, 150

catachetical form 57

character: blackening own 109; importance of 58, 61–2, 71, 80, 100; testing character 50, 64, 135

charity 25–6, 41–2, 143, 204; *see also* almsgiving

children, parental attitudes 21, 44, 80, 147–9

Chronicles, books of 8, 238; 1 Chronicles 109, 234–5; 2 Chronicles 95, 184, 238, 243, 245

civil rights 30

civil servants, training of 3, 49

cleverness, good and bad 99–100, 107–8

commandments: of God 78–9, 142–3, 179; =the Jewish law 13, 22, 24, 38, 56, 117–18, 139, 145, 158, 170, 220, 223; Ten Commandments 20, 88, 116–17, 164, 213, 221

corporal punishment 148–9
cosmology, ancient 10, 121
covenant, of God 139, 190–1, 204–5, 215; with Aaron 221; with Abraham 218–19; covenant-book of God (=law) 4, 124; with David 226–7, 234–5; with Noah 217–18; with Phinehas 224, 226, 253–5; at Sinai 88
cowards 179–80
craftsmen 52–3, 187–8, 191–2

Daniel, book of 89
daughters 44–5, 109–10, 129–30, 132–4, 207–8
David, king 18, 37, 109, 196, 224, 226, 232–7, 243, 245, 254; Davidic line of kings 122, 226–7, 234, 237, 241, 247
Dead Sea Scrolls, see Qumran manuscripts
death 84, 182, 198, 201–2, 217, 256; author's view 74; better than beggary 200, than misery 149; than scandal 132, 141; change of fortune at death 47, 60, 62–3, 89; early death as punishment 18, 93; fate for all 48, 198, 201–2; fear of death 52, 196, 201; finality of death, no life after death 5, 18, 43, 47, 54–6, 73–5, 90–1, 139, 150, 186, 215, 240; judgement at death 89, 94; originated from woman 200
debtors 145–6, 154
Deuteronomy, book of 25, 45–6, 51, 79, 82, 89, 95, 124, 128, 131, 144, 150, 164–5, 171, 196, 213, 236
Didache 32
discipline 106, 157; in family 44–5, 147–8, 206–8; in speech 101, 114–15; of wisdom 5–6, 13, 27, 37, 48, 84, 92, 110, 113, 125, 260
discrimination, need for 176–82, 188
dishonesty in trade 134–6, 143, 189, 204
divination 165–6
divisions of time 211
divorce 44–5, 130–1, 141–2

doctors 5, 54–5, 94–5, 183–5
double life of sinner 17–18
dreams 165–6
drunkenness 96, 132–3, 153–5
Duauf, Maxims of 3, 188
duplicity 33

Ecclesiastes, book of 1, 8, 61–2, 74, 80, 92–3, 95, 134, 150, 155, 261
Eden, garden of 43, 74, 87, 125, 130
Edomites 254
education 3, 28, 107–8, 147–8, 166, 190; in Judaism 261
Egypt: captivity and Exodus 82, 122, 174, 185, 195–6, 220; civil service 49, 189; conditions at time of Ben Sira 1, 6–7, 25–8; see also proverbial literature; Ptolemies
Elijah 4, 238–41
Elisha 239–42
enemies 65–7, 142, 144; being one's own enemy 57; gloating over misfortune 34, 96–7, 113, 207; making enemies 143, 181, out of friends 33, 35, 103, 178
Enoch 217, 248
Esther, book of 8
Euergetes, king of Egypt 6–7
Eve 130, 197; origin of evil and death 130
Exodus, book of 16, 20–1, 82, 116, 121, 123, 144, 164, 172, 175, 185, 195–6, 213, 219, 221, 224–5, 244, 248, 252
Ezekiel, book of 8, 23, 90, 149, 162, 246
Ezra, person 247; book of 8, 247

family: large families 56, 79–80, 82; as means of immortality 118, 203, relationships 18–21, 46, 148
fasting 20, 168–9, 224
fear of the Lord 56; Ben Sira's special use 4, 19–20, 45, 96, 99, 117, 127, 131, 134, 167, 191, 200, especially 10–14; =obedience to the law 53, 124, 158; =wisdom 106

festivals, religious 160–2, 211, 234–5
flood, the 198–9, 217
fools, unintelligent people 102–4, 107–8, 110–11, 136; dislike wisdom 37, 39, 76; ignorant 99–100, 151; not trustworthy 49, 97, 159; tactless 93, 101, 103
forgiveness, God's 31–3, 81, 90–3, 105–6, 168–9, 253; man's 20; relation between the two 139–40
fortune, change of 58, 62, 94
free will 78–9, 162
friends 35–7, 43, 65–7, 97–8, 112–13, 126–7, 137–8; false friends 34, 159, 178; new and old 51; turning into enemies 33, 35, 103, 140

gain, financial 33, 43–4, 64, 134, 145
Genesis, book of 43, 74–5, 79, 82, 85–7, 112, 121, 125, 130, 180, 195, 197–9, 210, 213, 217–19, 248
Genizah (of Cairo) 2, 260
Gerizim, mount 254
giants = nephīlīm 81–2; Goliath 233
Gideon 230
God: control of world 4, 42, 61, 79, 84–9, 118, 162, 194, 204, 214; creator of wisdom 9; ordering of creation 3, 184, 194, 209, 213; special love for Jews 10, 89, 122
Gog and Magog 246
gossip 33–4, 52, 66–7, 97–9, 115, 138, 140–2, 207
grandson of author (Greek translator) 1, 5, 7–8, 43, 217
greed 54, 113, 152–5, 182
Greek influence 23, 156, 166; biographical works 216; mercenary soldiers 177–8; rule in Palestine 174; thought 8, 85, 184, 214; way of life 7, 200, 254
greetings 25, 35, 204
guarantees for debtors 48, 50, 145–6

Haggai, book of 247
Hanukkah, feast of 134
health 11, 149–50, 167, 182–3

heathen, the 26–8, 158–9, 172, 174, 193
Hebrew manuscripts 1, 8
Hezekiah, king 242–5
high priest 176, 221–7, 247–51
Hillel 40
honesty: in business 135; to self 29
Horeb, mount 238–40
Hosea, book of 169
Hosea, prophet 242
hospitality 68, 72, 74, 104–5, 146
hosts at feasts 153, 156
hymns included in book 3, 91–2, 192–4, 209–14, 214–51

idolatry 149–50, 230, 236, 238
illness 182; punishment for sin 15, 18, 94–5; treatment by doctors 54–5, 183–5; visiting the sick 46; worse than death 149–50
imagination, human 23
immortality: through children 148, 215; through memory 56, 148, 181–2, 186–7, 190, 192; through reputation 203, 215
inclinations, Jewish doctrine of two, see tendencies
interest on money 144
international outlook 4, 166, 190
invitations: to one's own home 64; to other people's homes 69
Isaac 218–19
Isaiah, prophet 243–4; book of 8, 77, 85, 121, 175, 196, 244, 246
Israel, land 123; Jews as whole 119–20, 175, 181, 214–51; northern kingdom 237–8

Jacob = Israel, the Jewish people 119, 124–5, 173, 223, 225, 236, 239, 246; the patriarch 116, 218–20
Jeremiah, book of 8, 64, 165, 169, 175, 213, 245–6
Jeremiah, prophet 7, 245
Jeroboam I, king 237–8
Jerusalem: author's home 1; centre of Judaism 122, 173; destruction of 245; restoration after exile 247;

INDEX

Jerusalem (*cont.*)
Simon's renovations 251; wisdom's home 4, 119; *see also* temple
Jesus Christ 144, 261
Jews in Egypt 7; of Dispersion 8, 28, 125–6, 175
Job, book of 8, 10, 12, 15, 43, 61, 85, 93, 121, 199
Joel, book of 246
Johanan ben Zaccai 169
John, gospel of 27, 123, 156, 210
Jonah, book of 84
Joseph 112, 220, 248
Josephus ix, 8, 123; *Contra Apionem* 8; *Jewish Antiquities* 8, 251
Joshua, book of 8, 82, 229–30
Joshua, Moses' successor 227–9, 231, 234, 239
Josiah, king 16, 242–5
Judaism: of Ben Sira's time 5, 15, 43, 135, 145; later education 57, 261; later rabbinical teaching 4–5, 12, 21, 32, 51, 78–9, 90, 131, 169, 189, 217, 246, anticipated by Ben Sira 20–1, 25, 49, 131, 245; rabbis and trade 61, 261; threatened by Greek influence 23
judgement: of God *see* retribution; human discernment 22, 127–8, 179–81
justice 53, 112, 172, 205, 226

Kings, books of 8, 174, 242; 1 Kings 84, 236–42; 2 Kings 16, 238–45
Korah, rebellion of 81–2, 223, 225

law: civil 51, 215; of God 4, 52–3, 98, 117, 202, 218, 223; identified with wisdom 10, 40, 75, 99, 120–4, 165, 221; Jewish 28, 43, 51, 61, 75–7, 87–9, 157–9, 165–6, 189–90, =Pentateuch and Mishnah 17–23
lawcourts 29, 77, 188
lawsuits 145
lending money 48, 102, 142–5
Leviticus, book of 23, 46, 51, 98–9, 162, 169, 171, 225, 234, 251–3
Lot 81–2

Luke, gospel of 23, 53

Maccabean revolt 12, 134, 174
Maccabees, books of; 1 Maccabees 216, 219, 227; 2 Maccabees 12, 156–7
Malachi, book of 239–40
man, God-given authority of 86
manners at table 52–3, 204
manual work 3, 27, 42–3, 58, 187–9
Marah, miracle at 185
Mark, gospel of 26
marriage 45, 126–8, 142, 177, 207
Masada manuscript 2
Mattathias 216, 219, 227
Matthew, gospel of 26, 32, 40, 100, 115, 128, 139–40, 144–5, 152
medicine 5, 37, 95, 183–5
Meir, rabbi 61
merchants 134–5, 179
Messiah 175, 227; messianic expectation 224, 227, 248
miracles: of God 223; of prophets 229, 231, 238–44
misers 32, 72–3, 145
Mishnah 4, 17, 23, 32, 51, 117, 192, 224, 251–3, 262; *Aboth* 4, 5, 21, 40, 43, 69, 108, 144, 189, 192, 262; *Baba Bathra* 206; *Baba Metzia* 49, 169; *Eduyoth* 240; *Kiddushin* 184; *Sotah* 248; *Tamid* 252; *Yoma* 32, 224, 252–3
misreading of Hebrew by Greek translator 28, 37, 40, 63, 66, 125, 152, 221, 232
mocking 67–8
money 30, 47, 71, 135, 143–7, 151, 163, 206
Moses 46, 82, 123, 175, 222; as lawgiver 124, 191–2, 219–21
mourning 46–7, 110–12, 185–7, 202, 243–4

name, significance of 37, 39, 203, 215; sacred name of God 114, 252–3
Nathan 233–4
Nehemiah 47, 247

Nehemiah, book of 8, 21, 247
New Testament 5, 17, 21, 26, 27, 32, 40, 109, 115, 128, 130, 144–5, 192, 219, 254, 261
Noah 82, 217–18
northern kingdom 236–42, 254; Ephraim 236
Numbers, book of 40, 46, 82, 169, 175, 184, 224–6, 229, 252
numerical proverbs 116–18, 126–8, 131–5, 254

oaths 114–15
obedience: to God 19, 28, 243; to law 18, 106, 117–18, 140, 158–9; to parents 19; to wisdom 123
objectors' queries answered 78–9, 83–4, 88–9, 116–18, 193–5
old age 18–19, 21, 48, 80, 127, 154, 157, 206
opposites in nature 79, 160–2, 202, 209
oracle, divine 159–60, 223, 224
oral law 4, 17–18, 23, 160; see also Mishnah
oral repetition 17, 71, 192

Paneas, battle of 55, 175, 251
paradoxes 102–3
parents: duties of 20–1; respect for 18–21, 44–5, 115–16
Paul, apostle 32, 43, 166
Pentateuch 4, 7, 17–18, 23, 216, 224
Pharisees see Judaism, later rabbinical teaching
Phinehas 224, 226–7, 255
play on words: in Greek 12; in Hebrew 39, 213, 229
politicians, politics 29–30, 52–3, 174
polygamy 133, 180
prayer 41, 43, 180; answered by God 16, 19, 21, 25, 242, 257; for healing 183–5; Lord's Prayer 139; of repentance 90, 139
prayers in book 113, 172–4, 253
predestination 78, 161
priests 45–7, 221–7, 250
prohibitions 28–9, 41–2

property, distribution at death 74, 163
prophets 165, 173–5, 190, 229, 231, 238–42; books of canon 5, 8, 216; prophetical succession 234; twelve minor 8, 246
proverbial literature, in ancient Near East 3, 13, 17, 29, 68, 70, 98, 108, 117, 131; Babylonian 15; Egyptian 3, 15, 20, 29, 36, 49, 58, 93, 147, 155; Israelite 9, 120, 169; see also Proverbs; Ecclesiastes; Job
Proverbs, book of 3–4, 8–9, 11, 14–15, 20, 27, 29, 40, 51, 53, 58, 117, 120, 130, 134, 138, 146, 148, 155, 169, 180, 188–91, 216, 259
psalms, author's 174, 195, 256–8
Psalms, book of 8, 12, 16, 67, 76, 87, 91, 93, 123, 128, 167, 172, 175, 195, 199, 212–13, 216, 257
Ptolemies, kings of Egypt 7, 178; Ptolemy V 55
punishment for sin 32, 54, 74, 81–2, 138, 184; capital punishment 51, 147–8; leading to repentance 91; relation to forgiveness 139–40

quarrels 59, 140–2; private 112, 136, 154; public 35
Qumran: community 5, 109; manuscripts 2, 260

rabbinical teaching, later, see under Judaism
Rehoboam, king 237–8
repentance 4, 21, 32, 90–1, 94–5, 105–6, 118, 169, 184, 217
resurrection 12, 74, 230, 240; see also death
retribution, from God before or after death 11–12, 18, 32, 43, 62–3, 74, 91
revelation, divine 23, 124, 165
riddles 190–1, 200, 235–7; see also numerical proverbs
right time, importance of knowing 101, 156; for God's triumph 175; for speech 12–13, 101

ritual 223–6, 230
Romans, letter to 32, 130, 219
rumours about friends 97–8
Ruth, book of 20, 232

Saadia Gaon 36, 62, 78
sabbath day 11, 161
sacrifices 20–1, 41, 45–6, 73, 77, 168–72, 183–5, 222, 250
Samaritans 254–5
Samson 230
Samuel, books of 8; 1 Samuel 37, 89, 160, 165, 180, 232–3; 2 Samuel 18, 196, 227
Samuel, prophet 89, 231–2, 234, 239
Satan 160, 231–4, 236
secrets: betrayal of 137–8; of the future 243; of God 22, 208–9; of men 13–14, 69, 97, 112, 204; of wisdom 27, 75
self-control 12–13, 69, 156
self-discipline 113, 236
self-respect 30, 34, 57
Septuagint x, 7, 89, 221, 232
Seth 217, 248
Shammai 31, 40
Shem 217, 248
Sheol 74, 91
shopkeepers 134
Simon, son of Onias 77, 247–53
Sinai desert 82, 121–2, 219, 229; mountain 88, 213, 240
slavery, slaves 21, 44–5, 56, 163–5, 204
sleep 196–7
Sodom 195; and Gomorrah 82
Solomon, king 84, 235–7
southern kingdom (=Judah) 237, 240
speculation, mystical 22–3, 217, 246
Stoics 85, 87, 214
synagogues 17, 26, 57, 152, 261

Talmud, Babylonian 5, 20, 36, 43, 51, 93, 108, 117, 139, 150, 161, 169, 186
teachers 40, 87, 181, 261; methods of, 17; teacher–pupil relationship 15, 20, 85

temple, at Jerusalem 7, 16, 95, 134, 227, 238, 243–4; building of temple 234–6; destruction 169, 174; rebuilt 247; replica at Leontopolis 7; wisdom's home 4, 119–21, 223; worship 6, 20, 45–7, 77, 221–3, 249–53
tendencies, Jewish doctrine of good and bad 78–9, 106, 162, 178
tent, sacred 119–23
Testaments of the Twelve Patriarchs 255
testing: of Abraham 218–19; of friends 35, 53, 134–5, 178; of self 14–16, 69, 153, 182
Tobiah 47
Tobit, book of 20, 47, 150, 169, 171
trade 61, 135, 144, 189, 205, 261
translation, art of 5–6, 8; into Greek 1, 5–8, 28, 43, 47, 217, 253
travel 3, 106, 190–2, 259, 261

Urim 165; and Thummim 160, 224–5

verdict: of God 105; legal 25–6
vows 94–5

washing, ceremonial 168
wealth 56–8, 150–2
widows 171–2
wisdom 5–6, 13–14, 37–9, 100–1, 113, 128, 191, 199, 210, 214, 259; creative word 210; divine origin 9; feminine 4, 11, 260; human experience 9, 11, 49, 56–7, 76, 94, 99, 104–5, 110–11, 126–7, 154, 181–2; identified with Jewish law 10, 40, 75, 99, 120–4, 158, 165, 221; Israel's possession 119–20, 216; personified 4, 11, 26–7, 37–8, 75–6, 94, 119–23; pre-existent 9–11, 119–20; see also proverbial literature
Wisdom of Solomon, book of 8, 80, 210, 260–1

wives 43–5, 50–1; bad 129–32, 206, 208; good 126–7, 131–2, 177–8, 199; rival wife 132–3, 179–80; someone else's 204

women 50–1, 96, 110, 117, 129, 131–4, 177, 207, 236; as origin of evil and death 130, 162

worship 76–7, 121–2

wrath of God 31, 44, 223, 239

Zadok, Zadokites 224

Zechariah, book of 246–7

Zion see Jerusalem